D1028465

Nabokov's Canon

SRLT

NORTHWESTERN UNIVERSITY PRESS
Studies in Russian Literature and Theory

SERIES EDITORS
Robert Belknap
Caryl Emerson
Gary Saul Morson
William Mills Todd III
Andrew Wachtel

Nabokov's Canon

From *Onegin* to *Ada*

Marijeta Bozovic

NORTHWESTERN UNIVERSITY PRESS / EVANSTON, ILLINOIS

Northwestern University Press
www.nupress.northwestern.edu

Studies of the Harriman Institute
Columbia University

The Harriman Institute, Columbia University, sponsors the Studies of the Harriman Institute in the belief that their publication contributes to scholarly research and public understanding. In this way the Institute, while not necessarily endorsing their conclusions, is pleased to make available the results of some of the research conducted under its auspices.

Printed in the United States of America

10 9 8 7 6 5 4 3 2 1

Library of Congress Cataloging-in-Publication Data

Names: Bozovic, Marijeta, author.
Title: Nabokov's canon : from Onegin to Ada / Marijeta Bozovic.
Other titles: Studies in Russian literature and theory. | Studies of the Harriman Institute.
Description: Evanston, Illinois : Northwestern University Press, 2016. | Series: Northwestern University Press studies in Russian literature and theory | Series: Studies of the Harriman Institute | Based on the author's thesis (doctoral)—Columbia University, 2011.
Identifiers: LCCN 2015049346 | ISBN 9780810133143 (pbk. : alk. paper) | ISBN 9780810133150 (cloth : alk. paper) | ISBN 9780810133167 (e-book)
Subjects: LCSH: Nabokov, Vladimir Vladimirovich, 1899–1977—Criticism and interpretation. | Russian literature—20th century—History and criticism. Literature, Modern—20th century—Russian influences.
Classification: LCC PG3476.N3 Z5924 2016 | DDC 813/.54—dc23
LC record available at http://lccn.loc.gov/2015049346

To TN

Contents

Acknowledgments

Academic books, like most other forms of cultural production, undoubtedly owe their origins to psychological trauma. Looking back, it comes as little surprise that the first book I had to write was about geographical and cultural displacement—and how it could be made to look easy. The pleasure of reading Nabokov came early and has been colored and compounded along the way by the even greater pleasure of arguing about his works with remarkable mentors, colleagues, friends, and students.

The initial sparks flew at Harvard University in the inimitable Svetlana Boym's locally legendary Nabokov seminar. From that group of feisty undergraduates emerged academics, novelists, artists, and a variety of uncategorizable creative entrepreneurs: I have in mind Katharine Holt, Rob Dennis, Henry Moynahan Rich, Brooke Lampley, Matthew Gibson, and Jacob Rubin. For many of us, academic life began in Stephen Greenblatt's History and Literature concentration. *The Harvard Advocate* and Signet Society meanwhile were our cafés and cabarets, making possible connections both searing and lasting, including with Katharine Burgin (then Douglas), Angus Burgin, Dehn Gilmore, Jennifer Nelson, Min Lieskovsky, Cary McClelland, Cody Carvell, Jeremy Barnett Reff, Ezra Feldman, Lucy Ives, Reihan Salam, and others whose names I predict you will see more of in the years to come.

At Columbia University's Slavic Department, I found a mentor and a model of fierce intellectual integrity and passion in my Ph.D. advisor Valentina Izmirlieva, who shaped this project and my graduate years in more ways than I can express. The dissertation on which this book is based would have collapsed without the unfaltering wisdom of Irina Reyfman, an intellectual and *intelligent*. I am grateful to the teachers and friends I found along the way: to Boris Gasparov, Cathy Popkin, Stephanie Sandler, John Malmstad, William Todd III, Catherine Nepomnyashchy, Richard Gustafson, Robert Belknap, Lisa Knapp, Alan Timberlake, Frank Miller, Radmila Gorup, Tatiana Smoliarova, Rebecca Stanton, Gareth Williams, Joseph Massad, Lydia Goehr, Andreas Huyssens, Mark Lipovetsky, Anne Lounsbery, David Branderberger, Julia Bekman Chadaga, Alexandra Kirilchuk Lyons, Christopher

Ely, Galina Belaia, Dina Magomedova, Dmitrii Bak, Dragan Kujundžić, Tomas Longinović, Dubravka Ugrešić—not to mention the poets Jori Graham, Peter Sacks, Forrest Gander, D. A. Powell, and Janet Sylvester.

Comrades in arms in graduate school and beyond read countless chapters, abstracts, cover letters, talks, and drafts: Bella Grigoryan, Maksim Hanukai, Rossen Djagalov, John Cal Wright, and Jonathan Brooks Platt. I am equally indebted to the dose of perspective offered by friends in other fields, including Sergey Levchin, Maria Cristina Rueda, Catherine Burch Belkin, Robert Collier, Elyse Lightman, Timothy Dunne, Reif Larsen, Liam McCarthy, Halle Eaton, Tarun Chhabra; and more recently Matthew Miller, Anne Beggs, Jennifer Stob, April Sweaney, Greg Ames, and Yohei Igarashi.

This project was made possible by Yale University's Hilles Publication Subvention award and the Harriman Institute series, as well as earlier support from Columbia University's Slavic Department, the Columbia Core Curriculum, the New York Public Library, two Harriman Institute Junior Fellowships, the Ruth Hettleman Young Scholar award, a Foreign Languages and Area Studies fellowship, and Fulbright. The manuscript was reborn through the editing efforts of Roman Utkin, Kirsten Painter, and Michael Levine at Northwestern University Press. I found both support and invaluable critique from the Nabokov scholars Brian Boyd, Stephen Blackwell, Eric Naiman, Olga Peters Hasty, Robert Alter, Michael Wood, Michael Glynn, David Bethea, Siggy Frank, Lisa Wakamiya, Yuri Leving, Maksim Shrayer, Vladimir Alexandrov, Hilary Fink Kawall, Will Norman, Martin Hägglund, and Duncan White. At the eleventh hour, the talented Yale M.F.A. artist Mariya Vlasova generously created an original image for the cover of this book.

I owe a childhood among books and between languages to my sister Dolores and parents Ivan and Natasha Božović. Everything else I owe to the miraculous and mostly inexplicable love of Timothy Newhouse.

Nabokov's Canon

What Mad Pursuit: Nabokov and Canon Formation

> The existing monuments form an ideal order
> among themselves, which is modified by
> the introduction of the new (the really new)
> work of art among them. The existing order
> is complete before the new work arrives; for
> order to persist after the supervention of
> novelty, the *whole* existing order must be, if
> ever so slightly, altered; and so the relations,
> proportions, values of each work of art toward
> the whole are readjusted; and this is conformity
> between the old and the new.
> —T. S. Eliot, "Tradition and the Individual Tal-
> ent," 1919

> Human cultural evolution, in strong opposition
> to our biological history, is Lamarckian in
> character. What we learn in one generation, we
> transmit directly by teaching and writing.
> —Stephen Jay Gould, *The Panda's Thumb*, 1980

CONTROVERSIAL MONUMENTS

The veritable library of scholarship on Vladimir Nabokov, with few exceptions, still circles uncomfortably around two of his most ambitious works:
the voluminous annotated *Eugene Onegin* translation (1964) and the late
English-language novel *Ada, or Ardor* (1969). The controversy and the literary feud that followed the publication of Nabokov's eagerly awaited translation has become the stuff of legend.[1] Alexander Gerschenkron has said of
Nabokov's translation that it can and should be studied, but that it cannot be
read.[2] Many have responded similarly to *Ada*'s code-switching, trilingualism,
and many-layered allusions. Few novels aside from *Finnegans Wake* pro-

3

voke such critical divergence as *Ada*, acclaimed by some but viewed by many other readers as Nabokov's fall into self-indulgent irrelevance. Together, the two texts are often perceived as Nabokov's most solipsistic and disturbingly aristocratic; whereas *Lolita* has achieved full respectability and the status of a classic, *Onegin* and *Ada* remain problematic provocations, casting a shadow on the earlier works.

I will argue in this book that what the critical reaction points to and yet obscures is that these are also the most fraught and ambitious moments of Nabokov's career. *Eugene Onegin* and *Ada* are so attacked because of the threat they present, as attempts to shape and reform the dominant literary canon. My thesis is that Nabokov in the 1960s, after a series of grand successes and a dizzying rise to international fame, launched a campaign to promote a counter-canon to that of T. S. Eliot and the New Critics, encountered in the classrooms of American universities as in the pages of fashionable literary periodicals. Like Eliot, whom he detested, Nabokov intended to be that critic who, "from time to time, every hundred years or so . . . shall appear to review the past of our literature, and set the poets and the poems in a new order."[3] But how does a Russian émigré writer claim the cultural capital to reshape international modernism?

In opposition to the Anglo-American modernist canon, Nabokov attempted to reimagine a nineteenth- and twentieth-century canon of interpenetrating European traditions—with the Russian novel as a central, rather than marginal, strain. Nabokov's canon is pointedly transnational and translinguistic, continental but also specifically Russo-Franco-American-centric, and serves to legitimize his own literary practice. The discernable arc from *Onegin* to *Ada* describes an alternative romantic and modernist tradition, extending from Pushkin's early nineteenth-century Russian verse narrative to culminate unexpectedly in a late twentieth-century novel, written in English and after fifty years of emigration. In the one work, Nabokov sought to define a canon of suitable precursors; in the other, he meant to enter it himself.

What is perhaps especially threatening is that Nabokov argued for the primacy of his counter-canon in high modernism's own terms, privileging difficulty and the detail, exegetic close reading, and an understanding of literary sensibility based on its substitution for religious belief—evidenced in such terms as canon, genius, and masterpiece.[4] Frederic Jameson reads Nabokov (and his subsequent fall from grace) as reflecting "the misfortune to span two eras and the luck to find a time capsule of isolation or exile in which to spin out unseasonable forms."[5] One might even conjecture that American literary elites were more willing to change the rules of the game than to cede cultural authority.[6]

In my reading, *Eugene Onegin* and *Ada* emerge as Nabokov's key battle-sites for canon formation, in content and in form; far more so than the supporting texts *Strong Opinions* (1973) and the posthumously published Cornell lectures in *Lectures on Literature* (1980) and *Lectures on Russian Literature* (1981). Both *Evgenii Onegin*—I triangulate my texts with a look back at Pushkin's Russian novel in verse—and *Ada* serve as extraordinary allegories of cultural capital and its geographic, transnational distributions, as well as of the print medium and the novel's evolutionary struggles with other genres and media. Even the notorious awkwardness of Nabokov's "literal" translation of *Onegin* can be understood as an attack on the cultural hegemony of "correct" literary English and metonymically, on its gatekeepers.[7]

The canon traced in Nabokov's immense *Commentary* to *Onegin* and then animated in *Ada* rests on "great triads" of French, English, and Russian novelists: Chateaubriand, Byron, and Pushkin in the first generation; Flaubert, Dickens, and Tolstoy in the next; and finally Proust, Joyce, and Nabokov himself. Such precursors make Nabokov a legitimized authority and natural heir—rather than the outsider figure to *any* national tradition, with the cultural capital equivalent of a Nansen (Nonsense, he called it) passport, that he actually was. Mads Rosendahl Thomsen reminds us that "had it not been for *Lolita*, it is likely that Nabokov would not have been internationally canonized; one indication of this is that his early Russian novels were not translated until the 1960s."[8] Without *Lolita* and in fact popular, rather than high-brow success, Nabokov would have remained in the precariat as a teacher of Russian language in American Slavic departments, more Pnin than his tormenter V.V. from the eponymous novel of 1957. Once again, the very antagonism Nabokov later inspired speaks to the success of his self-fashioning: for the vaguely trans-European aristocracy Nabokov presented to the world was a construct of his own fictions and highly performative public persona.

Despite, or perhaps due to the controversy that he unfailingly inspired in the last two decades of his life, Nabokov has been acknowledged as the "first among Russian-born literati to attain the 'interliterary stature of a world writer.'"[9] Effectively, Nabokov tried to rescue his line of Russian literature by translating and annexing it to a hybrid, if English-dominant, canon. In this regard, he resembles less the other émigré writers (including Nobel Prize winners Ivan Bunin and Josef Brodsky) than the émigré artists, choreographers, and musicians (Wassily Kandinsky, George Balanchine, and Igor Stravinsky), who had a far easier time translating their life's work to European and American soil. Working within the medium of language, Nabokov managed not only to escape his own marginalization, but through his creative output and lifelong aesthetic propaganda campaign, to push for the reconfiguration of an international cultural playing field—conjuring in the minds of many readers an alluring vision of a transnational Antiterra.

It is ultimately the unexpected emancipatory dimension of Nabokov's canon reformation that interests me the most. Reading against the grain and according to a model of cultural studies that derives as much from Ernst Bloch as Theodor Adorno and Max Horkheimer, I turn to Nabokov as the inspiration for an unexpected and diverse array of transnational and world literature writers. The Iranian Azar Nafisi, Turkish Orhan Pamuk, South African J. M. Coetzee, and the German exile W. G. Sebald, among others, all in some sense see themselves as "Nabokov's children," producing works that build from and against Nabokov's fictions. Ever on the margins of Europe, simultaneously in- and outside, Russia's self-conscious cultural appropriations lend themselves to and provide seductive models for transnational literary practice.

Thus, for all the implied closure of Nabokov's counter-canon, the reforming gesture itself appears perversely productive.[10] The most useful and appealing readings of Nabokov in the twenty-first century, I argue, will continue to view him in relation to a cultural sea change, but as an advance guard of transnational and world literatures rather than high modernism's last stand.[11] Likewise, it seems more stimulating to interpret *Ada* than to evaluate it: as a novel *about* literary canons and cultural capital, *Ada* bares the device and shows up the game. In my reading, Nabokov's late fiction plays on the border of conceptualism.

My frame is fundamentally indebted to the sociology of literature: to the work of Pierre Bourdieu, John Guillory, and Pascale Casanova, especially in the opening chapters; with an adjustment of focus to media theory, in its relevance to the late twentieth-century novel, and to discussions of world literature(s) in the final chapters and conclusion. I ground my inquiries in readings and rereadings of three many-layered texts—Pushkin's *Onegin*, Nabokov's *Onegin* project, and Nabokov's *Ada*. In moving from the individual work to discussions of genre, medium, and cultural capital, I have found inspiration in the dense elegance of Guillory's formula, imagining the chain of mediation in diagrammatic form:

individual work] biographical oeuvre] genre] discourse] medium] social context] social totality[12]

By paying close attention to such layers of mediation, I try to see my texts as literary and cultural constructs; to avoid reading them as indexical; and to navigate between the Scylla and Charybdis of essentialism and reductive determinism.

PRE-TEXTS, LISTS, MAPS

It is still only recently that we have moved away from essentialist views of canon and canonicity, from signs taken for wonders in Franco Moretti's formulation, to think about how wonders—and traditions—are made.[13] What Bourdieu has called the "relatively autonomous" sphere of aesthetic production that emerged in the eighteenth century is driven by an economy, interacting with but irreducible to actual economic exchange: "Literature, art, and their respective producers do not exist independently of a complex institutional framework which authorizes, enables, empowers and legitimizes them."[14] The field of restricted cultural production (e.g., highbrow literature) is defined by agents and institutions competing for cultural authority; the symbolic value of cultural goods within a restricted field is inversely defined to material value. Thus, Bourdieu writes,

> In the most perfectly autonomous sector of the field of cultural production, where the only audience aimed at is other producers (as with Symbolist poetry), the economy of practices is based, as in a generalized game of "loser wins," on a systematic inversion of the fundamental principles of all ordinary economies: that of business (it excludes the pursuit of profit and does not guarantee any sort of correspondence between investments and monetary gains), that of power (it condemns honours and temporal greatness), and even that of institutionalized cultural authority (the absence of any academic training or consecration may be considered a virtue).[15]

The field of highbrow cultural production—the rules of the game—determines the possibilities for dissemination, canonization, in many ways all the stages of production itself.

The formalists were the first twentieth-century school to set aside impressionistic criticism and naive biographism in pursuit of studies of literature as a coherent system with internally consistent rules. As Moretti puts it, "Not surprisingly, Russian Formalism produced the most intelligent discussion of a literary exaptation ever written: 'How *Don Quixote* is Made,' by Viktor Shklovskij."[16] What pleases Moretti in Shklovsky's work is the insight that the noble Don's character must have originated from the novel's form. Once put into place by the structure of the growing text, the hero proved "useful in many other ways . . . and literary evolution could follow its course."[17]

The language used to describe literary apprenticeships, appropriations, and rebellions nearly inevitably involves metaphors of biological bloodlines and evolutionary or generational struggle.[18] Iurii Tynianov's first published work, "Dostoevsky and Gogol (Towards a Theory of Parody)" (1921), imagines a young Dostoevsky stylizing and producing variations on Gogolian fragments. In early works such as *Poor Folk* (1846), *The Double* (1846), and "The Landlady" (1847), it remained undecided what aspects of Gogol's work would prove fundamental to Dostoevsky's own practice, so he sampled different characteristics and techniques, piecing them together.

Stylization nearly unnoticeably turns to parody and to efforts to improve on Gogol, stylistically and ethically. In Dostoevsky's mature writing, "the subtle web of stylization-parody over a tragic and complex subject matter comprises Dostoevsky's distinctive grotesque."[19] Through symbolic struggle, Dostoevsky develops from a new or young Gogol into a singular adult literary identity.

Formalist criticism, however, tends to "defamiliarize the word and not world," to bracket off the referent as another artistic device: Shklovsky writes, "Art is a means of experiencing the artfulness of an object. The object itself is not important in art."[20] Bakhtin's corrective (for theory follows the same dialectic as the work it describes) in essence crosses the insights of the earlier school with Marxist theory. The 1928 essay "The Formal Method in Literary Scholarship" reintroduces the outside world without losing hold of art's artifice: "Every literary phenomenon . . . is determined simultaneously by external and internal factors; internally, by literature itself, and externally, by the other sphere of social life."[21] The Bakhtin circle thus moves beyond what Guillory calls formalism's "theoretical conclusion":

> The Formalists, much in advance of what came to be called "theory" in the 1960s, worked through certain hypotheses about the autonomy of the "linguistic system," and discovered at the end of this project that they were forced to affirm the inseparability of the linguistic from other aspects of the social . . . In this context the Bakhtinian response to Formalism makes available a strategic method . . . I refer to the Bakhtin circle's reformulation of the question of literary language as the question not of an *essentially* different kind of language (literariness) but of linguistic differentiation as a social fact.[22]

Bourdieu's sociology of literature, moving west and some decades ahead, in turn offers key concepts to parse the social facts of cultural differentiation. First and foremost, *cultural capital* is a "form of knowledge, an internalized code or a cognitive acquisition which equips the social agent with empathy towards, appreciation for or competence in deciphering cultural relations and cultural artifacts."[23] The terms "habitus," "strategy," and "trajectory" recognize the author as an agent without falling into reductive intentionality. Habitus describes the dispositions acquired through social context, schooling, and long exposure that become second nature, a feel for the game.[24] Strategy refers to orientation or practice, and is shaped relationally by the position of the agent in the cultural field; and trajectory suggests the changing positions and strategies of the same agent over time.[25] Bourdieu examines Gustave Flaubert and the French literary field: we might speak of Nabokov's mastery of modernist literary techniques and insistence on aesthetic autonomy; of the trajectory of his novelistic career and changing cultural status; and of his strategy, in the 1960s particularly, vis-à-vis an Anglo-American high modernist canon.

Guillory builds from Bourdieu to define literary canon formation as the "constitution and acquisition of cultural capital," linked specifically to the school syllabus as "the institutional form by means of which this knowledge is disseminated."[26] As a central case study, Guillory examines the New Critical revision of the university literary curriculum. T. S. Eliot used his authority as a literary figure to insist on an alternative tradition that, tautologically, had "a good deal to do with the legitimation of his poetic practice, with the emergence (somewhat belatedly in relation to the other arts) of a 'modernist' poetic."[27] Moreover, Guillory points out that "difficulty itself was positively valued . . . [as] a form of cultural capital, just by virtue of imparting to cultural objects a certain kind of *rarity*, the very difficulty of apprehending them."[28] This difficulty in turn demanded a particular mode of reading and exegesis that set the program for pedagogy, for the practice of the university classroom as for the syllabus.

> If the revisionist canon was the basis for a cultural jeremiad against modernity, a jeremiad in which the authority of literary culture was pitted against competing modern cultural authorities (whatever these may be), the programmatic attempt to demonstrate the continuity of every canonical English writer with the metaphysicals on the one hand, and the moderns on the other, was the strategic imperative of a more narrowly institutional campaign, a campaign for hegemony within the university.[29]

Pascale Casanova also follows in the footsteps of Bourdieu, but combines his understanding of cultural capital and its distributions with world systems theory, mapping out that distribution geographically according to centers and peripheries. She thus imagines a highly combative world republic of letters, where national canons compete for prestige and cultural capital. Casanova describes literary frontiers, "independent of political boundaries, dividing up a world that is secret and yet perceptible by all (especially its most dispossessed members); territories whose sole value and resource is literature . . . ; a world that has its own capital, its own provinces and borders, in which languages become instruments of power."[30] There have always been powerful centers of literary power with respective canons, and ideologies, to push.

Casanova's account of world literature is not without problematic oversights and assumptions: David Damrosch notes the "implicit triumphalism" in *The World Republic of Letters*, "which might be better titled *La République parisienne des lettres*."[31] And yet, with due correctives (for instance, Casanova takes little account of Russia and eastern Europe), the republic of letters proves a provocative and useful model for the cultural positioning of the Francophilic Pushkin and doubly Francophilic émigré Nabokov.

THE NOVEL, IMITATIVE DESIRE, AND THE RUSSIANS

"When a painter wants to become famous for his art, he tries to imitate the originals of the best masters he knows . . . In the same way Amadis was the pole, the star, the sun for brave and amorous knights, and we others who fight under the banner of love and chivalry should imitate him"; so opens René Girard's *Deceit, Desire, and the Novel* (1961), with an illustration of Don Quixote's imitative, or mimetic desire. Modeling his passions on chivalric literature, Quixote "surrendered to Amadis the individual's fundamental prerogative: he no longer chooses the objects of his own desire."[32] Girard's well-known study argues that, from its origins, the novel form has seen a marked preponderance of characters fashioning themselves openly after literary models. Girard concludes that novelistic insight has repeatedly unearthed a great psychological law, that all desire is fundamentally imitative. If earlier forms obfuscate the origins of desire, he writes, the greatest novels reveal its sources and hierarchy.[33]

If the novel as such betrays a particular affinity for imitative desire, the Russian novel was born with an extreme case. The political philosopher Marshall Berman, drawing from the literature of nineteenth-century St. Petersburg, has called this an early and powerful Russian modernism of underdevelopment, a peculiar self-conscious cast to the burgeoning literary tradition. In contrast to the modernization of rapidly advanced nations, he sees an emergent culture based on echoes and reflections, preserving itself "only through vast reserves of self-irony."[34] Like Casanova's model of competitive cultural centers and outsiders searching for ways to steal culture and to break in, Berman's view suggests that a sense of cultural belatedness, expressed through imitative and parodic characters, might lead to more innovative literary solutions.

Paradoxically, the marginality of St. Petersburg proves a cultural asset. The literature of a city itself imitative of European metropolises reflects alienation and acute historical self-awareness before these became dominant literary trends in Europe. By no coincidence, many of our terms and tools for the study of intertextuality emerge from studies of the literature of St. Petersburg: Tynianov's theory of parody and literary evolution stems from Dostoevsky's debt to Gogol, while Julia Kristeva's concept of intertextuality evolves from work on Bakhtin, who also looked to *The Double* as the fountainhead for Dostoevskian polyphony.

Yet Pushkin offers an even earlier prototype of a national poet characterized by "accelerated creative diversity and protean potential, full of promise for a Russian literature intent on catching up with centuries of European culture," as Monika Greenleaf summarizes.[35] What is by now a commonplace of Slavic studies—the notion that Russian literature is unusually and characteristically synthetic—owes a great deal to Pushkin's *Onegin* and its influential readers. *Evgenii Onegin* is a complex meta-literary fable: untimely or belated characters pursue one another, but also the latest French and English fashions, in a text that both performs and portrays anxieties about Russia's cultural position vis-à-vis the capitals of the West.

The body of critical and imaginative works that in some way reflect Pushkin's synthetic seminalism is so vast as to be virtually impossible to summarize: not least, Dostoevsky's Christian/nationalist variant discovered in Pushkin "the specifically *Russian* artist's ability to impersonate and incorporate any European nationality," testifying in turn "to the millennial role of Russian culture itself."[36] In the twentieth century, Iurii Lotman's and Nabokov's imposing annotated commentaries take *Onegin* in very different directions, yet both see meta-literary struggles and appropriations as crucial to its construction. An interesting play with temporality emerges across readings of Pushkin's seminal novel in verse: Russian literature, by virtue of being belated in the eighteenth and nineteenth centuries, anticipates the preoccupations of modernism—thereby catching up to and overtaking European literary fashions in one brilliant chess move.

Lotman finds in *Onegin* a distancing effect from the literariness of the preceding tradition: by exposing literary behavior and literary expectations as artificial and naive, Pushkin's verse novel appears realistic by contrast.

> The complex interlacing form of "foreign" and the author's own discourse constitutes the most important characteristic [of the work]. . . . In order to evoke in the reader a sense of simplicity, of natural spoken language, of the lifelike spontaneity of the subject matter and the artlessness of the characters, it was necessary to create a significantly more complicated formal construction than anything seen in the literature of those years. The effect of *simplification* was accomplished at the price of a marked *complication* of the text's structure.[37]

Lotman thus acknowledges the art and technical ingenuity of Pushkin's achievement, while simultaneously accounting for the tendency in Russian criticism to experience Pushkin's characters as psychologically realistic, or as social archetypes. Nabokov's variation from the 1960s, in contrast, emphasizes the artifice. But the peculiar interest of Nabokov's *Onegin* derives from the fact that *his* Pushkin was intended for international audiences and therefore posited as a "first poet" of a transnational Franco-Anglo-Russian literary tradition.

FROM *ONEGIN* TO *ADA*

This book rests on Nabokov's *Onegin Commentary* and novel *Ada* as case studies for transnational canon formation in the second half of the twentieth century; to do so, it necessarily reflects back on Pushkin's *Onegin*. In chapter 1, I reread with twenty-first-century eyes the allegory of centers and peripheries of cultural capital that came to serve as the foundation stone of the Russian canon. While Onegin's Breguet watch keeps time, Pushkin's Russian verse teems with anxieties about belatedness: what is fashionable in the provinces is already dated in Moscow or St. Petersburg, and hopelessly behind an imagined London or Paris. Untimely characters pursue one another and the latest foreign fashions in a text that brings to life anxieties over cultural borrowing and Russia's position vis-à-vis the West. Meanwhile, meta-literary digressions circle around questions of timeliness in literature: where does Russian literary fashion stand compared with European standards and innovations? The text confesses fears of being unfashionably late on the scale of national culture, yet it simultaneously aims to end the delayed development by providing Russian letters with an original chef d'oeuvre: a verse novel that proved ahead of its time in Russia for nearly a century. I turn to twentieth- and twenty-first-century theorists to think through Pushkin's temporal metaphors for cultural marginalization.

In chapter 2, I read Nabokov's controversial hybrid *Onegin*, three-quarters provocation to one-quarter translation, as an autonomous text. Nabokov's *Onegin* focuses on the Russian poet and his European sources, reading Pushkin's novel as a masterpiece of appropriation and adaptation. Nabokov's lengthy notes painstakingly trace echoes, allusions, and precedents, especially in the works of Lord Byron and Francois-René de Chateaubriand, and evaluate by comparison. When does Pushkin engage in conventional or derivative native imitations, and when in original and subtle parody? I argue that Nabokov carefully studies Pushkin's methods of linguistic/literary synthesis and cultural acceleration, finding in Pushkin a model for how to make new out of old, advanced out of belated, and central out of marginal. The *Eugene Onegin* project suggests Pushkin's novel in verse, not only as the point of origin for the Russian novel, but as Russia's entry into a transnational canon to which Nabokov could be both critical gatekeeper and creative heir. In Nabokov's *Onegin*, we trace the outlines of Nabokov's canon.

Chapter 3 turns to *Ada*, Nabokov's most complex work of fiction, as a modern allegory about literary canons and their geographical distribution. If Russian literature came late to the European stage, Nabokov feared it had been prematurely blighted by the tragedies of the twentieth century. Mourning what he saw as Russia's brief stretch of international cultural relevance, Nabokov tries to translate and annex his beloved works to the New World. The mysterious planet Antiterra, which reads as an idiosyncratic and personal world republic of letters, transplants and interbreeds Nabokov's beloved literatures. In this new self-conscious allegory, cultural capital *is* capital, and a cosmopolitan intellectual aristocracy coincides with the financial and political elite. To create this Russo-Franco-Anglophone world of literature, *Ada* steals lines, characters, and *fabulae* from *Onegin* but also from works by Byron and Chateaubriand. The transnational canon that emerges rests on great English, French, and Russian triads; the pattern repeats with Dickens, Flaubert, and Tolstoy; and the most fraught iteration involves Joyce, Proust—and Nabokov himself.

Chapter 4 focuses on Nabokov's pursuit of his French and English modernist rivals. In *Ada*, Joyce and Proust serve as secret signs by which great readers recognize one another; as carriers of World Culture; but also as source material, since *Ada* attempts to subsume its rivals. Even in this new struggle, Pushkin remains the model for how to bring off cultural grand theft: in essence, Nabokov tries to do with Joyce and Proust what he claimed that Pushkin had achieved with Byron and Chateaubriand. *Ada*, which like *Onegin* pursues its project simultaneously on the level of plot and meta-literary reflection, is rife with tongue-in-cheek literary genealogies. Despite the triumphalist overtones, the incestuous lovers Ada and Van Veen, heirs to the greatest traditions in the world, die childless. Perhaps the modernist novel shares a similar fate—is *Ada* a dead end, Nabokov's *Finnegans Wake*?

Chapter 5 takes on *Ada* in view of its working title, *The Texture of Time*. The exploration of time in *Ada* is more sustained and complex than in any of Nabokov's other works: how to make sense of time, how to remember?[38] The novel finds the root of modernist temporal obsessions in the philosophy of Henri Bergson. Bergson's seminal notions on the perseverance of the past into the present, on the falsity of models for time based on metaphors of space, as well as his cult of subjective and artistic thought, were hugely influential on international modernisms—and perhaps more central to Nabokov than he cared to admit. Van Veen, a great scholar of Bergson, aspires to an eternal present through his great immoral love, but the one-way time of ordinary mortality persistently threatens to take over the narrative. The structure of the novel mimics Zeno's paradox, famously refuted by the French philosopher: part 2 is roughly half the size of part 1; part 3 only half as long; and so on. While Van and Ada aim for immortality and to die into their book, the one-way arrow (Ardis in Greek, the name of the Veens' lost paradise) of time speeds toward death, the final target.

I conclude well after *Ada*, and after the author. Nabokov left behind more than the pleasures of his prose: he attempted to shift the literary landscape. His constant provocations—in the *Lectures*, in interviews, and in *Strong Opinions*, and embedded in his literary texts—tried to change both how and whom we read. James Wood has suggested that Nabokov's literary style may have infected several subsequent generations of English-language writers; but I close with Nabokov as the transnational precursor to a new generation of (often marginalized, often overtly political) world writers.[39]

Pushkin's *Evgenii Onegin*: The Breguet Keeps Time

> How the Romans Enriched Their Language:
> Imitating the best Greek authors, transforming
> themselves into them, devouring them; and after
> having well digested them, converting them into
> blood and nourishment, taking for themselves,
> each according to his nature, and the argument
> he wished to choose, the best author of whom
> they observed diligently all the most rare and
> exquisite virtues, and these like shoots . . . they
> grafted and applied to their own tongue.
> —Joachim du Bellay, *The Defense and Illustration
> of the French Language*, 1549

> Pushkin never broke the skeleton of
> tradition—he merely rearranged its inner
> organs—with less showy but more vital results.
> —Vladimir Nabokov, letter to Edmund Wilson, 1942

THE PURSUIT MOTIF

Evgenii Onegin was written and published between 1825 and 1832, in separate chapters and fragments "detailing (and willfully ignoring) events in its characters' lives between the late eighteenth century and 1825 . . . and addressing the central literary and ideological issues of the time."[1] Pushkin called the separately published first chapter a "description of the social [*svetskaia*] life of a young man from Petersburg at the end of the year 1819."[2] The completed work contained enough tantalizing detail to allow Vissarion Belinsky to read it as an encyclopedia of Russian life.

Nabokov's famously idiosyncratic readings seize on the art and artifice of Pushkin's *Evgenii Onegin* instead. In an intriguing structural analysis of chapter 1, Nabokov identifies what he calls "The Pursuit" motif:

The series of nineteen stanzas from XVIII to XXVI may be termed The Pursuit. In XXVII Pushkin overtakes his fellow hero and reaches the lighted mansion first. Now Onegin drives up, but Pushkin is already inside . . . Pushkin, the conventional libertine (XXIX) and the inspired preterist (XXX–XXXIV, ending on the initial flippant note), takes over so thoroughly that the troublesome time element in the description of Onegin's night is juggled away (since he is not shown wenching and gaming, the reader has to assume that seven or eight hours were spent by Onegin at the ball) by means of a beautiful lyrical digression, and Pushkin, after lagging behind at the ball (as he had lagged in Onegin's dressing room before it), must again overtake Onegin in his drive home (XXXV)—only to fall behind again while the exhausted beau goes to sleep (XXXVI). The pursuit that Pushkin started upon in XVIII–XX, when, on the wings of a lyrical digression, he arrives at the opera house before Onegin (XXI–XXII), is now over.

If the reader has understood the mechanism of this pursuit he has grasped the basic structure of Chapter One. (2:108)

In this chapter, I use Nabokov's insight as a springboard, and attempt to widen the pursuit theme as a way of grasping Pushkin's *Onegin*: in my reading, it is literary traditions and styles that pursue one another throughout the novel in verse. I thus return to and focus on Pushkin's *Onegin*, but with an eye to contemporary discussions of cultural capital and competition between national literatures. I reread Pushkin's *Onegin* as a narrative and meta-literary exploration of the processes of cultural competition and canon formation. In this light, *Onegin* seems less a story of unhappy love than of centers and peripheries, of fashions literal and literary; a novel preoccupied with timing, clocks, pursuit—and of course, in meter.

Through highly semioticized behavior, dress, and reading material, the heroes and heroines of Pushkin's text race and pursue one another. In the process, they grow painfully aware that fashions are relative, perceiving their distance from the trendsetting centers and cosmopolitan capitals in temporal terms. Like James Joyce's culturally colonized Irishmen in *Ulysses*, Pushkin's heroes gaze at each other, or are in turn examined by the narrator, with the growing suspicion that they are the crooked copies of foreign originals.

Meanwhile *Onegin* echoes with (parodic?) warnings to do things at the appropriate time, advice that the text itself seems unable or unwilling to follow. The novel begins with a death and ends in medias res, praising the writer wise enough to know when to stop. Only in chapter 7 does the narrator finally remember to include: "Bless my long labor, / O you, Muse of the Epic . . . Enough! The load is off my shoulders! / To classicism I have paid my respects: / though late, but there's an introduction."[3] Meta-literary digressions question the timeliness and adequacy of the elegy versus the ode, or the short lyric versus the novel; mourn the dearth of an adequately expressive Russian lexicon; and even lodge complaints about the poet's changing reception in the culturally conservative Russia of the 1830s.

Does the motif of timeliness reflect an outsider's anxiety that Russian letters lagged behind the developments of European romanticism, and an innovator's scorn for common sense and convention? *Onegin* performs sleights of hand across space and time: English, French, and German literary traditions clash, contradict, and seduce one another on Pushkin's pages, miraculously resulting in a great work of Russian literature.

The Russian literary canon in turn came to rest on Pushkin and *Evgenii Onegin* to such an extent that the poet and his most famous work can stand in metonymically for Russian culture in its entirety (hence the recurring avant-garde cry to throw Pushkin off the steamship of modernity).[4] Tome after tome of *Onegin* exegesis concludes that Pushkin is doing something with the Western literatures that he imitates and engulfs; and that something is often linked with Russia's late arrival on the international literary scene. By rereading the text with a focus on fashion and timeliness, we can recontextualize those insights in a coherent and productive framework.

TIME FLOWS DIFFERENTLY IN THE PROVINCES

Nineteenth-century Russia was hardly singular in suffering over perceived cultural backwardness, and Pushkin's attempt to enliven a national literature through meta-literary synthesis hardly the first of its kind. We might remember, for example, Herder's eighteenth-century dictum for German self-fashioning: "If we do not become Greeks, we will remain barbarians."[5] Similarly, the impulse on both sides of the East/West culture wars raging in Russian letters was "to locate the present in relation to (sacred) origins, to reinvent a national genealogy" both authentically local and rooted in authoritative models. But we might also compare Pushkin's work to various projects that shaped Europe centuries before. Pushkin's Russian does just what Joachim du Bellay proposed for sixteenth-century French: it imitates, transforms, and devours foreign sources, "and after having well digested them, convert[s] them into blood and nourishment."[6]

Pascale Casanova's *The World Republic of Letters* offers a global perspective for such national concerns. Casanova spatializes Pierre Bourdieu's concept of cultural capital: by combining Bourdieu with the geographical thinking of world systems, she models the distribution of literary capital around the world.[7] The central hypothesis is that there exists a world republic of letters, divided by literary frontiers into territories whose sole value and resource is literature . . . a world that has its own capital, its own provinces and borders, in which languages become instruments of power. . . . Rival languages compete for dominance; revolutions are always at once literary and political. The history of these events can be fathomed only by recognizing the existence of a literary measure of time, of a "tempo" peculiar to literature; and by recognizing that this world has its own present—the literary Greenwich meridian.[8]

Dominant languages and literatures violently suppress or consume minor ones, and a chasm separates capitals from the provinces. Casanova suggests that in all periods of Western history, an über-capital such as Rome or Paris emerges as the center of the cultural world and establishes the "now" of fashion. Distance from the capital reads as distance in time or backwardness; the aesthetic distance of a work from the center reads as a "temporal remove from the canons that . . . define the literary present." On the contrary, a work is said to be "contemporary, that it is more or less current (as opposed to being out of date—temporal metaphors abound in the language of criticism), depending on its proximity to the criteria of modernity."[9]

While necessarily reductive, the expansive global model for canon formation and cultural rivalries remains very useful in the case of Russian (and émigré) literary experiences in the nineteenth and twentieth centuries. While granting the literary world a relative independence, Casanova politicizes what is too often depicted as "peaceful internationalism, a world of free and equal access in which literary recognition is available to all writers, an enchanted world that exists outside time and space and so escapes the mundane conflicts of human history."[10] (Franco Moretti, in the *Atlas of the European Novel 1800–1900*, similarly argues that "geography is not an inert container . . . but an active force, that pervades the literary field and shapes it in depth.")[11]

Casanova draws particular attention to the agonizing decision that writers from culturally colonized spaces are often called on to make: to assimilate to a foreign ideal and perpetuate an oppressor culture's dominance, or to work as national writers with a limited local audience, languishing in the obscurity of their minor (forgotten, neglected, or newly reinvented) native tongue. The Algerian writer Mohammed Dib in "Thief of Fire" rawly describes the dilemma of such a cultural outsider:

> The poverty of the means granted to him is so impossible to imagine that it appears to defy all credibility. Language, culture, intellectual values, scales of moral values, none of these gifts that one receives in the cradle are of any possible use to him . . . What to do? The thief gets hold at once of other instruments, ones that have been forged neither for him nor for the ends that he means to pursue. What matters is that they are within his reach and that

he can bend them to suit his purposes. The language is not his language, the culture is not the heritage of his ancestors, these turns of thought, these intellectual, ethical categories are not current in his natural environment. How ambiguous are the weapons at his disposal![12]

Only the greatest writers escape their immediate context for a hard-won creative autonomy: "The modern work is condemned to become dated unless by achieving the status of a classic, it manages to free itself from the fluctuations of taste and critical opinion . . . by being declared timeless and immortal."[13]

Eastern Europe figures little in *The World Republic of Letters*: most of the territories discussed are either western European or former colonies.[14] For Casanova, the paradigmatic twentieth-century writers to escape the national/collaborator aporia are Joyce and Beckett.[15] Unwilling to remain in Dublin or to out-English the English in London, Joyce and Beckett both found refuge in the international capital of Paris. Beckett famously chose to write in French or to self-translate into English, seeking a language that felt non-native, while Joyce found an English idiom that was his alone. However, as I will argue in this and subsequent chapters, the longing for autonomy and timeless status marks nineteenth- and twentieth-century Russian culture's conscious negotiations and competition with western European centrality. In strikingly similar terms, the Francophile Pushkin, and Nabokov a century later, prove archetypal members of the intellectual International.[16]

Marshall Berman looks specifically to Russian literature to suggest another model for cultural appropriation. He draws from Pushkin, Gogol, Dostoevsky, and others to find in nineteenth-century St. Petersburg a prescient "modernism that arises from backwardness and underdevelopment":

This modernism first arose in Russia, most dramatically in St. Petersburg, in the nineteenth century; in our own era, with the spread of modernization—but generally, as in old Russia, a truncated and warped modernization—it has spread throughout the Third World. The modernism of underdevelopment is forced to build on fantasies and dreams of modernity, to nourish itself on an intimacy and a struggle with mirages and ghosts. . . . It turns in on itself and tortures itself for its inability to singlehandedly make history—or else throws itself into extravagant attempts to take on itself the whole burden of history. It whips itself into frenzies of self-loathing, and preserves itself only through vast reserves of self-irony. But the bizarre reality from which this modernism grows, and the unbearable pressures under which it moves and lives—social and political pressures as well as spiritual ones—infuse it with a desperate incandescence that Western modernism, so much more at home in the world, can rarely hope to match.[17]

19

Berman emphasizes the self-ironizing imitation arising from political and cultural backwardness, and from the paradox or double marginalization of the Russian writer. However, if Casanova's thief of fire only rarely escapes his circumstances and breaks into a state of autonomy, Berman argues that the unbearable pressures of belatedness may in fact lead to better literature. He considers Russian literature the paradigmatic modernism of underdevelopment, something of an unofficial movement to spread from St. Petersburg through much of the Third World in the course of the next century.[18]

Taken together, Casanova and Berman offer politically charged models for mapping literary patterns, and draw our attention to the anxieties and paradoxical opportunities available to the local writer working from a position of cultural and economic belatedness. It is the potentially marginalized members of the world republic of letters who are most aware of the "literary Greenwich meridian" and of their own fraught relationship with literary fashion: to avoid being provincial and backward, they must become cosmopolitan and timeless.

"BLEST WHO WAS YOUTHFUL IN HIS YOUTH"

On the narrative level alone, that is to say, on the level of romantic *fabula*, Pushkin's *Onegin* reads as a veritable parable about the untimely man. The eponymous hero seems to do everything at the wrong time, affecting blasé cynicism in his youth and falling in love too late. The poem's narrative digressions and didactic asides reinforce the building anxiety over belatedness and poor timing, as we shall see. The most striking and memorable stanza on the topic of timeliness occurs late in the novel:

> Блажен, кто с молоду был молод,
> Блажен, кто во-время созрел,
> Кто постепенно жизни холод
> С летами вытерпеть умел;
> Кто странным снам не предавался,
> Кто черни светской не чуждался,
> Кто в двадцать лет был франт иль хват,
> А в тридцать выгодно женат;
> Кто в пятьдесят освободился
> От частных и других долгов,
> Кто славы, денег и чинов
> Спокойно в очередь добился,
> О ком твердили целый век:
> N. N. прекрасный человек.

> Blest who was youthful in his youth;
> blest who matured at the right time;
> who gradually the chill of life
> with years was able to withstand;
> who never was addicted to strange dreams;
> who did not shun the fashionable rabble;
> who was at twenty fop or blade,
> and then at thirty, profitably married;
> who rid himself at fifty
> of private and of other debts;
> who fame, money, and rank
> In due course calmly gained;
> about whom lifelong one kept saying:
> N.N. is an excellent man. (8:X)[19]

Here are the practical man's beatitudes, parodying the Gospel of St. Mark: blessed are the reasonable and the conformists, for theirs is the kingdom here and now on earth. The stanza's repetitions and list structure enhance the commonsensical authority of the content. Internal sound echoes hint at an innate reasonableness to such logic; round dates punctuate a philosophy of civilized normality; and the second line's "matured" (*sozrel*) links the timely human life to natural rhythms. Characters are likened to flora throughout this novel in verse, and nearly always in the context of portraying timeliness: Onegin is prematurely withered; Lensky is blighted on the vine; whereas Tatiana ripens when her time comes.

The list offered in the "Blest who" stanza thus offer a natural timeline and a template for the timely life. However, there is noticeably no room for childhood in this scheme. We meet Pushkin's characters only at a marriageable age and as budding participants in society. The reader is tricked into sharing the point of view of the provincial matchmakers who see in any new bachelor an opportunity: "Wealthy, good-looking, Lenski / was as a suitor everywhere received: / such is the country custom" (2:XII).[20] The lines are reminiscent of Jane Austen's equally tongue-in-cheek opening to *Pride and Prejudice*: "It is a truth universally acknowledged, that a single man in possession of a good fortune must be in want of a wife."[21]

On the surface, at least, Pushkin's stanza suggests that the accoutrements of age are to be acquired sequentially: fashionable society, wife, money, status. Life is a straight line, a clear and comprehensible trajectory, and time can be measured and broken into controlled intervals. The repeated sounds *"Blazhen, kto," "kto," "o kom,"* are reassuringly liturgical, and the rhymes are simple: nouns mainly rhyme with nouns, verbs with verbs of the same masculine past tense ending, one genitive plural with another. The final *rime riche* (*vek/chelovek*) or compound rhyme (*tselyi vek/chelovek*) ends the stanza with the same suggestive logic: the duration of life and man himself are equivalent and mutually containing. The model life even stops short with summarizing definition, avoiding the less pleasant logical conclusion—a model death.

An earlier stanza in the novel, predicting what Lensky's life might have been like, were it not for the fatal duel, evokes a very different mood:

> А может быть и то: поэта
> Обыкновенный ждал удел.
> Прошли бы юношества лета:
> В нем пыл души бы охладел.
> Во многом он бы изменился,
> Расстался б с музами, женился,
> В деревне счастлив и рогат
> Носил бы стеганый халат;
> Узнал бы жизнь на самом деле,
> Подагру б в сорок лет имел,
> Пил, ел, скучал, толстел, хирел,
> И наконец в своей постеле
> Скончался б посреди детей,
> Плаксивых баб и лекарей.

> And then again: perhaps, the poet
> had a habitual lot awaiting him.
> The years of youth would have elapsed:
> the fervor of the soul cooled down in him.
> He would have changed in many ways,
> have parted with the Muses, married,
> up in the country, happy and cornute,
> have worn a quilted dressing gown;
> learned life in its reality,
> at forty, had the gout,
> drunk, eaten, moped, got fat, decayed,
> and in his bed, at last,
> died in the midst of children,
> weepy females, and medicos. (6:XXXIX)

Again we find life presented as a list, but this time dull enough to make us envy Lensky his early exit. This stanza complements and completes the "Blest who" verses in a sense, filling in what happens at forty (gout), and after a successfully normal life.

Yet the moral of the novel, if such a thing exists, or at least the way that *Onegin* is most often read, condemns the hero's failure to conform to such lists. Onegin is not "youthful in his youth," despite his outward appearance: in imagery, he is prematurely withered, a blighted bud. Initially this artificiality seems dashingly demonic and original, but the last chapter sums him up mercilessly:

> Онегин (вновь займуся им),
> Убив на поединке друга,
> Дожив без цели, без трудов
> До двадцати шести годов,
> Томясь в бездействии досуга
> Без службы, без жены, без дел,
> Ничем заняться не умел.

> Onegin (let me take him up again),
> having in single combat killed his friend,
> having lived without a goal, without exertions,
> to the age of twenty-six,
> oppressed by the inertia of leisure,
> without employment, wife, or business,
> could think of nothing to take up. (8:XII)

Onegin has merely survived (*dozhiv* rhymes and pairs visually and grammatically with the *ubiv* of the previous line) until the age of twenty-six. His life is already a list of missed opportunities and of all he has failed to accomplish. The narrator thus seems to project the vector of a socialized, teleological life span and then to judge the characters according to that pattern. Onegin was neither youthful when young, nor has he ripened with age. He has failed to acquire the signs and symbols that demonstrate progress in life, such as service, spouse, and rank. Worse yet, his ennui is no longer in fashion.

But are we taking *Onegin* dangerously literally? Pushkin's novel in verse, in Lotman's words, "does not only mean what it 'means,' but something else as well."[22] Greenleaf suggests that it is precisely in such didactic moments as the above stanzas that the text evades our attempts to attribute the represented worldview:

[The] well-nigh proverbial lines represent not mature wisdom, but the ironically "mentioned" common sense of the "collective". . . . Unexpectedly, the process of maturation . . . is itself ironized as an attribute of the crowd into which "we" as readers have been integrated.[23]

There is no consistent dialectical development, not even to an ironic and mature viewpoint: "Demystified clear-sightedness, which would seem to be the logical end of an ironic 'sentimental education,' is actually the starting point, which in retrospect will turn out to have been a form of blindness."[24] The additional twist is that the demystified viewpoint and the sentimental education are themselves borrowed western European topoi that already seem dated by the end of the novel.

Most of the satisfying readings of *Onegin* find its governing principle to be meta-literary maturation—that it is a story about how we tell stories, trying on more or less successful genres and styles. Jan Meijer argues that *Onegin* outgrows lyric poetry, leaving behind the eponymous hero and allowing Pushkin alone to go forward.[25] I try to tease out the interplay between narrative and meta-literary levels in the following sections. Certainly the characters read, write, and misread each other's "texts," allowing for a subtle play with the conventions of literature and interpretation. In Lotman's words, "the heroes themselves are drawn into the same literary world as the readers. Their self-interpretations and their grasp of the essence of events are often predicated by various literary clichés."[26]

Todd elaborates that the "characters, like the poet, must reckon with their audience and reach that audience through, and only through, the conventions of their culture."[27] Todd's most appealing contribution is to read the novel as Tatiana's bildungsroman, with the heroine as the author's closest stand-in, a Pushkin-in-skirts:

> The final step in Tatiana's cultural maturation occurs when she becomes the hostess of a Petersburg salon and, as a "legislatrix" (8:28) and "goddess" (8:27), imposes what her age considered an aesthetic order upon reality. . . . This achievement [is] almost equal in its emotional range to the novel as a whole . . . The author-narrator underscores the parallels between her creation and his.[28]

Tatiana takes the "less than inspiring materials of her social situation and [shapes] them in brilliant fashion" into a recognizably European cultural product.[29] In this reading, Tatiana is the timely woman to Onegin's untimely man: unlike Onegin but like their author, she catches up to fashion, overtakes it, and even sets it.

Coming back to the leitmotif of life as a list, we can turn to the novel's final stanza:

> Блажен, кто праздник жизни рано
> Оставил, не допив до дна
> Бокала полного вина,
> Кто не дочел ее романа

И вдруг умел расстаться с ним,
Как я с Онегиным моим.

Blest who life's banquet early
left, having not drained to the bottom
the goblet full of wine;
who did not read life's novel to the end
and all at once could part with it
as I with my Onegin. (8:LI)

Why cut off there, prematurely, without giving us the expected end of the teleological trajectory of such a novel—Onegin's marriage or death? We end with "my Onegin," but the hero, heroine, author, and reader are all left in limbo: it remains fundamentally unclear whether the story, or even the text itself, is finished.[30] Untimely Onegin even fails to find his proper ending: just as he grew cynical too early and fell in love too late, now he parts ways with his author before the end of the narrative.

The "Blest who" structure of these final lines echoes the earlier recipe for timeliness, now openly parodic and inverted so as to implicate the reader. For the author, knowing when to stop and ending early is even better than being on time, for he scorns his own lists, surprises his audience, and proves ahead of fashion. Dropping life's novel or leaving life's banquet early sound grimly like metaphors for dying young, yet by refusing plot closure, Pushkin leaves open the possibility of continuing his story and thus defers another kind of death. Onegin lingers on, unchanging, unfinished, as if vampirically undead. Paradoxically, Onegin's failure to do things at the right time provides Russian literature with a productively open-ended fairy tale, a model for an ambiguous relationship with time, fashion, and the authority of cultural centers.

PROVINCIAL MISSES, DANDIES, AND TRENDSETTERS

Another word for "timely" is "fashionable." Pushkin's heroes run into trouble when they act out of time, affecting ennui too young and loving too late, but their poor timing is even more evident when the characters fail to master the vicissitudes of fashion—a kind of applied timeliness. In *Onegin*, the "shaping force of history manifests itself in the characters' lives not in the guise of a rapacious Cossack horde . . . but as change in cultural possibilities and, most importantly, as 'fashion.'"[31] Pushkin's characters read, interpret, and evaluate one another as provincial, affected, or stylish according to the prevailing tastes that they follow; there is a distinct and unforgiving Greenwich meridian in fashion. At this moment, as some but not all of Pushkin's heroes realize, to be a member of Russian high society means to dress "according to the latest London fashion, speak and write French, dance the Polish mazurka, and bow with cosmopolitan grace."[32]

What makes Pushkin's text so fascinatingly ambiguous and polyphonic, to borrow from Bakhtin's writings on Dostoevsky, is the refusal to espouse fully any of the represented styles and ideologies. Some are privileged over others: the timely local life, a "humdrum country idyll," is not only boring but virtually unnarratable—happy families are all alike, but every unhappy family is unhappy in its own way. Pushkin's heroes are violently liberated from provincial rhythms through an encounter with foreign customs, but then these too are quickly spent and discarded.

From the perspective of the provinces and country customs, the timeliest character of all is Olga. Perfectly natural, Olga "bloomed like a hidden lily of the valley / which is unknown in the dense grass / either to butterflies or bee" (2:XXI).[33] To the point of banality, she is exactly what a country maiden should be: "Always as merry as the morn" (2:XXIII).[34]

But Onegin, the narrator, and the reader have long moved on from this ideal:

> . . . но любой роман
> Возьмите и найдете верно
> Ее портрет: он очень мил,
> Я прежде сам его любил,
> Но надоел он мне безмерно.

> . . . but any novel
> take, and you'll surely find
> her portrait; it is very winsome;
> I liked it once myself,
> but it has palled me beyond measure. (2:XXIII)

Onegin later rankles Lensky with the observation, "In Olga's features there's no life, / just as in a Vandyke Madonna" (3:V).[35] The fresh and natural younger Larina is too familiar a type, the clichéd beauty of a certain kind of novel or painting. The Russian country maiden is but a representation, the dated copy of well-known foreign originals.

Olga hardly needs warnings to be young in her youth: she plays with dolls and other children, and at marriageable age falls in love with her intended. Olga's timeliness, in fact, will not be delayed or swayed by particular attachments to individuals: "Poor Lensky! Pining away, / she did not weep for long" (7:X).[36] Since it was simply time for her to love, she replaces one groom with another, marrying soon after Lensky's death.

The pseudo-German romantic Lensky idealizes all that is natural and un-spoiled, and expresses his dismay over Olga's coquetry precisely in terms of her youth: "Scarce out of swaddling clothes— / and a coquette, a giddy child! / Already she is versed in guile, / already to be faithless has been taught" (5:XLV).[37] Lensky has his own conventional timeliness. Also consistently marked by the epithet "the young" or "the youthful Lensky," he is "in the full bloom of years" (2:VI),[38] and "from the world's cold depravity / not having yet had time to wither" (2:VII).[39] Despite a foreign education and the influence of his danger-ous older friend, no premature blight darkens Lensky's bloom. The affected melancholy of his verse remains purely literary; he hardly seeks a Svetlana (the sentimental heroine of Vasily Zhukovsky's 1813 ballad) in cheerful Olga.

But Lensky is already behind the times in his imitations of German verse. Attributing the rebuke to a stern critic, the narrator complains of ele-gists: "always the same thing / regretting 'the foregone, the past'; / enough! Sing about something else!" (4:XXXII.)[40] Yet Lensky has his charm, and even Onegin hesitates to cut short his youthful naiveté:

> И без меня пора придет;
> Пускай покамест он живет
> Да верит мира совершенству;
> Простим горячке юных лет
> И юный жар и юный бред.

> without me just as well that time will come;
> let him live in the meanwhile
> and believe in the world's perfection;
> let us forgive the fever of young years
> both its young glow and young delirium. (2:XV)

After all, Lensky is happy: "Blest hundredfold who is to faith devoted; / who, having curbed cold intellect, / in the heart's mollitude reposes," the narrator intones (4:LI).[41] Again we see the telltale formula "blest who" (*blazhen, kto*) linked with a warning about the well-timed life and the dangers of a cold and arrogant intellect in the next lines: "but pitiful is he who foresees all" (4:LI).[42]

The ability to see too far ahead suggests the bitter gift of prophecy in classical tragedy: divination haunts *Onegin* in parodic echoes of the thinking man's foresight. The over-aware hero and the narrator both, "enemies of Hymen, / perceive in home life nothing but / a series of wearisome images, / a novel in the genre of Lafontaine" (4:L).[43] This is the life for which Lensky was intended, a boring novel à la Lafontaine.[44] Poor Lensky was born to live and die in poetry or prose: whether his story ends in a wedding and funeral is less relevant, for both end the possibility for a continued narrative.

Lensky duels in the name of youth itself, lest "a flower two morns old / wither while yet half blown" (6:XVII).[45] Such is the clichéd language of his verse, but death comes to the poet as that same premature blight: "The youthful bard / has met with an untimely end! / The storm has blown; the beauteous bloom / has withered at sunrise" (6:XXXI).[46] Unexpectedly however, Lensky's language becomes suddenly appropriate as the plot shifts to accommodate and legitimize the elegiac style. This is only the first of many twists and transformations in *Onegin* that problematize the evaluation of good taste.

Olga and Lensky are straw figures, foils for the more complicated heroine and hero. Like Onegin in the first chapter, Tatiana is introduced through negation and contrast: if country girls are golden and rosy, Tatiana is their photographic negative. "Neither with her sister's beauty / nor with the latter's rosy freshness" is she blessed; "She was not apt to snuggle up"; and "wished not to play and skip" (2:XXV).[47] The list of negations and expectations that Tatiana fails to fulfill continues for stanzas. Even after her transformation into an ideal St. Petersburg beauty, Tatiana remains characterized by the qualities she lacks, but now she is sans any affectation or vulgarity.[48]

As a girl Tatiana avoids Olga and her companions, and shows no inclinations toward sewing, embroidery, or dolls.[49] For all the subsequent life of Pushkin's Tatiana as a model of Russian womanhood, the character never has children: there is something sterile—even blighted—in the kind of adulthood she eventually achieves.[50]

Romantic novels are to blame for the heroine's dangerous ideas: "She early had been fond of novels; / for her they replaced all" (2:XXIX).[51] Her father did nothing to prevent her passion, seeing little harm in books, since "he, never reading, / deemed them an empty toy" (2:XXIX).[52] The good reader knows better: it was a book that led Paolo and Francesca into Dante's *Inferno*, and the seduction topos spread quickly from there. It is no surprise then that Tatiana reads a "delicious novel" with such attention, and "with what vivid enchantment / drinks the seductive fiction!" (3:IX).[53] As René Girard reminds us, dangerous novels are akin to Tristan and Isolde's love potion, preparing the way for emotions as fatal. And so it is with Tatiana: "Long since had her imagination, / consumed with mollitude and yearning, / craved for the fatal food" (3:VII).[54]

Tatiana follows her literary models to make the inappropriate and untimely move of declaring love to a man she has met only once. It is true that young Tatiana merely falls in love when her time comes, and in that sense behaves as naturally as Olga; but fashion—and Onegin—do not condone her actions.[55] Only the narrator defends his heroine by stressing her natural, childish inexperience: "Tatiana in dead earnest loves / and unconditionally yields / to love like a dear child" (3:XXV).[56] Her subsequent sentimental education takes place in Onegin's castle, where she raids the dandy's bookshelves and grows in leaps and bounds: "To reading fell / Tatiana with an avid soul; / and a different world revealed itself to her" (7:XXI).[57] The provincial miss learns to read the reader, parsing Onegin's nail-marks and marginalia until she understands the hero better than he understands himself:

> Что ж он? Ужели подражанье,
> Ничтожный призрак, иль еще
> Москвич в Гарольдовом плаще,
> Чужих причуд истолкованье,
> Слов модных полный лексикон?..
> Уж не пародия ли он?

> Who's he then? Can it be—an imitation,
> an insignificant phantasm, or else
> a Muscovite in Harold's mantle,
> a glossary of other people's megrims,
> a complete lexicon of words in vogue? . . .
> Might he not be, in fact, a parody? (7:XXIV)

Catching up on her reading, Tatiana grasps that her misread beloved has modeled himself after Byron rather than Richardson—but that he is no more original for it.

Increasingly timely in literature, as once in youthful love, Tatiana is no longer the misplaced duckling of the early chapters by the time that she arrives in the city and is evaluated by "Moscow's young graces." The cosmopolitan charmers find her a bit provincial and pale, but "on the whole not bad at all" (7:XLVI).[58] In the final chapter and before her next meeting with Onegin, Tatiana metamorphoses fully into a St. Petersburg swan. She remains a list of negations, but how different the sense:

> Она была нетороплива,
> Не холодна, не говорлива,
> Без взора наглого для всех,
> Без притязаний на успех,
> Без этих маленьких ужимок,
> Без подражательных затей . . .
> Все тихо, просто было в ней,
> Она казалась верный снимок
> *Du comme il faut* . . . (Шишков, прости:
> Не знаю, как перевести.)

29

> She was unhurried,
> not cold, not talkative,
> without a flouting gaze for everyone,
> without pretensions to success,
> without those little mannerisms,
> without imitational devices . . .
> All about her was quiet, simple.
> She seemed a faithful reproduction
> *du comme il faut* . . . (Shishkov, forgive me:
> I do not know how to translate it.) (8:XIV)

The next stanza continues to praise her divine lack of flaw:

> Никто б не мог ее прекрасной
> Назвать; но с головы до ног
> Никто бы в ней найти не мог
> Того, что модой самовластной
> В высоком лондонском кругу
> Зовется *vulgar*. (Не могу . . .

> Люблю я очень это слово,
> Но не могу перевести;

> None could a beauty
> have called her; but from head to foot
> none could have found in her
> what by the autocratic fashion
> in the high London circle
> is called "vulgar" (I can't—

> much do I like that word,
> But can't translate it. (8:XV–XVI)

Olga Vainshtein writes that "the good taste, 'comme il faut,' commanded by Pushkin's heroine imparts a surprising paradox: by adhering completely to worldly convention, a person seems maximally natural. This is the truest sign of the absence of vulgarity."[59] In these few years, Tatiana has mastered the faithful reproduction of the manners in the height of fashion. Coming full circle, she now appears original and real, the highest compliment that can be paid to urban artifice.

Tatiana and Onegin are capable of far subtler play with literary patterns than are the other characters: the hero and heroine choose what fashion to follow, drawing on their models with some awareness. As a result they are more interesting and volatile than those who progress peacefully through life stages—and hence make suitable subjects for a romantic novel. Initially guided by the belated trends that reach the countryside, Tatiana speeds up her development and moves ever closer to the cultural centers: in the end, the sophisticated salon hostess is in a position to define fashion in the Russian capital.

In Tatiana's last encounter with Onegin, she criticizes her former beloved for being so terribly late: "But *now*! . . . / How, with your heart and mind, / be the slave of a trivial feeling?" (8:XLV).[60] For if Tatiana moves from risky untimeliness to learn the full importance of appropriate action, Onegin makes the reverse journey.[61] Born and raised in a stanza and a half, Onegin in essence begins as a St. Petersburg dandy, defined exclusively by the fashions of his time and set. A confident player in *le monde*, he negotiates five or more social events in an evening with the help of his trusty Breguet. The ticking foreign watch serves as his guide.[62]

On the surface all is highly directed motion in such a world and life: Onegin "like an arrow, / has flown up the marble stairs" (1:XXVIII) to some ball or other.[63] Yet nothing happens at all. The narrator, who shares Onegin's early excesses, summarizes: "He will awake past midday, and again / till morn his life will be prepared, / monotonous and motley" (1:XXXVI).[64] "Like a London *Dandy*" (1:IV) and like many a Byronic hero before him, Onegin burns out prematurely.[65] An unnatural and premature spleen besets him: "feelings early cooled in him"; "toward life he became quite cold" (1:XXXVII–XXXVIII).[66] The hero and lyric persona nurse their regrets side by side on the banks of the Neva, but the plot only begins with Onegin's move to the country—for what interests Pushkin is the clash of sensibilities that ensues:

> Eugene begins, like the others, by shaping his life along a literary pattern: that of the dandy—cold, scornful, amorally destructive. . . . His life is, on the social plane, analogous to a work of art understood as an end in itself, an object of aesthetic contemplation. . . . [but] Eugene's Byronic redaction of dandyism, which makes his life an aesthetic object, finds an audience in the country which is unprepared to appreciate it or even to accept it.[67]

By the time Onegin meets Tatiana, much like the lyric persona, he thinks of his youth as over: "this was the way he killed eight years, / having lost life's best bloom" (4:IX).[68] Predicting years of suffering after a moment of happiness as their future, he explains it to Tatiana, again in temporal terms: "For dreams and years there's no return; / I shall not renovate my soul" (4:XVI).[69] Instead, Tatiana should follow the country customs and bloom with the seasons:

Chapter One

Сменит не раз младая дева
Мечтами легкие мечты;
Так деревцо свои листы
Меняет с каждою весною.
Так видно небом суждено.
Полюбите вы снова: но . . .

A youthful maid more than once will exchange
for dreams light dreams;
a sapling thus its leaves
changes with every spring.
By heaven thus 'tis evidently destined.
Again you will love . . . (4:XVI)

The chiasmic reversal of desire and fortunes that takes place between Tatiana and Onegin in the final chapter has been commented on innumerable times, but suffice to say that the restraint of one is motivated and genuine by the logic of the novel, whereas the other's is *only* fashion. Tatiana's mature wisdom comes through experience and a series of events shared with the reader: the loss of love, Lensky's death, disillusionment, and compromise. Onegin is a sphinx with no mystery, as Tatiana learned from his library, an imitation tilting into unintended parody. His Byronic pose is now behind the times.

If Onegin read Tatiana as a provincial miss, unfashionable in her sincerity, now he finds that his dandyism has gone out of style. Too late, he attempts to mimic her earlier manner, writing letters and longing for love: "Spring quickens him: for the first time . . ." (8:XXXIX).[70] But time, fashion, and Tatiana have moved on. The narrator responds with another didactic stanza, the sequel to the "Blest who" verses. Now we see what happens to the untimely man:

Любви все возрасты покорны;
Но юным, девственным сердцам
Ее порывы благотворны,
Как бури вешние полям:
В дожде страстей они свежеют,
И обновляются, и зреют—
И жизнь могущая дает
И пышный цвет и сладкий плод.
Но в возраст поздний и бесплодный,
На повороте наших лет,
Печален страсти мертвой след:

Так бури осени холодной
В болото обращают луг
И обнажают лес вокруг.

All ages are to love submissive;
but to young virgin hearts
its impulses are beneficial
as are spring rains to fields.
They freshen in the rain of passions,
and renovate themselves, and ripen,
and vigorous life gives
both lush bloom and sweet fruit.
But at a late and barren age,
at the turn of our years,
sad is the trace of a dead passion . . .
Thus storms of the cold autumn
into a march transform the meadow
and strip the woods around. (8:XXIX)

Thus is Onegin tried and condemned as hopelessly behind. Tatiana belittles his passion; then even the author and readers abandon Onegin.

The Muse and the Narrator remain not-quite-characters, but mysterious doubles or even triple-shadows to Tatiana and Onegin, providing a link between the world of the novel and the meta-literary concerns to which I turn next. The divine Muse breathes fresh air into a work so concerned with irreversible consequences. Her story opens chapter 8 in one of *Onegin*'s most charming digressions. Immortal and ever young, the Muse shifts shape according to changes in fashion and philosophy.

The narrator, a lyric persona who shares Pushkin's biography, seems to have suffered all of his characters' combined disappointments in the fashionable world.[71] He overtakes Onegin in every frivolity and dissipation; their friendship is born of shared disillusionment:

Я был озлоблен, он угрюм;
Страстей игру мы знали оба;
Томила жизнь обоих нас;
В обоих сердца жар угас;
Обоих ожидала злоба
Слепой Фортуны и людей
На самом утре наших дней.

> I was embittered, he was sullen;
> the play of passions we knew both;
> both, life oppressed;
> in both, the heart's glow had gone out;
> for both, there was in store the rancor
> of blind Fortuna and of men
> at the very morn of our days. (1:XLV)

The morally poisonous and empty *monde* has ruined both young men. But the crucial difference between the two is again one of fashion: Onegin's dated ennui pales before Pushkin's innovative and productive poetics. The author's only chance of escaping the eternal return of fashion is to set it, to somehow become timeless.

LITERARY PURSUITS

As Pushkin's characters pursue one another and the latest St. Petersburg, Paris, or London fashions, *Evgenii Onegin* itself enacts anxieties over literary fashion, changing tastes, and cultural borrowing. Plot and meta-literary untimeliness merge and infect one another: how is a writer to be recognizably modern, and yet to forge ahead and set the trends? The famously protean text mimics the abrupt reversals and peculiar dialectic of the world of fashion.

> The metaphor of the chameleon best expresses the culture of European dandyism in the nineteenth century. . . . The aesthetic side of dandyism above all presupposes good taste and a sophisticated responsiveness to everything beautiful, an ability to orient quickly and to discern fashionable trends. . . . [As Goncharov writes, the dandy] is given to eternal chameleonism; his taste is ever in motion; he plays the role of a clock hand, and all check their taste by him as if synchronizing watches to some single regulator, but all are slightly behind.[72]

Pushkin's polyphonic text leaps from one trend to another: while his characters are left ever behind, the tastemaker author changes shape following subtle currents discernible only to him.

Olga represents one quickly and long-abandoned old-fashioned literary ideal. Lensky, the straw poet, allows Pushkin to satirize sentimental lyric poetry and his own early apprenticeship to the Germanophile Zhukovsky. In passing, the lyric persona puts the professional critics in their place, seeming to float above their fray:

—Одни торжественные оды!
И, полно, друг; не все ль равно?
Припомни, что сказал сатирик!
. . .
«Но всё в элегии ничтожно;
Пустая цель ее жалка;
Меж тем цель оды высока
И благородна . . .» Тут бы можно
Поспорить нам, но я молчу:
Два века ссорить не хочу.

Nothing but solemn odes!
Oh, come, friend; what's the difference?
Recall what said the satirist!

"But in the elegy all is so null;
its empty aim is pitiful;
whilst the aim of the ode is lofty
and noble." Here I might
argue with you, but I keep still:
I do not want to set two ages by the ears. (4:XXXIII)

But of course he does precisely that throughout, setting the fashions of one epoch against another. Moving quickly through Tatiana's sentimental phase, Pushkin spends the bulk of the novel satirizing Onegin's demonic romantics: Byron, Chateaubriand, Constant, and others blend to form Onegin's affected spleen. The first is his especial target, for Byron is the fountainhead of all this fashionable cruelty: "Lord Byron, by an opportune caprice, / has draped in glum romanticism / even hopeless egotism" (3:XII).[73]

Having mastered and discarded so much, it is no wonder that the writer considers switching to prose as next in line for literary fashion:

Быть может, волею небес,
Я перестану быть поэтом,
В меня вселится новый бес,
И, Фебовы презрев угрозы,
Унижусь до смиренной прозы;
Тогда роман на старый лад
Займет веселый мой закат.

Perhaps, by heaven's will,
I'll cease to be a poet;

A new fiend will inhabit me;
and having scorned the threats of Phoebus,
I shall descend to humble prose:
a novel in the old mood then
will occupy my gay decline. (3:XII)

There are not only right and wrong times to love, but right and wrong eras
for genres and forms. Literary fashions come and go: is there an appropriate time in life for short lyrics, and a moment for a longer masterwork? Is
youth best suited for poetry, and the mature years for prose? The narrator
admits, "The years to austere prose incline; / the years chase rhyme, the
romp, away, / and I—with a sigh I confess— / more indolently dangle after
her" (6:XLIII).[74] But perhaps lost youth coincides with a lost cultural moment; the lyric sensibility itself has eroded. The narrator must move on to
more contemporary ambitions: "and soon, soon the storm's trace / will hush
completely in my soul: / *then* I shall start to write / a poem in twenty-five
cantos or so" (1:LIX).[75] As early as the first chapter, *Onegin* signals that it is a
meta-novel, about the difficult process of writing *Onegin*.

Pushkin's verse novel has been read as transitional, marking a progression from poetry to prose. Craig Cravens writes that by combining
verses with a long narrative form, "Pushkin exploits the capacity of lyric
poetry to express a state of mind and combines it with a fictionally created
character and world. . . . In short, by mixing the genres of lyric and novel,
Pushkin created an unprecedented type of psychological narration."[76] The
destroyed chapter 10 would have been the most prosaic and certainly the
most historical, but even as is *Onegin* suggests a stylistic and aesthetic authorial trajectory. The momentum picks up and the work grows increasingly plot-driven: most of the action takes place in the second half. The
first chapter is essentially all digression, but the sixth, seventh, and eighth
chapters are packed with narrative events: "Forward, forward, my story!"
(6:IV).[77]

Cravens bases his contrastive parallelism of timeless lyric and chronologically driven narrative prose on a dichotomy familiar from Roman Jakobson: "narrative foregrounds sequence and metonymy, and lyric foregrounds
simultaneity and metaphor."[78] However, *Onegin*'s painstakingly constructed
verse powerfully enacts the thematic concern with timeliness throughout.
What captures the progress of time better—and more relentlessly—than
regularly metered verse? Pushkin's iambic tetrameter pounds on, ever teleological: each line progresses toward its inevitable end, as does each tightly
structured Onegin stanza. Even the well-known "little feet" digression reads
as an index to meter. When the narrator exclaims, "Ah little feet, little feet!
Where are you now?" (1:XXXI),[79] he links little feet with metric feet, and

the lightly pounding meter with *le temps perdu*. If the narrative drive of any novel is based on the passage of time, the novel in verse might be read as an attempt to control and aestheticize that passage.[80]

Meijer reads *Onegin* as so transforming the "array of forms out of which it grew, and which it outgrows, that it cannot continue. It . . . can only lead beyond itself to something new. This is a developmental model in both *fabula* and form: in fact, the plot thematizes the same forward-moving development that the form displays."[81] Serial publication and the work-in-progress sensibility only encourage the reader to remain aware of the text's composition. We are left with a novel about the effects of time on literature, illustrating those temporal effects, and attempting simultaneously to outrace time and to stop it, interrupt it, or confuse it altogether. The paradox of fashion is that one must be timely to be stylish; one must be ahead of time to set the style; and to escape the whirl of fashion altogether one must become immortal. What better way to gesture toward immortality than to refuse an ending?

Pushkin's audience remained with him up to a certain point: however, "the hostile and bewildered reviews . . . of the final chapters of *Eugene Onegin* reveal a new impatience with 'fragmentariness,' an unwillingness on the part of the reader to grapple with a discontinuous, polymorphous structure, to make the effort to connect one semantically or stylistically disparate scene with another."[82] Pushkin was too far ahead of his time: he had lost his audience. At the end of the last chapter, among the other fruitless reading Onegin turned to in despair, we find:

> И альманахи, и журналы,
> Где поученья нам твердят,
> Где нынче так меня бранят,
> А где такие мадригалы
> Себе встречал я иногда:
> *E sempre bene*, господа.

> both "almanacs" and magazines
> where sermons into us are drummed,
> where I'm today abused so much
> but where *such* madrigals
> to me addressed I met with now and then:
> *e sempre bene*, gentlemen. (8:XXXV)

Even aspiring immortals hear the ticking of fashion's fancy watch, for tastes can always change.

Several years later, when Pushkin thought again of taking up *Onegin*, he wrote:

Итак, еще роман не кончен—это клад:
Вставляй в просторную, вместительную раму
Картины новые—открой нам диораму:
Привалит публика, платя тебе за вход—
(Что даст еще тебе и славу и доход).

So, the novel's still not finished—that's treasure:
Insert into the roomy, spacious frame
New pictures—show us a diorama:
The public will come, paying you for entrance
(Which will bring you more fame and income). [83]

Perhaps his novel could be expanded further still, like the modish diorama. The poet might learn from and incorporate still newer forms and media into his famous meta-story, for the only way to win back the public is to set the fashion once again.

The final untimely hero of *Onegin* is Russian literature itself, ever in ambivalent pursuit of English, French, and German traditions. Plot and metaliterary untimeliness interpenetrate in *Onegin*. The three principal readers—Lensky, Onegin, and Tatiana—enter the novel formed by their respective western European reading lists. Lensky is such an evident Germanophile that country neighbors consider him the "the half-Russian neighbor" (2:XII). He powerfully imagines himself to be the poet/hero of a romantic elegy and so dies senselessly in a duel with his closest friend.[84] Tatiana, fittingly the main reader of novels in *Onegin*, mimics various sentimentalist heroines from Samuel Richardson's Clarissa (in French translation) to Jean-Jacques Rousseau's Julie. Tatiana expresses herself in French and writes to Onegin in her native literary language. Onegin in turn fancies himself a Muscovite Childe Harold, keeps the economics of Adam Smith on his shelf, and dresses like a London dandy: Tatiana is the last to realize that he is a Byronic parody. If Lensky, Onegin, and Tatiana misread one another, it is because their borrowed literary fashions clash, and cannot but lead them astray on Russian soil.

Pushkin's lyric persona, like his characters, is forced to rely on foreign material whenever he finds the Russian language lacking. He is presumably well ahead of literary trends, but he nonetheless constantly and mockingly draws attention to his reliance on foreign languages and cultures. The novel begins with an epigraph from a French private letter and foreign words pepper the text, often at line ends, to draw even more attention as rhyme pairs with Russian (e.g., *"dysha/entrechat,"* 1:XVII). And of course there is Tatiana's enigmatic French letter, preserved only in the narrator's "incomplete, feeble translation / the pallid copy of a vivid picture" (3:XXXI).[85]

In chapter 1, the narrator issues a mock apology for his polylingualism:

> Но *панталоны, фрак, жилет,*
> Всех этих слов на русском нет;
> А вижу я, винюсь пред вами,
> Что уж и так мой бедный слог
> Пестреть гораздо б меньше мог
> Иноплеменными словами,
> Хоть и заглядывал я встарь
> В Академический словарь.

> But "pantaloons," "dress coat," "waistcoat"—
> in Russian all these words are not;
> whereas, I see (my guilt I lay before you)
> that my poor style already as it is
> might be much less variegated
> with outland words,
> though I did erstwhile dip
> into the Academic Dictionary. (1:XXVI)

Playful references to foreign words crop up accompanied by faux apologies to the conservative philologist A. S. Shishkov. These Cyrillicized terms for foreign apparel are in touch with the times in a way that the ponderous Academic Dictionary cannot be.[86]

Anything to do with fashion may force the narrator to resort to a foreign language. Thus Tatiana is "comme il faut," and not at all "vulgar." After using the latter term in English, Pushkin continues with a striking enjambment over the stanza break: "I can't— // —much do I like that word, / but can't translate it; / with us, for the time being, it is new" (8:XV–XVI).[87] He twice repeats his inability to translate the word and then rhymes "*slovo*" with "*novo*," highlighting the reliance of the former upon the latter. Words must be new; literature must be modern; Russian must have more of both. The writer/narrator of *Onegin* deliberately invents a new Russian style even as he complains about untranslatable foreign terms. By transliterating borrowed words into Cyrillic and rhyming others with Russian, he is in effect Russifying this transplanted language. Sometimes he translates with an explanatory phrase; sometimes the meaning is evident only in context; sometimes he culturally "translates" a type or context. More grandly, he introduces entire romantic archetypes, such as the Byronic antihero into Russian literature, transfigured as the Russian Onegin.

Pushkin's romantic novel breathtakingly creates new cultural possibilities through synthesis, parody, and innovation. Pushkin imports and appropriates western European models, but by wittily calling attention to the fact, and exploring the fears of being unfashionably late through plot, meta-literary digressions, and structure, he avoids coming across as derivative. Through the "vast reserves of self-irony" that Marshall Berman found to be characteristic of St. Petersburg's literary culture, Pushkin distances himself from and complicates his creations. At any given moment, it is one of his characters or some facet of Russian society that espouses a provincially imitative or affected style—the author himself remains one step ahead, and out of reach. In Pascale Casnova's terms, he declares himself a member of the intellectual International.

As a result, *Onegin* easily reads as less early romantic than presciently modernist. Pushkin's forced acceleration of Russian literature was astonishing and seemed premeditated: he wrote in an appended note to the text, "Our destiny, certainly a fortunate one in all regards, is characterized by a kind of extraordinary velocity: we mature not in the course of centuries, but in the course of decades."[88] His effort to overtake European trends resulted in a verse novel felt to be ahead of its time, and that would inspire Russian writers for the following two centuries.

Andrei Tarkovsky's 1975 classic film *Zerkalo* (*The Mirror*) includes a lengthy quotation from the famous unsent letter that Pushkin wrote to Pyotr Chaadaev in 1836. Chaadaev had decried Russia's tragic divide from and lag behind Europe in the first of his "Philosophical Letters." Although the original addressee never saw it, Pushkin's impassioned reply—that Russia had a unique, if as yet unclear destiny in world history—was to captivate the Russian imagination for centuries.

Here is the oft-quoted segment in the original French, the language to which both Pushkin and Chaadaev turned for philosophical discourse:

Il n'y a pas de doute que le schisme nous a séparé du reste de l'Europe et que nous n'avons pas participé à aucun des grands événements qui l'ont remuée; mais nous avons eu notre mission à nous. C'est la Russie, c'est son immense étendue qui a absorbé la conquête Mongole. Les tartares n'ont pas osé franchir nos frontières occidentales et nous laisser à dos. Ils se sont retirés vers leurs déserts, et la civilisation chrétienne a été sauvée. Pour cette fin, nous avons dû avoir une existence tout-à-fait à part, qui en nous laissant chrétiens, nous laissait cependant tout-à-fait étrangers au monde chrétien . . . Vous dites que la source où nous sommes allé puiser le christianisme était impure, que Byzance était méprisable et méprisée etc.—hé, mon ami! Jésus Christ lui-même n'était-il pas né juif et Jérusalem n'était-elle pas la fable des nations?

*l'évangile en est-il moins admirable? . . . Quant à notre nullité historique, dé-
cidément je ne puis être de votre avis . . . et (la main sur le coeur) ne trouvez-
vous pas quelque chose d'imposant dans la situation actuelle de la Russie,
quelque chose qui frappera le futur historien? Croyez vous qu'il nous mettra
hors l'Europe? Quoique personnellement attaché de coeur à l'Empereur, je
suis loin d'admirer tout ce que je vois autour de moi; comme homme de lettre,
je suis aigri; comme homme à préjugés, je suis froissé—mais je vous jure sur
mon honneur, que pour rien au monde je n'aurais voulu changer de patrie, ni
avoir d'autre histoire que celle de nos ancêtres, telle que Dieu nous l'a donnée.
(October 19, 1836)*[89]

Such a letter, with its admixture of national pain and pride, sheds a poignant
light on Pushkin's relationship to Russian language and belles lettres. He
writes in French, at the same time as he insists on Russian cultural singular-
ity, and predicts that the historian of the future will certainly include Russia
in the cultural map of Europe. All that is needed is a feat, "*quelque chose
qui frappera,*" something astonishing to reconfigure the world. Juxtaposed
with such a letter, Pushkin's translations, imitations, and variations on European literary themes readily suggest a strategy to accelerate Russian literary
time—that is to say, Russia's cultural pursuit of Europe.

PUSHKIN NASHE VSE

"Pushkin is our everything," asserted Apollon Grigoriev in 1859, coining a
well-nigh liturgical phrase. It would be the subject of another study (and has
been of several) to investigate Pushkin's eminent appropriability: the uses
to which Pushkin has been put are nearly innumerable.[90] We are familiar
with Pushkin the literary revolutionary of Belinsky's social criticism; Pushkin
the conservative populist of the Slavophiles; Pushkin the Western-leaning
aristocrat; Dostoevsky's universal Pushkin from the 1880 speech; the "My
Pushkins" of so many Russian modernists; the 1937 Pushkin signaling a neo-
classicist turn in Soviet art; the African Pushkin; and these are only a few of
his better-known incarnations. Countless Russian writers have paid obliga-
tory homage to Pushkin for the sake of their own literary credentials—even
those, as Tynianov has noted, that seemed to be writing in an entirely different key.[91]

How did Pushkin's novel, after a limited impact on its contemporaries
and even on the development of nineteenth-century Russian literature,
come to be accepted as the cornerstone of Russian culture in the twentieth
century and today?[92] Greenleaf situates the poet's cult in the larger context
of romantic canon-building projects:

Like Shakespeare, or for that matter Goethe, Dante, Mickiewicz, or any of the other "first poets" venerated by Romanticism, Pushkin had to be shown to be seminal, the origin without origin, pregnant with all the forms of his culture. Indeed in Dostoevsky's Christian/Russian variation on this model, not only is the artist's ability to transcend himself as a man reinterpreted as kenosis, but the specifically *Russian* artist's ability to impersonate and incorporate any European nationality testifies to the millennial role of Russian culture itself.[93]

The Russian first poet offers a variation on the romantic trend: Pushkin opens the fount of Russian letters by performing an alchemical transformation of his western European sources. As latecomers to the European cultural scene, Russian writers shared with the German romantics a "fascination with European fashions and an ironic talent for conflating or stepping outside of them."[94] The putative millennial role of Russian culture—the idea of Russia as an all-encompassing redeemer nation—owes a great deal to Pushkin's *Onegin* and to its powerful later readers.[95]

Pushkin in turn proved brilliantly suited to appropriation. A prime candidate for the origin of the Russian literary tradition, the conveniently ambiguous Pushkin could be interpreted to prefigure the desired current trend. His protean authorial persona evades readers from text to text and his oeuvre covers a broad range of genres and styles, leaving tantalizing gaps for heirs and an impression of the accelerated pursuit of literary innovations.[96] Lotman stresses the leap forward that *Evgenii Onegin* presented formally as "a phenomenon so innovative, that the literature of Pushkin's time, for the most part, was incapable of evaluating the scale of his artistic breakthrough."[97]

Subsequent generations not only recognized the achievement but selected facets of Pushkin's work to invent the Russian tradition that they needed. The modernists read Pushkin as one of their own, temporally misplaced and speaking to them over the heads of his contemporaries.[98] The poet-Pushkinists Valerii Briusov, Vladimir Khodasevich, Marina Tsvetaeva, Anna Akhmatova, and Osip Mandelstam all wrote beautiful essays in which they worked out the theories and praxes of their own poetics, projecting Pushkin

against the background of modern poetics and modern poetics against the background of Pushkin, as the combination of possessive adjective and proper name suggests. They testify to the compulsive, perhaps apocalyptic urge of Pushkin's readers to "finish speaking for Pushkin" [*dogovarivat' za Pushkina*], to fill the structural gaps, supplement the allusions and historical or literary context, and halt the semantic oscillation of his works.[99]

The great critics of the early twentieth century followed suit. Tynianov, his eye conditioned by new media as well as aesthetics, inverted value systems to find meaning in rupture and the "juxtaposition of heterogeneous elements." The terminology available to literary criticism began to borrow from that of cinema and montage: the romantic fragment, as a similar principle with a long history in verbal art, was suddenly central both to Pushkin's greatness and to future Russian poetics.[100]

My reading suggests that Pushkin's monument was always already about Russian literature's relationship to its imagined West. The threat of cultural marginalization, of cultural colonization and literary provincialism—a major concern of Russian literature throughout subsequent centuries—reaches an apotheosis and becomes a veritable obsession in the works of the émigré Nabokov, as subsequent chapters will show. Nabokov painstakingly studied Pushkin's work in order to wage his own cultural capital wars: in precisely the "Commentary" to his "transfiguration" of *Onegin*, to which I turn next, and in his own meta-literary monument, *Ada*.

Nabokov's *Eugene Onegin*:
The Chateaubyronic Genre

> Nowadays—an unheard of case!—the foremost
> French writer is translating Milton word for
> word and proclaiming that an interlinear
> translation would be the summit of his art, had
> such been possible.
> —Aleksandr Sergeyevich Pushkin on Chateaubri-
> and's *Le Paradis perdu*, 1836

> The pursuit of reminiscences may become a
> form of insanity on the scholiast's part, but
> there can be no doubt that, despite Pushkin's
> having by 1820–25 practically no English,
> his poetical genius managed somehow to
> distinguish in Pichot, roughly disguised as Lord
> Byron, through Pichot's platitudes and Pichot's
> paraphrases, not Pichot's falsetto but Byron's
> baritone.
> —Vladimir Nabokov, *Commentary to Eugene
> Onegin* (2:33), 1964

NABOKOV AND *ONEGIN*

The peculiar blend of humility and arrogance, of passionate scholarship
and creative ambition that is Nabokov's *Eugene Onegin* finds no equivalent
in twentieth-century literary history. Nabokov threw down a four-volume
gauntlet with his notorious annotated translation of Pushkin's novel in verse,
defending himself with Pushkin's own aphorism (prose, in pencil, scribbled
on a draft of chapter 8, upper-left corner): "Translators are the post horses of
enlightenment" (*Commentary to Eugene Onegin*, 3:229). The literary scan-
dal and feud that followed in the wake of Nabokov's translation have become
legendary.

Nabokov thought of translating *Onegin* as early as 1948, and suggested a joint "scholarly, copiously annotated prose translation" to Edmund Wilson. Nothing came of the endeavor, and by 1950 he informed Roman Jakobson that he was working on a translation alone. When a Guggenheim fellowship in 1952 allowed him to research full-time at Harvard and Cornell, he planned to finish in little over a year; instead he continued to work on the expanding, exploding commentaries until 1957, adding a final revision before the Bollingen Press released the work in 1964.[1]

Such formidable opponents as Wilson, Anthony Burgess, and Robert Lowell responded by going for the jugular. Wilson in particular denounced the "bald and awkward language that has nothing in common with Pushkin." Wilson's surprisingly personal attacks spoke of "the perversity of [Nabokov's] tricks to startle or stick pins in the reader" and of "his sado-masochistic Dostoevskian tendencies so acutely noted by Sartre—he seeks to torture both the reader and himself by flattening Pushkin and denying to his own powers the scope for their full play."[2] Wilson was certain that this *Onegin* was deliberate treason, for as he complained, "It had always seemed to me that Vladimir Nabokov was one of the Russian writers who, in technique, had the most in common with Pushkin."[3] The battle raged on, fueled by reviews, attacks, and counterattacks. Nabokov took months to edit and revise an even more aggressively literal translation, and in turn accused Lowell of "mutilating defenseless dead poets" and "doubly martyring" Mandelstam; Lowell and George Steiner responded and the feud continued for years.[4]

Steiner, whose pioneering 1975 *After Babel* argued that all of human communication can be considered translation and that literal translation between different systems of sense-making is a priori impossible, considered Nabokov's experiment a curio. Steiner writes that "literalism of this lucid, almost desperate kind, has within it a creative pathology of language . . . [the translator] produces an 'interlingua,' a centaur-idiom," neither English nor Russian. However, he adds in a footnote, "Taken together with the Commentary, Nabokov's production is a masterpiece of baroque wit and learning."[5]

Yet the *Commentary* is what so complicates the project. By adding three elaborately worded tomes to his awkwardly literal translation, Nabokov released his *Onegin* into the world as an aesthetic project and not just a practical tool after all—a very peculiar hybrid. In the time that it cost him and judging by his usual rate of production, Nabokov could have written three or four more novels. Why spend a decade on a project that threatened to dim an already considerable reputation with an unpleasant brand of notoriety?

Like Eliot, Nabokov fully believed that the literary past shapes and haunts the present. As a younger man Nabokov had spoken of his poetry "borrowing on the strength of the tradition." Long before he began work on *Onegin*, he stated that "Pushkin's blood" ran in his veins, as could be said of all Russian writers (Nabokov uses the metaphor of literary evolution frequently); with *Eugene Onegin*, therefore, he battles for the supremacy of his Russian literary bloodline. Furthermore, Nabokov clearly intended to wrest himself a space in the canon: he aimed quite openly for literary immortality.[6] This project was a key component of that struggle, one of the works for which he expected to be remembered.[7]

An agonistic struggle with the literary father, as in Harold Bloom's violent vision, only partially describes Nabokov's *Onegin*. Nabokov was more interested in championing Pushkin to Western audiences than in clandestinely demonstrating his own superiority.[8] Instead, to make a mischievous comparison, Nabokov's stakes in winning posthumous recognition for Pushkin resemble feminist revisionist projects: we might think of Virginia Woolf's passion on the subject of Jane Austen. Every pioneer needs a predecessor, a point of origin that speaks to the legitimacy of the current project: Nabokov is something of a Russianist revisionist. If to read Nabokov's 1964 *Eugene Onegin* is to read Pushkin not *with* Nabokov but *as* Nabokov, the commentaries allow unprecedented access to the latter's strategy regarding cultural capital and canon formation.[9] Now that the controversy of Nabokov's translation has faded, we can examine the annotated *Eugene Onegin* as a whole and with entirely different interests than its first critics.

What we find is that Nabokov's *Onegin* delivers a feint and jab against numerous and diverse rivals simultaneously. The *Onegin* translation grew out of Nabokov's pedagogical frustrations: by the end of the 1950s, Nabokov had made a tour of the American Ivies. As a professional Russianist at and around Wellesley, Harvard, and Cornell, he had practical experience and direct insight into what kind of Russian literature was reaching American readers, and in what form. He had endured a number of slights from Roman Jakobson and other Slavists. (Jakobson famously overturned Nabokov's nomination for a faculty position at Harvard University with the poisonous rhetorical question, "Gentlemen, even if one allows that he is an important writer, are we next to invite an elephant to be Professor of Zoology"?)[10] According to Brian Boyd, Nabokov was even convinced that Jakobson was a Soviet agent; in 1957, he broke off their relations definitively, writing to Jakobson after a visit to Moscow, "Frankly, I am unable to stomach your little trips to totalitarian countries, even if these trips are prompted merely by scientific considerations" (*Selected Letters*, 216).[11]

Eugene Onegin was an attack on American Slavists and Soviet scholars—but also on reigning Anglo-American literary elites.[12] For a start, Nabokov's "literal" translation betrayed Pushkin far less than it did the English language, or expectations to cleave to standard literary and lyrical usage. In *Writing Outside the Nation*, Azade Seyhan reconsiders Walter Benjamin's and Rudolf Pannwitz's theories of translation, critical of translations that "appropriate the soul of another language and subject it to the rule of the language into which it is translated."[13] Building on Pannwitz, Seyhan asks whether

> the fundamental error of the translator is that he is fixated on the arbitrarily defined higher status of his own language. Translation should be neither a full linguistic reconstruction nor an appropriation. Rather, it should incorporate the original language's mode of signification. Both the original and the translation should be recognizable "as fragments of a larger language" [*als Bruchstück einer größeren Sprache*]. (*Writing Outside the Nation*, 155)

This, I would argue, is just what Nabokov's translation and *Commentary* sought to do. As Nabokov had readily demonstrated his ability to write critically acclaimed English-language prose, his *Eugene Onegin* by implication expressed disdain for standard literary usage—and for the higher status of English. His purposefully awkward rendition was quite correctly perceived as an assault on English-language poetry, and as a personal blow to other translators, critics, and American intellectual elites. Wilson's response, in this light, proves that the challenge was immediately taken and so understood.

The three tomes of *Commentary*, however, provide even richer material for analysis than the actual translation, reflecting Nabokov's own investment and the respective size of the two components of the hybrid project. The very existence of the *Commentary* implies that Nabokov had the authority to write a scholarly treatise on the foundational text of the classic Russian canon—an authority wrenched from the Slavists and Soviets alike. But Nabokov used the *Commentary* to write not only about Pushkin and Russian nineteenth-century literature, but about inter- and transnational romanticisms as well. Nabokov's *Onegin* reaches past a personal genealogy to claim Pushkin's relevance beyond a national tradition. Nabokov dwells on Chateaubriand as well as Byron, insists on his interpretation and natural authority as heir to form a transnational canon of the romantic and modernist novel (and not, as we shall see, of poetry). Effectively, he redraws the Western canon to include the Russian strain in a central position.

John Guillory, analyzing Eliot's canon-reformation in the early twentieth century, writes that Eliot's

> shadowy, alternative "tradition" of minor poets has a good deal to do with the legitimation of his poetic practice, with the emergence (somewhat belatedly in relation to the other arts) of a "modernist" poetic. The status of Eliot's "canon" (if it can be called that) corresponds exactly to the status of a minority *within* literary culture, that minority of poets and writers who can be associated with the practices of Eliot and Pound, and who are at the time Eliot's

essays are written still relatively marginal to literary culture, a coterie whose work will only later come to define modernism in poetry.[14]

Nabokov conversely used his *Onegin Commentary* to put forward an international romantic tradition as the precursor to his particular style of modernism.

As Guillory writes, "Canonicity is not a property of the work itself, but of its transmission, its relation to other works in a collocation of works," institutionalized in the school or university syllabus, or other privileged lists.[15] Nabokov's very index in *Eugene Onegin* serves as a counter-list to the academic syllabus, the privileged site of canon formation in Guillory's analysis of New Criticism. Nabokov's strategy remains quite similar to that of T. S. Eliot, even in the essentialist claims and mystification of his insistence on categories like genius and masterpiece: Nabokov too posits as central and natural a tradition that had hitherto seemed marginal.[16]

Of course, Nabokov's canon is a counter-response not only to an Anglo-American modernist canon but to an international leftist one. Another possible transnational canon accommodating Russian literature could well include Dostoevsky, Freud, Woolf, and Sartre, among others, not to mention the vast global influences of socialist realism.[17] The trick is not only to include Russian literature, but to determine *which* Russian literature was to be included. In a sense, Nabokov's canon was the more threatening for using the logic of New Criticism against it: in keeping, it is the position of relative cultural autonomy, gained by an outsider, that has made Nabokov a powerful example to other writers. His translation project veers into "transnation," asserting authority and a counter-canon in terms both comprehensible and threatening to many sets of intellectual elites.

REASONABLE PUSHKINS

Nabokov's Pushkin joins a long list of "My Pushkins" in Russian belles lettres. If Dostoevsky made Pushkin into a prophet of the millennial role of Russian culture, the subsequent generation of modernist Pushkinist-poets emphasized their unique personal visions in poetic essays. Valerii Briusov, Marina Tsvetaeva, Anna Akhmatova, Osip Mandelstam, and Vladimir Khodasevich used Pushkin as the background for their own poetic practices—refuting in the process the crudely institutionalized national monument of the imperial and then Soviet regime.[18] The Russian modernist poets seized on Pushkin's fragmentariness and ambiguous irony: their musings were often pieced together from memory (most dramatically so in the case of Tsvetaeva) to combine personal ruminations with explorations of literary tradition as cultural or even linguistic memory. Nabokov, who was nearly of the same generation as the youngest of these modernist Pushkinists, follows in a very similar vein in some respects, but ultimately distances himself through his international focus.

Like the formalist critics, Nabokov sought to scrape away the accumulated banalities from a reified and kitschified Pushkin in order to build his revised Russian canon on a cleaner foundation. Pushkin was not only modern but timeless, a paradigm of the heights reached by Russian literature and the eternal model for any Russian writer. Nabokov's Pushkin emerged out of modernist readings and the modernist sensibility, and in turn proved so provocatively authoritative as to force all subsequent Pushkinists to contend in one way or another with Nabokov's encyclopedic tomes.[19]

Like most of these other twentieth-century Pushkins, Nabokov's Pushkin stands for liberty and innovation, and marks the beginning of great Russian literature. Nabokov saw the literature that preceded Pushkin as ignorable or regrettable, including the eighteenth-century traces still discernible in Pushkin's work: he deemed the eighteenth century a "pedestrian age," that "most inartistic of centuries," which glorified the generic and betrayed a "pathological dislike" for detail. Not even Pushkin could shed entirely neoclassicism's odious conventionality ("a glorification of the derivative, an affront to originality") but the "intuitive genius of freedom" made quite a bound with *Onegin*.[20] For Nabokov, the Russian canon clearly begins with *Onegin*, a long narrative claiming autonomy and relevance beyond its context. Out of a long and derivative eighteenth century suddenly blossoms a timeless masterpiece, a text with its own gravitational pull.

However, Western readers remained at best shakily convinced. A deity second only to Shakespeare on Nabokov's Olympus, Pushkin remained widely under-read outside the Russophone world. Worse yet, the available channels distorted him to their own ends.[21] Nabokov fumes over the academic reading on both sides of the Atlantic, the "special term for Onegin's distemper" (*Oneginstvo, Oneginism*) and "thousands of pages of type" devoted to turning Onegin into an archetype, the superfluous man of Russian letters. Stealing from literature for sociological clichés strikes him as the most shameless of appropriations:

> Thus a character borrowed from books but brilliantly recomposed by a great poet to whom life and library were one, placed by that poet within a brilliantly reconstructed environment, and played with by that poet in a succession of compositional patterns—lyrical impersonations, tomfooleries of genius, literary parodies and so on—is treated by Russian pedants as a sociological and historical phenomenon. (*Commentary*, 2:151)

Nabokov defends *Onegin* from one kind of immortality and passionately calls for another. The world is to admire Nabokov's Pushkin, not the Pushkin of Soviet philology or of American Slavic studies.[22] At stake is Pushkin's place in a rarified, aesthetically unquestionable list of greats—and implicitly, Nabokov's own right as *arbiter elegantiarum* to define that canon.

As harsh as he could be with rival readings and competing translations, adaptations of *Onegin* fare even worse. It is for bad adaptations that Nabokov consistently reserves the epithets "criminal" and "insane." When invited in 1954 to translate Tchaikovsky's libretto for NBC, Nabokov refused to have anything to do with that opera's "criminal inanities."[23] A decade later in the *Commentary*, he refers mockingly to the "incredible Italian libretto of Chaykovski's silly opera *Eugene Onegin*," the "lunatic scenes" of which he describes as follows: "in Act I 'Signora Larina' is seated under a tree, 'making candy' (with Olga in a tree and Tatiana in a swoon)" (2:333–34).

Tchaikovsky's opera was one of several adaptations readily available to international audiences through visual or musical media, and threatening to overshadow the poetry of Pushkin's original. Nabokov equally deflates Ilya Repin's "most famous and most execrable picture of the Lenski-Onegin duel, in which everything, including the attitudes and positions of the combatants, is ludicrously wrong." The painting offers only a double lie, the distorted echo of a distorted echo: "It is doubtful that the 'great' Russian painter had read Pushkin's novel (although he certainly had seen the opera by the 'great' composer) when he painted his *Duel of Onegin and Lenski* (1899)." Nabokov scoffs: "As in the opera, everything in the picture insults Pushkin's masterpiece" (*Commentary*, 3:42). His *Onegin* vies explicitly with these contending transfigurations.[24]

Wilson and others accused Nabokov of trying to upstage his great precursor (a classic case of anxiety of influence), but Nabokov grapples less with Pushkin as rival than with rival Pushkins. One such threatening impostor is the hero of Dostoevsky's "Pushkin Speech":

> In the published text of a famous but essentially clap-trap politico-patriotic speech, pronounced on June 8, 1880, at a public meeting of the Society of Amateurs of Russian Letters before a hysterically enthusiastic audience, Fyodor Dostoevski, a much overrated, sentimental, and Gothic novelist of the time, while ranting at length on Pushkin's Tatiana as a type of the "positive Russian woman," labors under the singular delusion that her husband is a "venerable old man" . . . all of which goes to show that Dostoevski had not really read *EO*. (*Commentary*, 3:191–92)

Dostoevsky is especially dangerous because "Dostoevski the publicist is one of those megaphones of elephantine platitudes (still heard today), the roar of which so ridiculously demotes Shakespeare and Pushkin to the vague level of all the plaster idols of academic tradition" (3:191–92).[25] The game is to determine the canon but also its terms.

Nabokov's first published essay on Pushkin, the 1937 "Pouchkine, ou le vrai et le vraisemblable" ("Pushkin, or the Real and the Plausible"), happens also to be one of the rare pieces he wrote in French. A first pass at the subject and aimed at European audiences, it is the starting point of the campaign that culminates in the monumental *Commentary* of 1964. (The piece gains gravitas from the story that James Joyce was in the audience on the night that Nabokov delivered a version of the paper as a talk.[26] It is tempting to think of Joyce—or someone with his equivalent level of erudition, versed in all things literary in English and French, but with no Russian—as Nabokov's ideal audience for all of his subsequent writing about Pushkin.)

"Pushkin, or the Real and the Plausible" opens with an incongruous case study of the "pearl of some lunatic asylum," a man whose madness induces him to write himself into history, no matter how far removed, with fictitious personal anecdotes and recollections. And yet, despite the imaginative potential of this scenario,

> sad to say, my chap was fundamentally uncultured and woefully underequipped to profit by this rare psychosis, and was reduced to nourishing his imagination with a hodgepodge of banalities and general ideas that were more or less erroneous. Napoleon's crossed arms, the Iron Chancellor's three lone hairs, or Byron's melancholy, plus a certain number of those so-called historical anecdotes historians use to sweeten their texts, provided, alas, all the detail and color he needed, and all the great men he had known intimately resembled each other like brothers.[27]

Nabokov's lunatic is the double of all false interpreters: translators, writers of "those curious books customarily called 'fictionized biographies,'" or other bad rewriters. When such charlatans turn on his favorite, Nabokov calls for incarceration: "It is fruitless to reiterate"—and yet he does, he will—"that the perpetrators of the librettos, sinister individuals who sacrificed *Eugene Onegin* or *The Queen of Spades* to Tchaikovsky's mediocre music, criminally mutilated Pushkin's texts. I use the term 'criminally' because these really were cases that called for legal action."[28]

But look at what Nabokov will do with his poet only paragraphs later:

> The life of a poet is a kind of pastiche of his art. The passage of time seems inclined to evoke the gestures of a genius, imbuing his imagined existence with the same tints and outlines that the poet had bestowed on his creations. . . . Here, then, is this brusque, stocky man, whose small swarthy hand wrote the first and most glorious pages of our poetry . . . it is but imagination that bestows a certain elegance on Pushkin, who, incidentally, in keeping with a whim of the period, liked to disguise himself—as a gypsy, a Cossack, or an

English dandy. A fondness for the mask, let us not forget, is an essential trait of the true poet.

. . . It is not my fault if I get carried away by these images, images common to Russians who know their Pushkin, and a part of our intellectual life in the same inextricable sense as multiplication tables or any other mental habit. These images are probably false, and the true Pushkin would not recognize himself in them. Yet if I inject into them a bit of the same love that I feel when reading his poems, is not what I am doing with this imaginary life somehow akin to the poet's work, if not to the poet himself?[29]

Nabokov also imagines and fictionalizes a masked bohemian behind the beloved verse. Yet he implies that there is the devil of a difference between his own illusionism and the thievery of opera house, soapbox, and lunatic asylum transfigurations. The difference lies in the stark admission that this is at best a plausible Pushkin; the difference is measured in precise knowledge, imagination, and love. Nabokov never claims to be saner than his committed competitor, only a good deal more erudite and fastidious.

The early essay beautifully illustrates the paradoxes of cultural heritage and translated originality. Nabokov, well aware of the difficulty of breaking through to French audiences, may not be speaking for Pushkin alone when he writes:

It is always harder for a poet than for a proseman to cross borders. But in Pushkin's case there is more profound cause for that difficulty. "Russian champagne," a refined litterateur said to me the other day. For let us not forget that *it is precisely French poetry, and an entire period of it*, that Pushkin put at the service of his Russian muse. As a result, when his verse is translated into French, the reader recognizes both the French eighteenth century— rose-tinted poetry thorny with epigrams—and the artificially exotic romanticism that lumped together Seville, Venice, the Orient with its babooshes, and sweet-honeyed Mother Greece. This first impression is so wretched, this old mistress so insipid, as to discourage the French right away. It is a platitude to say that, for us Russians, Pushkin is a colossus who bears on his shoulders our country's entire poetry. Yet, at the approach of the translator's pen, the soul of that poetry immediately flies off, and we are left holding but a little gilded cage.[30]

The observation is moving and quite subtle, an early illustration of brilliant theft or reflected fire. Decades later in the four volumes of *Eugene Onegin*, Nabokov is still tracing what Pushkin "put to the service of his Russian muse," to determine where fashionable borrowing ends and timeless genius begins: 1964's hybrid monster bursts out of 1937's little gilded cage.

Equally striking is the intense modesty of this introduction to Nabokov's Pushkin scholarship. Nabokov wrote then that he nurtured "no illusions about the quality of these translations." He offers only a "reasonably plausible Pushkin, nothing more; the true Pushkin is elsewhere. Yet, if we follow the riverbank of this poem as it unfolds, we do note, in the bends I have managed to comply with here and there, something truthful flowing melodiously past, and that is the sole truth I can find down here—the truth of art."[31] For all the austere rules of Nabokov's later translation, for all the perverse purity and painstaking research behind his elephantine notes, he codes in from the start the humorous, the slightly fantastical, and the personal. *Eugene Onegin* too is only Nabokov's best: a reasonably plausible Pushkin.

PUSHKIN AND HIS PRECURSORS

Within a more or less autonomous literary field, or what Bourdieu calls the limited field of cultural production, it is the influential writers, scholars, literary prizes, journals, and institutions with sufficient cultural capital that re-imagine and reformulate the working canons. In his essay on Kafka, Jorge Luis Borges writes that we choose our literary, if not biological ancestors.[32] Not unlike their characters, Pushkin and Nabokov load personal bookshelves with literary relations. *Evgenii Onegin* is famously rife with foreign novels: Pushkin seized on excuses to include long lists of authors and books. With near-perverse insistence on the irrelevance of all but style, Nabokov archly suggests that Pushkin did it only for the sake of rhyme: first, "These tabulations of names of authors and titles of works were well known in French and English literature"; and second, "What amused Pushkin was to iambize and rhyme them" (*Commentary*, 3:96).

Yet some authors recur far more than others. How amusing could it be to repeatedly iambize "Bayron"? When Nabokov does address Pushkin's precursors and international competitors in his *Commentary*, the two that emerge glaringly are Byron and Chateaubriand. The former is a clear choice: it is more or less impossible to write on *Onegin* without discussing the presence of the English bard. But Nabokov idiosyncratically insists on and inserts Chateaubriand into the commentary, while ignoring and downplaying or even belittling more evident influences. A closer reading of the *Commentary* reveals a project that goes beyond mere exegesis of Pushkin's text.

My previous chapter invoked Pascale Casanova's *World Republic of Letters* to examine the *Onegin*-influenced critical commonplace that Russian literature is unusually synthetic. Pushkin incorporated foreign sources into his own work and attempted simultaneously to catch up to and move beyond their accomplishments. But the *Onegin* project, to give the screw another turn, allows Nabokov to assert *his* Pushkin's sources. We choose our predecessors, but Nabokov claims the right to choose Pushkin's as well—and hence to handpick his own literary grandfathers. Nabokov's *Onegin* is more than a translation and more even than an extensive study of Pushkin: Nabokov uses the excuse and the space to construct an international canon dating from the early nineteenth century, and in which Russian, French, and English literature freely interpenetrate. Byron thieves from Chateaubriand and is preyed on by Pushkin; in the next generation the pattern repeats with Flaubert, perhaps Dickens, and certainly Tolstoy; and then ultimately Proust, Joyce, and the humble author himself.[33] These are the "greats" of the novel form, the pillars of the canon proposed by Nabokov. Crucially, this particular genealogy of the novel stresses how easily literary bloodlines cross national borders—and how present the Russian cousins were from the start.

Voltaire and Rousseau are among those missing or downplayed in this account of Pushkin's genesis; Constant is acknowledged but put in his minor place, alongside the entire French classical tradition and the German romantics. Vicomte de Parny and other poets are mentioned but also curiously deemphasized.[34] Nabokov could have easily chosen to focus on the verse side of Pushkin's novel in verse: instead he primarily scrutinizes the novel form, even anachronistically looking forward to Tolstoy, Dickens, Flaubert, even Joyce.[35] It is always more difficult for a poet than a novelist to cross borders, and Nabokov means to prove Pushkin's international relevance. Moreover and more subtly, he positions Pushkin, Byron, and Chateaubriand as precursors to his own poetic novels.

The vast majority of Nabokov's comments on sources and similarities in *Onegin* center on Lord Byron:

> The reader should be reminded of the fascination that Byron exercised on Continental minds in the 1820s. His image was the romantic counterpart of that of Napoleon, "the man of fate," whom a mysterious force kept driving on, toward an ever-receding horizon of world domination. Byron's image was seen as that of a tortured soul wandering in constant quest of a haven beyond the haze. (*Commentary*, 2:85; 3:85)

Even the *baletmeyster* in 1800s Petersburg, Nabokov notes, was "dubbed the 'Byron of the Ballet' for his 'romantic' fancy."

As Nabokov carefully documents, Pushkin alternately welcomed and parried the comparison. In a much-cited 1825 letter to Petr Viazemsky, Pushkin described *Evgenii Onegin* as "not a novel—but a novel in verse—a deuced difference" (or "the devil of a difference," *diavol'skaia raznitsa*) "in the genre of *Don Juan*." In a draft that he addressed to Aleksandr Bestuzhev-Marlinksy he wrote of the new work: "Its stanzas are perhaps even more licentious [*vol'nee*] than those of *Don Juan*" ("Translator's Introduction," 1:69–70). He assumed publication in Russia to be impossible. When the publisher I. V. Slenin made an unexpected offer, Pushkin wrote back to Viazemsky, "What say you about Russia—verily she is in Europe, and I thought it was a mistake of the geographers" ("Translator's Introduction," 1:70). In the fragment of yet another letter, he called *Onegin* a romantic poem after Byron.[36] In a published introduction, the oft-quoted preface to chapter 1, after summarizing his piece as "the description of a St. Petersburg young man's fashionable life at the end of 1819," he continues, it "recalls *Beppo*, somber Byron's humorous production" (*Commentary*, 2:10–11).

On the one hand, Byron provides both a model and material for *Onegin*'s structure and parodic play.[37] On the other, Pushkin very quickly tried to differentiate himself and to move past the prototype. Critics have been quick to seize on this thread: V. M. Zhirmunsky proves "the fact of Pushkin's youthful Romantic 'apprenticeship' to the fashionable English poet" and then argues that "the Romantic influence had been conclusively overcome before Pushkin's major works were written."[38] Monika Greenleaf tries to pinpoint the difference:

> At first identified with Byron's notorious practice of stitching together narrative poems out of lyrical outbursts, nature descriptions, and garishly lighted fragments of plot, with a self-conscious emphasis on the open-ended process of his improvisation, the rubric "fragmentary" stuck to Pushkin and came to stand for more than stylistic eccentricity. No one could pretend not to know what a Byronic poem meant, where its center of value lay. Pushkin's poems, however, were genuinely ambiguous.[39]

Pushkin emphasized similarities with Byron when it seemed useful to do so: if readers questioned his hole-riddled work, Pushkin retorted, "Pardon me, I am much too lazy. Moreover, I humbly submit that two stanzas are left out of *Don Juan*" (*Commentary*, 3:128).[40] But when he realized the dangers of being considered overly Byronic, he turned in the other direction. He wrote to Bestuzhev-Marlinksy, "None esteems *Don Juan* . . . more than I, but it has nothing in common with *Onegin*. You speak of a satire by an Englishman, Byron, and you compare it with mine, and demand one like it from me! No my dear old fellow, you ask too much. . . . There is not a ghost of it in *Eugene Onegin*" ("Translator's Introduction," 1:72). However, the comparisons kept coming, and usually not in Pushkin's favor: in an 1832 letter Evgenii Baratynsky, who disliked *Onegin*, deemed the work a "brilliant but juvenile imitation of Byron" (*Commentary*, 2:381).

How Byronic was Pushkin? Nabokov inherits the polemic and tries to differentiate fact from romantic fiction. Most famously, and in the increasingly vehement polemic with Edmund Wilson, he insisted that Pushkin knew Byron only through French filters:

> By 1820, eager Russian readers had already at their disposal the first four volumes of Pichot's and de Salle's first edition (1819) of Byron's works in French, and it is in these prose versions, pale and distorted shadows of the original, that Pushkin read for the first time. . . . *Le Corsaire, Manfred*, and the first two cantos of *Le Pèlerinage de Childe-Harold* . . . . It should be noted that while turning the entire poetic production of Byron into easy French prose, Pichot not only made no attempt to be accurate, but methodically transposed the text into the most hackneyed, and thus most "readable," French of the previous age. ("Translator's Introduction," 1:159)

We note that this is precisely what Nabokov's English tried not to do.

Edmund Wilson understood Nabokov's insistence that Pushkin only read in French as prompted by a desire to belittle and one-up the seminal Russian poet. I will dodge that debate, but point out a curious side effect: Nabokov's claim that Pushkin read Byron through the French shows the two Western traditions crossing even before coming to Russian shores. Nabokov writes: "Mark this curious and significant case: a reminiscence tainted by the influence of a hack coming between two poets" (*Commentary*, 2:176). Since Nabokov's *Onegin* posits an English-French-Russian canon and a multinational origin for the romantic (and neo-romantic) novel, this side effect works rather well, marking the beginnings of an attack on traditional studies of national literature.

Byron is everywhere in Pushkin's, and in Nabokov's, *Onegin*. In Pushkin's *Onegin*, Byron is mentioned directly, by name or through one of his memorable characters, no fewer than six times. Byron intervenes in the plot as well as inspires the structure and style. Nabokov reminds us that in chapter 7 "Tatiana discovers Byron (and through Byron, glimpses Onegin's mind)" (*Commentary*, 2:352). He retells Pushkin's absurd claim as to why he did not publish *Onegin's Journey*: "The thought that a humorous parody might be taken for disrespect in regard to a great and sacred memory also restrained me. But *Childe Harold* stands so high that whatever the tone in which it is spoken about, the thought of a possible offense to it could not have arisen in me" (quoting Pushkin, *Commentary*, 3:127). Nabokov in turn decides not to call the missing chapter *Onegin's Pilgrimage*, concluding that it would "crudely emphasiz[e] a resemblance that Pushkin himself tried to avoid" (*Commentary*, 3:258).

A mere glance at the index suggests the importance of Byron to Nabokov's Pushkin: a full column and a half is given over to Byron, or more than two hundred individual page references. The discussion of what is and is not Byronic in *Onegin* starts as early as the "Translator's Introduction" in Nabokov's translation; the key structural element of chapter 1 is, according to Nabokov, anti-Byronic: "In LVI the difference between a stylized Pushkin, blissfully dreaming in idyllic wilds, and Onegin, moping in the country, is used to mark the fact that our author does not share the Byronic fad of identifying himself with his hero" ("Translator's Introduction," 1:26).

For many of the key characterizations, plot developments, or leitmotifs of the book, Nabokov finds an explicitly romantic and usually Byronic genealogy:

> French literature of the eighteenth and early nineteenth centuries is full of restless young characters suffering from the spleen. It was a convenient device to keep one's hero on the move. Byron endowed it with a new thrill; René, Adolphe, Oberman, and their cosufferers received a transfusion of demon blood. (*Commentary*, 2:152)

Earlier Pushkin works, such as *The Gypsies*, he calls "frankly Byronic," and writes of *The Caucasian Prisoner* that the hero "traveled to the distant Caucasus . . . in a Byronic search for inner 'liberty,' and found captivity instead. He is a vague and naïve prototype of Onegin" (*Commentary*, 2:167). Other tidbits from the commentaries offer fascinating marginalia: "In a MS note of 1835 Pushkin carefully computed that Byron's father squandered, at twenty-five rubles to the pound sterling, 587,500 rubles in two years" (*Commentary*, 2:39). Or we learn that on the first anniversary of Byron's death, "Pushkin and Anna Vulf, in the province of Pskov, had Greek-Orthodox rites performed in commemoration of 'the Lord's slave Georgiy' at the local churches on their lands" (*Commentary*, 3:231).

All of this is fair enough, but Nabokov mentions Byron even when it seems less relevant, comparing works that Pushkin could not have known, such as Byron's "MS variant (unknown to Pichot or Pushkin)" (*Commentary*, 2:35). Nabokov finds an almost supernatural example of mirrored rhyme-riche linking the two poets: "in can. VII of *Don Juan*, among bungled Russian names that had already been misspelled in their passage through German transliteration into French and English," there is a "'Mouskin-Pouskin' (Musin-Pushkin) rhyming with 'through skin' and 'new skin.' (The counts Musin-Pushkins are distantly related to the plain Pushkins)" (*Commentary*, 2:477). Perhaps Nabokov found this detail too eerie to ignore, but when describing Lensky's last days, he offers the following equally unmotivated digression: "It is amusing to examine what live Byron was doing while Pushkin's creature danced, dreamed, and died" (went to the Corso; wrote in his diary about the passing of time; fired pistols) (*Commentary*, 2:546). Nabokov is willing to devote pages to such details, which is particularly striking since he has virtually nothing to say about Pushkin's own favorite classical authors, even when they are referred to explicitly in the verse novel.

This is not to suggest that all the notes laud the demonic Lord: Nabokov is quick to defend the disciple against the master. He suggests that one ought to look again, and critically, at "Byron's famous and mediocre stanzas, *Fare Thee Well*" (*Commentary*, 3:129). Or he informs the reader that, as Pushkin scribbled in his own manuscript notes, "Byron used to say he would never undertake to describe a country he had not seen with his own eyes. Nevertheless in *Don Juan* he describes Russia; in result, certain errors can be detected" (*Commentary*, 2:478). To this Nabokov adds his own complaint that "Russians on the whole had less trouble with Byron's and his character's name than Byron had with Russian ones" (*Commentary*, 2:479). And when Pavel Katenin conjectured in his *Recollections* that *Onegin's Journey* "contained an imitation of *Childe Harold* canceled by Pushkin presumably because the inferior quality of places and things had not allowed him to compete with the Byronian model," Nabokov responds to this "ridiculous remark" with the following comment: "Our poet's respect for Katenin remains inexplicable" (*Commentary*, 3:254). Nothing could prevent Pushkin from competing with Byron: he did so openly, and in Nabokov's eyes, he won.

Another French presence, far more significant than that of Pichot, lurks behind Byron. When Tatiana discovers Onegin's library and quickly catches up on her reading, Pushkin gives merely the lines:

> Хотя мы знаем, что Евгений
> Издавна чтенье разлюбил,
> Однако ж несколько творений
> Он из опалы исключил:
> Певца Гяура и Жуана,
> Да с ним еще два-три романа,
> В которых отразился век,
> И современный человек
> Изображен довольно верно
> С его безнравственной душой,
> Себялюбивой и сухой,
> Мечтанью преданной безмерно,
> С его озлобленным умом,
> Кипящим в действии пустом.

Although we know that Eugene
had long ceased to like reading,
however, several works
he had exempted from disgrace:
the singer of the Giaour and Juan,
also with him, two or three novels
in which the epoch is reflected
and modern man
rather correctly represented
with his immoral soul,
selfish and dry,
to dreaming measurelessly given,
with his embittered mind
boiling in empty action. (7:XXII)

Nabokov unearths two variants in Pushkin's draft. The second lists specific titles instead of "two or three novels": it includes "*Melmoth, René*, Constant's *Adolphe*." Nabokov leaps on the opportunity to speak about "*René*, a work of genius by the greatest French writer of his time" (*Commentary*, 3:98), Nabokov's beloved French romantic author Chateaubriand.

Nabokov's hunt for French precursors may have ulterior motives, and his singular fixation upon Chateaubriand quickly becomes evident. Chateaubriand remains a precursor rather ignored by most *Onegin* commentators: the importance Nabokov attributes to Chateaubriand bears little resemblance, for example, to Iurii Lotman's take on the same subject. Chateaubriand has just under fifty index references in Nabokov's *Commentary*, although he is mentioned exactly once in the text of *Evgenii Onegin* and once more in Pushkin's appended notes. For Nabokov, however, this is no minor ghost, but a serious and beautiful presence haunting the text more profoundly than we might otherwise realize. In fact, I would suggest that one of the side goals of Nabokov's *Eugene Onegin* is to restore Chateaubriand to his proper international fame.

Whenever Chateaubriand's name comes up, Nabokov attaches a suitably grandiose epithet to it: "The French writer of genius, Chateaubriand, is mentioned—somewhat irrelevantly" in chapter 4 ("Translator's Introduction," 1:38). Onegin's mood in chapter 7 warrants another note and a quoted passage from Chateaubriand's *Mémoires d'outre-tombe*: "*Ce qui enchante dans l'âge des liaisons deviant dans l'âge délaissé un objet de souffrance et de regret. On ne souhaite plus le retour des mois . . . une belle soirée de la fin d'avril . . . ces choses qui donnent le besoin et le désir du bonheur, vous tuent*" (*Commentary*, 3:71).[41] Elsewhere Nabokov inserts him almost wildly: "Speaking of poets, Chateaubriand says through René '*Leur vie est à la fois naïve et sublime . . . ils ont des idées merveilleuses de la mort'"* (*Commentary*, 2:276–277).[42] And for little immediately apparent reason, Nabokov translates "*i nechto, i tumannu dal*'" into French in the commentaries, adding: "Cf. Chateaubriand's note on '*le vague de ses passions*,' 'the haze of his emotions'" (*Commentary*, 2:241).

Even when forced to discuss other novels of the period that are directly referenced in the poem, Nabokov throws Chateaubriand back into the discussion. Glossing *Werther* he writes, "A faded charm still clings about this novel, which artistically is greatly inferior to Chateaubriand's *René* and even to Constant's *Adolphe*" (*Commentary*, 2:345); or again on Richardson: "Chateaubriand, by far the greatest French writer of his age, very admirably said in 1822: '*Si Richardson n'a pas de style . . . il ne vivra pas, parce que l'on ne vit que par le style*'" (*Commentary*, 2:346–47).[43] When noting some number of analogies between *Onegin* and Senancour's *Obermann*, he even concludes that these are "probably coincidental or going back to Chateaubriand" (*Commentary*, 3:71). Nabokov only allows, not to mention dwells on, certain comparisons and literary echoes. Naturally, he chooses to include a discarded variant of stanza 1:IX with the lines:

> The fervor of the heart torments us early.
> Enchanting fiction:
> not nature teaches us love,
> but Staël or Chateaubriand.
> We thirst to learn life in advance—
> we learn it from a novel. (*Commentary*, 2:62)

Discussing a variant draft of 4:XXVI, Nabokov suggests, "Pushkin does not seem to have been quite sure of his ground here in using Chateaubriand's great name" (*Commentary*, 2:440). Another cut variant is given on the same page: "And, says Chateaubriand, / not nature teaches us love, / but the first nasty novel."

Nabokov also goes out of the way to retell and critique Aleksandr Shishkov's conservative charge that the "monstrous French Revolution, having trampled upon all that was based on the principles of Faith, Honor, and Reason, engendered in France a new language, far different from that of Fénelon and Racine." Nabokov explains:

This is presumably a reference to Chateaubriand, whose genius and originality owed nothing, of course, to any "revolution"; actually, the literature produced by the French Revolution was even more conventional, colorless, and banal than the style of Fénelon and Racine; this is a phenomenon comparable to the literary results of the Russian Revolution, with its "proletarian novels," which are, really, hopelessly bourgeois. (*Commentary*, 3:171)

Lest we miss the parallel to the humble translator, another political exile fond of racy themes, Nabokov's "Translator's Introduction" opens with an epigraph from Pushkin, on Chateaubriand.[44] Clearly, Chateaubriand forms an important part of the heritage that Nabokov is claiming throughout his *Onegin* project.

In fact, the very first note of the *Commentary*, on the origins of the word *pétri* in the master motto, mentions Chateaubriand's usages. (In *Mémoires d'outre-tombe* he refers to himself as an *"androgyne bizarre pétri des sangs divers de ma mère et de mon père"*; in *René*: *"Mon coeur est naturellement pétri d'ennui et de misère."*)[45] Nabokov then traces the further descent of *pétri*: "In Russian literature the next *pétri* (half a century after Pushkin's) occurs, with a literal sense, in the famous French phrase spoken by the repulsive homunculus in Anna Karenin's fateful dream (*Anna Karenin*, pt. IV, ch. 3)" (*Commentary*, 2:5–6). Like a tangible heirloom or a recognizable family trait, this peculiar word passes from Chateaubriand to Pushkin, to Tolstoy, and then to Nabokov: as early as the first note, we glimpse the beginnings of Nabokov's projected literary genealogy.

Almost like Charles Kinbote, the villain-victim of *Pale Fire*, Nabokov forces Chateaubriand into the exegesis of an entirely different work.[46] He analyzes Pushkin but seizes on any excuse to bring up the "greatest French writer of that time." Constant's *Adolphe* is a more immediate presence in Pushkin's *Onegin*, but Constant does not really enter Nabokov's canon; thus he merely writes, "The analogies with *Onegin* are several, all of them obvious: it would be a great bore to go into further details" (*Commentary*, 3:101). He quotes from Pushkin's unsigned note on Viazemsky's translation of *Adolphe*: "Constant was the first to bring out this character, which later the genius of Lord Byron popularized." Nabokov then continues, "Neither Chateaubriand nor Constant seems to have been highly appreciated by English critics. Of Chateaubriand's *Atala*, *The Edinburgh Review*, an influential sheet of the period, wrote . . . 'The subject, conduct, and language of it, are, to our apprehension, quite ludicrous and insane'" (3:102). Nabokov seems to say that yes, *Onegin* alludes to Constant, but let us return to the far more interesting Byron and Chateaubriand.

One implication is that we should look beyond the obvious reference: Chateaubriand is the genuine and noteworthy source for many of the paradigmatic themes and motifs of European romanticism. Furthermore, Byron and Chateaubriand go hand in hand in Nabokov's *Commentary*, granted a near-mystical connection as the greatest writers of their time, a status and connection to which Pushkin will also claim a share: "*René*, a work of genius by the greatest French writer of his time, François (Auguste) René, Vicomte de Chateaubriand . . . was, he says, thought up under the very elm at Harrow, in Middlesex, England, where Byron *'s'abandonnait aux caprices de son âge'"* (*Commentary*, 3:98). Byron and Chateaubriand are likewise linked in a lengthy note on the origins of *ennui*.[47] Under the pretext of demonstrating the French fashion of hyphenating Childe Harold's name, Nabokov includes Béranger's 1855 note "to couplets inscribed to Chateaubriand: '. . . *le chantre de Child-Harold est de la famille de René* '" (*Commentary*, 2:157).[48] It is as if Nabokov takes up the gauntlet on the side of Chateaubriand, who paraphrased "with grim satisfaction" some of Byron's more clichéd Venetian imagery in *Childe Harold*, for he "bore Byron a grudge for his never mentioning René, the Pilgrim's prototype" (*Commentary*, 2:183).

In his classic study *The Romantic Agony*, Mario Praz has suggested that it is difficult to calculate how much Byron may have owed to Chateaubriand, and that French critics, following the example set by Chateaubriand himself in *Mémoires d'outre-tombe*, tend to exaggerate the debt. (Praz notes that some "even go so far as to say that Byron's incest with his half-sister was a plagiarism, because Byron committed in reality the crime of which René had conceived the horrible possibility.")[49] Instead, Praz argues it much more likely that both drew from a common source, the prevalent demonic and darkly erotic strain in romanticism.

Nabokov prefers a model of literary history where the greats steal directly from each other, to an attribution of their common themes to a general climate of thought. If he is to write about *ennui* in the *Onegin Commentary* (or about incest in *Ada*), he turns at once to specific works and to the most sparkling representatives. Finally, Nabokov offers a telltale crossed-orchid of a reference: he describes Charles Nodier's *Jean Sbogar* as "a short French novel of a Chateaubyronic genre . . . smuggled in by Pushkin" (*Commentary*, 2:358). His concern is not with the romantic novel, but with the transnational Chateaubyronic genre. In the final analysis, it is Chateaubyron whom Pushkin smuggled into Russian literature, and Chateaubyron whom Pushkin must best.

INNOVATION AGAINST HISTORY

Few works are quite so temporally self-conscious as Pushkin's *Onegin*; fewer grow that much more so in their subsequent exegesis. Nabokov's composite text and commentary form an apotheosis of temporal concerns.[50] He traces structural and thematic temporality, and finds for example that the "time element" dominates chapter 7 "rather obsessively, with rhetorical transitions depending on the establishment of this or that season or hour or of the passage of time." Rhetorical transitions ("Now is the time") predominate, picking up the "youth-is-gone" theme with which chapter 6 ends (*Commentary*, 2:49). But Nabokov is not always complimentary: when Pushkin waxes philosophical in chapter 8, ruing the passage of time and his unseasonal hero, the notes grumble, "Sts. XXVII–XXIX belong to the didactic philosophizing order, and the seasonal metaphors with which XXIX is crammed are repetitious and conventional" ("Translator's Introduction," 1:56).

If Pushkin's *Onegin* explores anxieties of belatedness on plot, structural, and meta-literary levels, Nabokov adds an evaluative mood. He not only translates and annotates Pushkin, but assesses every line. Even when we evaluate the transitions in a work, he writes, we pass "esthetic and historical judgment upon them" (*Commentary*, 2:18). Quality is conveyed through another set of temporal terms: Pushkin is a great writer because he overtakes French and English authors, because he leaps ahead of his time, because he somehow as a result becomes eternal, entering a canon outside of ordinary human temporality.[51]

Time and again, Nabokov judges Pushkin's original contribution against what was already familiar at the time, or worse yet, was already dated; his metaphors for literary progress are akin to those of cumulative scientific knowledge. I have discussed the meta-literary fear of belatedness visible even on the surface of Pushkin's *Onegin*: while the characters fret about fashion and the timing of life choices, Pushkin worries about literary trends and the timeliness of Russian poetry and prose. But meta-literary timeliness is the only kind that interests Nabokov. He dismisses Pushkin's didactic stretches as literary clichés carried over from eighteenth-century convention: after all, Pushkin began writing elegies to his blighted youth at the ripe old age of seventeen. At twenty-one, Nabokov adds, in a poem beginning "I have outlived my aspirations," Pushkin wrote such pseudo-profound lines as "Under the storms of cruel fate / My bloomy wreath has withered fast" (*Commentary*, 3:64). Nabokov has unapologetically little interest in the philosopher or ethicist Pushkin, whom he considers to be largely critical inventions.

Nabokov's *Commentary* consistently moves the reader away from the plot and toward meta-literary patterns: he argued vehemently that *Onegin* "is not a picture of 'Russian life'" and that the novel "would disintegrate at once if the French props were removed and if the French impersonators of English and German writers stopped prompting the Russian-speaking heroes and heroines" (*Commentary*, 2:7–8). Again like the Russian formalists or American New Critics, Nabokov contends that literature—a novel in verse especially—is made up of language forced and cajoled into doing things. If we forget the medium for the distracting story, we have missed everything:

> Pushkin's composition is first of all and above all a phenomenon of style . . . It is not "a picture of Russian life"; it is at best the picture of a little group of Russians, in the second decade of the last century, crossed with all the more

obvious characters of western European romance and placed in a stylized Russia, which would disintegrate at once if the French props were removed and if the French impersonators of English and German writers stopped prompting the Russian-speaking heroes and heroines. The paradoxical part, from a translator's point of view, is that the only Russian element of importance is this speech, Pushkin's language, undulating and flashing through verse melodies the likes of which had never been known before in Russia. ("Translator's Introduction," 1:7)

He drives the point home brutally, glossing Pushkin's most beloved aphorisms as filler, transition, and purely functional literary devices. Alas, Nabokov adds, "Pushkin was a brilliant wit (especially in his correspondence), but he did not shine in the didactic genre, and his indebtedness to the elegant generalities of his time, or more exactly of a period just previous to his time, is sometimes painfully evident in the rather trivial observations of the Social Whirl, Women, Custom, and Mortality that occur throughout *EO*" ("Translator's Introduction," 1:20). So much for the Russian ethicist Pushkin of Dostoevsky's famous speech. The only thing Nabokov finds brilliant in *Onegin* is the Russian verse: the so-called content is French and English anyway.

Drastically, he even posits that Pushkin wrote about time and belatedness only for the sake of handy rhymes: "In a work where 'novelty' [*novizna*] and 'fashion' [*moda*] are constantly referred to, their juxtaposition with the old, the dismoded, the old times, is inevitable. Moreover, *starina* belongs to the rhymes-on-*na* group, for which Pushkin had a special predilection" (*Commentary*, 2:212). Nabokov frequently chooses English translations that will emphasize the borrowing, italicizing as it were the cliché. "Social hum" is glossed as "an old French cliché, *le bruit, le tumulte, le fracas du monde* . . . I have gone to English formulas, e.g., Byron's 'the gay World's hum'" (*Commentary*, 2:148). These choices seem paradoxical, given Nabokov's 1937 fears that Pushkin inevitably sounded derivative in French. Now he even translates "*Kuda, kuda vy udalilis*'" as "Whither, ah! whither are ye fled" in a rare and marked departure from his literal translation method. "Quite literally, 'Whither, whither have you receded,'" he concedes, "but I have preferred to echo the cry so often heard in English seventeenth- and eighteenth-century poetry" and he gives several examples from Alexander Pope to the nineteenth-century John Keats (*Commentary*, 2:25). The only thing more important than fidelity to the original Russian text is a fair exposition of its foreign sources—even to Pushkin's apparent disadvantage.

Nabokov is fascinated by the various kinds of timeliness and pursuits explored in Pushkin's *Onegin*. However, since he means to dissuade readers from viewing the characters as real individuals, he dismisses as irrelevant such questions as whether Onegin withered on the vine, or fell in love long after the springtime of his years. Instead, Nabokov emphasizes meta-literary timeliness. Throughout the *Commentary*, he evaluates Pushkin as well as his western European near-contemporaries in the tribunal of posterity, to determine where they are innovative, where derivative, and when they become immortal.

The missing link between Pushkin's "Blest who" stanzas lauding the timely man, explored in my first chapter, and Nabokov's emphasis on literary mastery is once again fashion. For once, Nabokov agrees with the critical mainstream in comparing Onegin to Beau Brummell, London's leading dandy from 1800 to 1816, although he quibbles with the terms, striving even here for precision: since "glaring extravaganzas in dress constitute dandyism, Brummell most assuredly was no dandy. He was a *beau*. . . . His chief aim was to avoid anything marked." Nabokov concludes, "Onegin, too, was a beau, not a dandy" (*Commentary*, 2:44).[52]

A detailed analysis of contemporary fashion fills the commentaries, despite Nabokov's protests of ahistoricism; however, the discussion remains grounded in or linked to literary style. When Nabokov argues that Onegin, for all his vague, impersonal ennui (plundered from Lord Byron, who stole it from the Vicomte de Chateaubriand) is less flat a character than Benjamin Constant's Adolphe, he notes that Onegin is a man with a wardrobe. Each mention of Onegin's enviable Breguet warrants a gloss from Nabokov, here to a literary echo (the timepiece of Pope's *Rape of the Lock*) and there to a disapproving aphorism: "Those who have the least value for their time have usually the greatest number of watches and are the most anxious about the exactness of their going" (*Commentary*, 2:69, 76).[53] If we must think of Onegin as any kind of "type" at all, then he is the fashionable type of the moment.[54]

These echoes of Brummell, Constant's Adolphe, and Pope (Pope is often invoked in connection to his student and Pushkin's more immediate influence, Byron) show how closely Moscow and Petersburg fashions aped Paris and London:

> Liberal French fashions, such as haircuts *à la* Titus (short, with flattened strands), appeared in Russia immediately after the lifting of various preposterous restrictions dealing with dress and appearance that had been inflicted on his subjects by tsar Paul (who was strangled by a group of exasperated courtiers on a March night in 1801). (*Commentary*, 2:43)

Fashion is as crucial to duels as it is to dress: like dancing, dueling offers a perfectly semioticized form of social behavior.[55] While Onegin and Lensky face off, Nabokov untangles the origins of the code so ubiquitous to the Russian nineteenth-century novel: "The hostile meeting described here is the classical duel *à volonté* of the French code, partly derived from the Irish and English pistol duel, for which the basic code duello was adopted in Tipperary about 1775" (*Commentary*, 3:43).

From literal to literary fashion is a small step. The most elegant fusion occurs in the commentary notes to chapter 8, where Tatiana's perfect social demeanor wins the following frame of reference from Nabokov: Lady Frances wrote to her son Henry Pelham, as quoted in the "tedious *Pelham; or, Adventures of a Gentleman*," a work that "Pushkin knew well from a French version," that "whatever is evidently borrowed becomes vulgar. Original affectation is sometimes good *ton*; imitated affectation always bad" (*Commentary*, 3:168). Lady Frances's advice for bon ton is precisely what Nabokov demands of literature. Brilliant artifice is one thing, but when caught by the wary reader, whatever is evidently borrowed becomes vulgar and embarrassing.

In Nabokov's analysis, the plot twists and character portraits of *Onegin* are excuses to muse on literary fashion. Lensky, the straw poet, dies to the accompaniment of a "deliberate accumulation of classical and romantic metaphors" ("Translator's Introduction," 1:47). Pushkin describes

> the nature of that young and mediocre poet in the idiom Lenski himself used in his elegies . . . an idiom now blurred by the drift of unfocused words, now naively stilted in the pseudoclassical manner of minor French songsters. Even the closest translation is prone to tough up with some applied sense the ambiguous *flou* of Pushkin's remarkable impersonation. (*Commentary*, 2:232)

Tatiana's and Onegin's respective reading lists afford a similar opportunity. We make sense of these characters and grasp their relative positions through what is on his shelf or underneath her pillow. They read each other quite similarly: Tatiana conducts herself like a provincial miss as long as her tastes are a step behind St. Petersburg fashion. What Nabokov calls the "rather professional" explanation of Onegin's library in turn gives us his favorite books: "*The Giaour, Don Juan*, and two or three novels depicting the man of the time." Snooping Tatiana "from the marks of his pencil and thumbnail . . . reconstructs the man, and when three years later they meet again she will know he is not a fascinating demon or angel but an imitation of fashionable freaks" ("Translator's Introduction," 1:51).

Pushkin's lyric persona reveals more writerly anxieties. Nabokov calls these moments Pushkin's professional digressions: for example, "Pushkin confesses he now dallies more sluggishly with mistress rhyme and inclines toward prose" ("Translator's Introduction," 1:48). Elsewhere, in some canceled stanzas reinserted by Nabokov, Pushkin frets that his book

> will finish belowstairs its shameful span
> like last year's calendar
> or a dilapidated primer.
>   . . .
> Well, what? In drawing room or vestibule
> readers are equally plebeian
> over a book their rights are equal;
> not I was the first, not I the last
> shall hear their judgment over me,
> captious, stern, and obtuse. (*Commentary*, 2:313)

Critical reception was changing, as the fashion-conscious Pushkin was acutely aware. And as many critics have noted, the digressions on Lensky's old-fashioned elegies serve as a distancing mechanism from Pushkin's own early work. Nabokov points out that these asides were a response to Wilhelm Küchelbecker's provocative essay, which "correctly criticized the Russian elegy for its colorless vagueness, anonymous retrospection, trite vocabulary, and so on." Pushkin doubtless grasped that "the vocabulary of his own elegies, despite their marvelous melodiousness, was well within the range of Küchelbecker's attack" (*Commentary*, 2:445). Approximately halfway through the serial publication of *Evgenii Onegin*, fashion turned against the poet. Pushkin wrote in one letter, "For a long time reviewers left me in peace. This did them honor: I was far away, and in unfavorable circumstances. They became used to considering me still a very young man. The first inimical reviews began to appear after the publication of *EO*, Four and Five" (*Commentary*, 2:484).[56] The witty but vicious reviewer Faddei Bulgarin, for example, "welcomed the appearance of a new personage" in the churring beetle of chapter 7 "and expected him to prove a better sustained [*viderzhanniy*] character than the others."[57]

Pushkin closely followed his negative reviews. Bulgarin wrote that chapter 7 was nothing but "two small printed sheets—variegated with such verses and such clowning that even *Eugene Velskii*," an anonymous travesty of 1828–29, "appears in comparison to be something having a semblance of common sense. . . . Not one idea in this watery Chapter Seven, not one sentiment, not one picture worthy of contemplation!" (*Commentary*, 3:125–26). Pushkin, sounding very much like a nineteenth-century Nabokov, exploded in response that *what* is not important at all: literature's only concern is *how*. Nabokov translates and includes Pushkin's self-defense in the *Commentary*:

> The most insignificant subject may be selected by the author for his poem. Critics need not discuss what the author describes. They should discuss *how* he describes it.

In one of our reviews it was said that Chapter Seven could not have any success because the age and Russia go forward whereas the author of the poem remains on the same spot. This verdict is unjust (i.e., in its conclusion). If the age may be said to progress, if sciences, philosophy, and civilization may perfect themselves and change, poetry remains stationary and neither ages nor changes. Her goal, her means remain the same, and while the conception, the works, the discoveries of the great representatives of ancient astronomy, physics, medicine, and philosophy have grown obsolete and are daily replaced by something else, the works of true poets remain ever fresh and young. (*Commentary*, 3:126–27)

The irony of the claim that Russia was leaving Pushkin behind is that the next centuries would imagine so powerfully the reverse narrative: Russian letters were not yet ready for Pushkin. In other words, if Pushkin was untimely, he was more premature than belated. But this passage also beautifully illustrates the tension between a supposedly eternal canon and the vagaries of aesthetic fashion. Pushkin, who mocked Derzhavin's faith in the immortality of his verses in "Exegi monumentum," states plainly that poetry has no teleology: he saw personally that literary tastes followed trends and went the way of haircuts and hemlines. And yet Pushkin, like Nabokov, would like to believe that talent is eternal—as Mikhail Bulgakov would write a century later, that manuscripts do not burn.

Where in *Onegin*, according to Nabokov, is Pushkin innovative and where is he merely fashionable? When original and when derivative? The *Commentary* brims with elaborate judgments, the tone set by the "Translator's Introduction": "The structure of *EO* is original, intricate, and marvelously harmonious, despite the fact that Russian literature stood in 1823 at a comparably primitive level of development, marked by uncontrollable and perfectly pardonable leanings toward the most hackneyed devices of Western literary art still in use by its most prominent exponents" ("Translator's Introduction," 1:16). *Onegin* rests on eighteenth-century European props, or leans "pardonably" toward hackneyed devices, but the ultimate triumph of the work lies in transcending Russia and the early nineteenth century.

Clearly Pushkin's innovative brilliance lies in his virtuosity with the Russian language. But given the translator's paradox, as Nabokov puts it, what remains when that play with language is removed? A different reader might concentrate on the characters or on the plot, on the "climate of thought" or on Pushkin's ideology; Nabokov has forbidden himself all of it.[58] Another translator might instead mimic the wordplay and look for English equivalents; but this too is against Nabokov's principles. His own charming, erudite, and fanciful commentaries shimmer with a different kind of English-language virtuosity;

but that is all Nabokov, with no pretense of directly conveying Pushkin. Reading somewhat generously, we might decide that the sheer joy in language and erudition of Nabokov's notes reflect the equivalent in Pushkin's verse—that Nabokov's *Commentary* is the real, or at least plausible, translation of *Onegin*.

However, what Nabokov writes about is Pushkin's source material: the best way that he can show *his* Pushkin is to trace what and how Pushkin borrows, and how wittily he thieves, adapts, and improves. Nabokov's *Commentary* brims with elaborate evaluations. A dazzling example is the analysis of the independent short poem "Exegi monumentum," which Nabokov otherwise inexplicably includes:

> In 1836, in one of the most subtle compositions in Russian literary history, Pushkin parodies Derzhavin stanza by stanza in exactly the same verse form. The first four have an ironic intonation, but under the mask of high mummery Pushkin smuggles in his private truth . . . The last quatrain is the artist's own grave voice repudiating the mimicked boast. His last line, although ostensibly referring to reviewers, slyly implies that only fools proclaim their immortality. (*Commentary*, 2:310)

All of Nabokov's key words are here: Pushkin "parodies" rather than imitates; he "smuggles in truth" under the mask of mummery. The parody must be supremely conscious, masterful in execution, and spun through with the unique and individual sensibility of the later artist. Pushkin works with and against his precursor to create subtle meaning that only a reader familiar with both texts can follow.[59]

In contrast, less graceful or self-conscious borrowings warrant a rebuke: "All this is embarrassingly close to a passage in Kozlov . . . and is only a slight improvement"; "A curious rewording of Baratinsky's *Spring*"; this "stems from Virgil and not from direct observation" (*Commentary*, 2:83, 70, 84). Elsewhere, Nabokov is even more specific in his accusations of careless influence: "The recurrent intonations in the listing of the participants of this noble rout [8:XXIV–XXVI] are too close to those in Byron's *Don Juan*, XIII, LXXXIV–LXXXVIII." On the same page as he gives the last reproach and hardly by accident, Nabokov quotes from a letter by Count Mikhail Vorontsov that characterized Pushkin as *"un faible imitateur d'un original très peu recommandable: Lord Byron"* (*Commentary*, 3:194). The crucial difference is that in these verses Pushkin appears to be more generally and vaguely influenced by the style of his precursors: rather than engaging in a controlled and conscious parody or response, Pushkin seems to lean on the intonations and formulations that were already accepted as poetic at the time.

What peculiar aesthetics/ethics of literary theft do Nabokov's evaluations reflect? Pushkin is allowed to use previous models: he must, for in literature as in music there is nothing entirely outside of tradition and form. However, he must do so consciously; he must innovate or play inventively on the brink of parody. For, as Lady Frances warned, imitated affectation is never good *ton*.

Pushkin, as a non–western European outsider, was quite cynically aware of literature's dependence on fashion: his *Onegin* is a whirl of conscious pursuit, a bid to imitate brilliantly (and hence to catch up to) but also to innovate, adapt, and thus to overtake his distinguished competitors. Nabokov in turn positions himself as a cultural insider, the natural authority and guardian of a canon no longer defined along national lines. The criteria for evaluation are to be inspired innovation and conscious mastery; English language and literature are always already infected with French; and Pushkin and the Russian greats are central, not marginal to *his* Western canon—an idealized and glamorous Anglo-Franco-Russo blend.

How did *Onegin* finally enter an international tradition and come to influence English-language literature, inspiring the English Onegin stanzas of such works as Vikram Seth's *The Golden Gate* (1986) and Diana Burgin's *Richard Burgin: A Life in Verse* (1989)? Nabokov's *Eugene Onegin* intended not only to bring Pushkin back to life, and to promote "his Pushkin" over other readings of the romantic poet, but even to rewrite history, as George Steiner has claimed that powerful translations can do.[60] The translated *Onegin*, shown through Nabokov's notes to be thoroughly interpenetrated with English and French literature, gave Pushkin's original the world literature status it had hitherto never quite achieved. Pushkin's belated foreign triumph came after the Nabokov translation and the subsequent controversy. English-language audiences accepted—whether believing that Nabokov had done so satisfactorily or not—that *Evgenii Onegin* must be worth translating. The *Onegin* stanza entered English-language poetry, and after the publication of Nabokov's last six books the international novel would never be the same.

As a creative writer, Nabokov held up *Onegin* as a standard and a challenge. The late English-language novel *Ada, or Ardor* (1969), seen by many critics as his other overextension and self-indulgent failure, brings his transnational canon to fictional life. From Pushkin and the Chateaubyronic genre to the meta-literary, incestuous modernist games of Nabokov's *Ada* is only a small step.

Nabokov's *Ada, or Ardor*: Translating the Russian Novel

> Poetry can only be made out of other poems;
> novels out of other novels. Literature shapes
> itself and is not shaped externally: the forms
> of literature can no more exist outside of
> literature than the forms of sonata and fugue
> can exist outside of music.
> —Northrop Frye, *Anatomy of Criticism*, 1957

> One can borrow on the strength of a legacy.
> —Vladimir Nabokov, *Dar* (*The Gift*), 1938

TREMORS OF *ADA, OR ARDOR*

Moving forward simultaneously a century and a half and a mere few years, we come to Nabokov's 1969 English-language novel *Ada, or Ardor*, one of his last and certainly his most demanding work. Nabokov had planned to write a fictional meditation on time as early as 1958. Shortly after finishing *Eugene Onegin* and his burlesque of the art of annotation in the 1962 novel *Pale Fire*, he returned to his notes for *The Texture of Time*. The project began to grow and take on new dimensions; in interviews, he described the new work as above all technically ambitious:

> The difficulty about it is that I have to devise an essay, a scholarly-looking essay on time and then gradually turn it into the story I have in mind. The metaphors start to live. The metaphors gradually turn into the story because it's very difficult to speak about time without using similes or metaphors. And my purpose is to have these metaphors breed to form a story of their own, gradually, and then again to fall apart, and to have it all end in this rather dry though serious and well-meant essay on time.[1]

In those same years, reviews of *Eugene Onegin* continued to come in, and Nabokov revised *Speak, Memory*, working from both his English original

71

and the Russian expansion. The memoir's themes of idyllic childhood and exile found their way into *Ada*, alongside parodies of his own genealogical research. In a sense, *Ada* is to *Speak, Memory* as *Pale Fire* is to *Eugene Onegin*: one gets the impression that Nabokov found these mischievous novelistic inversions of his ostensibly sincere nonfiction works especially pleasurable and productive.

But what he called the "first flash of *Ada*" came in 1966:

> Sea crashing, retreating with shuffle of pebbles, Juan and beloved young whore—is her name, as they say, Adora? is she Italian, Roumanian, Irish?— asleep in his lap, his opera cloak pulled over her, candle messily burning in its tin cup, next to it a paper-wrapped bunch of long roses, his silk hat on the stone floor near a patch of moonlight, all this in a corner of a decrepit, once palatial whorehouse, Villa Venus, on a rocky Mediterranean coast, a door standing ajar gives on what seems to be a moonlit gallery but is really a half-demolished reception room with a broken outer wall, through a great rip in it the naked sea is heard as a panting space separated from time, it dully booms, dully withdraws dragging its platter of wet pebbles.[2]

This early passage already reveals something of the strange and experimental novel to come: a tightly controlled structural frame (the description begins and ends with sea and pebbles) sets off an image that could be a painting or a movie still, but for the slight movement and sound—conveyed in prose. The decaying Villa Venus introduces the motifs of the "rose" and "sore" of Eros, anagrams that will plague the book. The parodic play with the motifs and imagery of romanticism is also firmly in place: the decidedly Byronic Van Veen was even originally named Juan.

The Nabokovs hunted for the butterflies and the artwork of *Ada* and summered in Italy. By now, there was a constant barrage of interviewers, photographers, and publishers making the pilgrimage to Montreux, Nabokov's Yasnaya Polyana. In the span of one decade, as Brian Boyd reminds us, Nabokov's life had changed inconceivably:

> Although in 1958, reviewers, readers, and writers across America had hailed *Lolita*, Nabokov himself was not well known. . . . A decade later, his literary reputation was at its height. The publication of his Russian fiction had revealed the depth and breadth of his oeuvre, while *Pale Fire* showed he could produce another surprise as great in scale as *Lolita* yet wholly different in kind. By the second half of the 1960s he was often acclaimed as the greatest writer alive, the standard against which other writers should be measured, the one certain choice for a Nobel Prize.[3]

Nabokov had the attention of the world. Hollywood began nosing around *Ada* as early as 1968: it was decided that the asking price for movie rights would be no less than one million dollars.

However, the film never happened and the call from Stockholm never came. Instead *Ada* provoked such critical discord as have few novels aside from *Finnegans Wake*. Devotees hailed the work, while others viewed it as Nabokov's fall into indulgent irrelevance. Steiner wrote in an early review, "At a first reading *Ada* . . . seems to me self-indulgent and at many points irredeemably overwritten. . . . But with a writer of this reach, first readings are always inadequate. Lived with, the layer cake in *Ada* may prove a culinary find."[4] Richard Rorty concluded that if Nabokov's middle period found a balance between the "initial maximum difficulty of synthesis and eventual transparency," with *Ada* "he becomes *merely* idiosyncratic."[5] Michael Wood, evoking Edward Said's and Adorno's notions of late style, sees *Ada* as an odd mix of mastery and apparent ineptness, and points out that Nabokov was seventy by the time of publication. For Wood, *Ada* is "a sickly and elaborate world, a sort of hell which parades as paradise."[6] In a more recent reading Eric Naiman summarizes wittily: "More than any other book by Nabokov, *Ada* equates complexity with complicity . . . do we want to be the type of person who appreciates this type of writing?"[7]

Alexander Gerschenkron has said of Nabokov's *Onegin* translation that it can and should be studied, but that it cannot be read.[8] Many have responded similarly to *Ada*'s code-switching, trilingualism, and many-layered allusions, dubbing it Nabokov's most "aristocratic" work. What the critical reaction simultaneously points to and obfuscates is that these texts are critical sites of formation and the battlegrounds of Nabokov's alternative literary canon, rival to what dominated the American campuses he had recently left behind. After laying the foundations of his transnational canon in the *Eugene Onegin* project, rife with interjections like "'our national poet' (as if a true poet could be 'national')!" (*Commentary*, 2:361), Nabokov attempted to go much further with *Ada*.

Fiction afforded him greater liberties. The project of illustrating how his favorite works of literature (not to mention the flood of paintings, films, and other media present in the novel) might come together determines the very form and *fabula*. *Ada* is a work of "physics fiction" in which Russia's poets have not been "squandered" but safely transported to the New World.[9] The utopian aspirations of the fantasy—the rescue of Russian literature through literal and figurative translation and cultural interbreeding—are right on the surface.[10] If *Speak, Memory* presented us with a portrait of the artist, or as much as he is willing to show, *Ada* offers a landscape of the artist's canon.

On Antiterra or Demonia, as the alternate world of the novel is called, "sleight of land" and time allow literatures to intermingle and the nineteenth and twentieth centuries to coexist. Nabokov's new planet *is* the world of literature: relatively autonomous from the tragedies of Terra but in no way decoupled, rather haunted by and oddly reflecting our world. The diminishing structure of the novel's five parts and the incestuous love story of Van and Ada Veen, who contend that morals are for mortals and not exceptionally intelligent and talented beings, meanwhile reflects the equal and opposite anxiety of excessive stylistic inbreeding, as I shall explore in subsequent chapters.

Like the *Onegin* project, *Ada* reads quite differently from the perspective of the twenty-first century. Moving against the grain of critical discourse, we can mine Nabokov for unexpectedly emancipatory elements and recast *Ada*'s new world as a forerunner of transnational and world literatures.

TRANSLATIONS AND TRANSFIGURATIONS

While struggling with *Ada*'s early stages, Nabokov completed his translation of *Lolita* into Russian. The experience was not wholly positive: if the afterword to the English *Lolita* emphasized the private tragedy that "I had to abandon my natural idiom, my untrammeled, rich, and infinitely docile Russian tongue for a second-rate brand of English,"[11] the new Russian afterword revealed an equally strong but opposite reaction:

> Alas, that "marvelous Russian language" that I thought awaited me somewhere, blossoming like a faithful springtime behind a tightly locked gate whose key I had kept safe for so many years, proved to be nonexistent, and beyond the gate are nothing but charred stumps and the hopeless autumnal vista, and the key in my hand is more like a jimmy.[12]

Nabokov's laments ring somewhat false, or require decoding. It seems unlikely that his rusty Russian was to blame, and his contention in the melancholy afterword, that Russian is "a good 'From' language but a terrible 'Into' one," is unconvincing.[13]

The bleak landscape behind the garden gate suggests two possible changed circumstances: one is the natural passage of time from "blossoming" and "faithful springtime" to "hopeless autumnal vista"; the violence of "charred stumps" suggests the other. As Nabokov repeated many times, everything that he had loved in Russia had been shot through the heart or burnt to the ground. Nostalgia longs for a lost time rather than merely for a lost place: Nabokov's enchanted garden is not only the Russian language, but the Russian language of a different era. In translating 1950s Americana "back" into his native tongue, the writer faced the linguistic repercussions of the turbulent twentieth century. Should Lolita speak pre-Revolutionary Russian in 1965?

Can the American preteen's maddeningly average slang come across in the archaic lexicon of an émigré bluestocking? (Worse yet, can it be sexy?)

Another translator might have been tempted to interpolate contemporary Russian and hence Soviet jargon, shading Lo into a delinquent pioneer. By translating *Lolita* himself, Nabokov forestalled such cleverness. The Russian *Lolita* is instead recognizably a translation, unmistakably a novel from *tam* ("over there," or abroad). Michael Cummins notices a strange kinship precisely with Nabokov's *Onegin*, "that indefatigably clumsy, 'literal' translation of Pushkin's masterpiece." In both, Nabokov the translator "gives us a reading of a great classic of literature, a literal copy 'rendering as closely as the associative and syntactical capability of another language allows, the exact contextual meaning of the original.'"[14] The result is more anachronistic than archaic, even blurring into a cultural collage. Nabokov remained deliberately vague about the intended audience for a Russian *Lolita*, mentioning that it might find the same readers as had Osip Mandelstam's verse. Yet anxiety over the readership is embedded into this newly Russian prose: as Cummins notes, "the new *Lolita* has exegesis right in the body of the text. The reader is coached in English poetry, taught the mechanics of the Bronx cheer (36) and hopscotch (12)."[15]

If the decline of *his* Russian literary tradition had not sufficiently preoccupied Nabokov before, the Russian *Lolita* illuminated matters starkly—there was no returning to the garden. However, the oddly hybrid-sounding Russianized American place names and cultural landscapes must have suggested a creative escape. If the Eden was no more, he could write a new Garden into existence by translating culture in the other direction. The Russo-American world of *Ada* would resurrect the grand tradition of the Russian novel, but in English and on the soil of the New World.

Not least among Nabokov's sources for the expanding new novel was the notoriety and acclaim of the 1962 film adaptation of *Lolita*, and the experience of working with Stanley Kubrick on the screenplay. In the same few years, Nabokov finished *Speak, Memory*, translated Bulat Okudzhava, and read an edition of Mandelstam's verse sent to him by Gleb Struve. He found Mandelstam's poems "marvelous and heart-rending," but as Vera wrote to the *New Yorker*, "V's blood boils when he sees what purports to be translations from the Russian of, say, poor, defenseless, doubly murdered Mandelstam by some of our modern practitioners." Nabokov was more direct, writing in *Encounter* that Robert Lowell should "stop mutilating defenseless dead poets—Mandelstam, Rimbaud and others," and privately to Struve that somebody needed to attack Lowell "for his illiterate and cretinic reworkings."[16] Translations, adaptations, and transfigurations were very much on his mind.[17]

Nabokov's longest novel, though written in English, is littered with references to the Russian literary tradition. For the most part, Nabokov keeps the markers and signposts to his Russian subtexts in plain view: *Ada* is his only novel where characters from *Onegin* appear on the page to mingle with Nabokov's own.[18] Nevertheless, in 1970 Nabokov appended the "Notes by Vivian Darkbloom" section, to patiently identify lines and echoes that the first readers may have missed. As both the text of the novel and the added notes readily show, equally direct references to Chateaubriand and Byron occur side by side with those to Pushkin: in *Ada*, Nabokov seemingly put all of his material from the *Onegin* project to use.

In seven pages and at breakneck speed, the opening chapter introduces the reading experience to follow. *Ada* opens with an infamous inversion:

> "All happy families are more or less dissimilar; all unhappy ones are more or less alike," says a great Russian writer in the beginning of a famous novel (*Anna Arkadievitch Karenina*, transfigured into English by R.G. Stonelower, Mount Tabor Ltd., 1880). That pronouncement has little if any relation to the story to be unfolded now, a family chronicle, the first part of which is, perhaps, closer to another Tolstoy work, *Detstvo i Otrochestvo* (*Childhood and Fatherland*, Pontius Press, 1858).

We begin with a parody of mistranslation, attributed to a cross between George Steiner and Robert Lowell (the latter guilty of re-martyring Mandelstam, the former of theorizing away the crime). This first two-sentence paragraph is ominously dense, with the preposterous verb "transfigured," the title in Russian and in gross English mistranslation, and even that initial provocation that part 1 may be "close to" Tolstoy. After assessing the response, Nabokov added in the first of Vivian Darkbloom's notes that this opening alluded to the "transfigurations (Mr. G. Steiner's term, I believe) and betrayals to which great texts are subjected by pretentious and ignorant versionists" (*Ada*, 591).

In the mid- and late 1960s, the Nabokov-Wilson feud over Nabokov's *Eugene Onegin* translation exploded to include Lowell and Steiner. In 1966 Steiner published the essay "To Traduce or Transfigure: On Modern Verse Translation" in *Encounter*, an evident response to Nabokov's manifesto for literal translation in the "Translator's Introduction" to *Onegin*, and in defense of Lowell's translations of Mandelstam. Steiner argued that the "unfaithfulness inevitable in translating into verse is more than compensated for" by the translator's equivalent achievement. Moreover, a "creative insurgence" forms the start of any new poem. For this reason, Steiner concluded that "a great poetic translation—Hölderlin's Sophokles, Valéry's restatement of Virgil's *Eclogues*, Robert Lowell's readings of Osip Mandelstam—is criticism in the highest sense."[19] Nabokov wrote a letter to *Encounter* in response, prompting Lowell to write a piece, "In Defense of George Steiner" (*Encoun-*

ter, 1967); to which Nabokov replied in turn with "On Adaptation" in the *New York Review of Books* (1969), and again in the pages of *Ada*.

But is *Ada* another transfiguration? Is it a parody of transfiguration, a trap for influence-hunting scholars, and a labyrinth for readers that proves definitively that Nabokov is always one step ahead? "Old storytelling devices," says Van, "may be parodied only by very great and inhuman artists, but only close relatives can be forgiven for paraphrasing illustrious poems. Let me preface the effort of a cousin—anybody's cousin—by a snatch of Pushkin, for the sake of rhyme—" (*Ada*, 246). Lowell and Steiner are presumably neither great and inhuman artists nor "close relatives" of the writers they disfigure: Nabokov, however, claims to be both.

So soon after the highly public *Onegin* feud, *Ada* opens with a jab, announcing with the first lines that it will play all manner of games with the Russian literary tradition. In the next breath, we realize that matters are more complicated still, for "our great and variegated country" joins

> lands in the Severn Tories (Severnïya Territorii), that tessellated protectorate still lovingly called "Russian" Estoty, which commingles, granoblastically and organically, with "Russian" Canady, otherwise "French" Estoty, where not only French, but Macedonian and Bavarian settlers enjoy a halcyon climate under our Stars and Stripes.

If Russian, French, and American territories intersect "granoblastically" on Antiterra, the following four pages covertly introduce all the main characters in several generations of "organically" intermingled Veens and Zemskis, as becomes apparent on rereading. The themes of adultery and incest are present long before we recognize them.[20]

Next we see two children in an attic, in a parody of an exposition scene. Nabokov viciously critiqued the reliance on artificial expositions, such as are occasionally found in Chekhov or Austen. (Here Darkbloom adds the note: "Jane Austen: allusion to rapid narrative information imparted through dialogue, in *Mansfield Park*, 592.") But in the place of an artificially transparent, reader-friendly exchange, Van and Ada serve us an exaggeratedly opaque improvisation à deux. The little Veens' patter demonstrates their precocious intelligence and intensely private world. Ada challenges Van with a luxuriant biological monologue that ends with a comparison to the "Stabian flower girl," an "'allusion, which your father, who, according to Blanche, is also mine, would understand like this' (American finger-snap)" (*Ada*, 8). Camouflaged in their dense exchange is the information that they are brother and sister, as the gossipy maid has already told Ada. Nabokov turns the family chronicle on its head in content as well as style: cheerfully explicit incest replaces the oblique hints at *"cousinage, dangerous voisinage"* in Tolstoy.[21]

The challenge and the key to reading *Ada* is also stated outright: the reader must catch allusions as quickly and accurately as possible to keep up with the Veens. Certain seductive characters, including Ada, Van, and their father Demon, are wonderful allusion-hunters. Will readers fall on the inside or the outside of the Veen circle? The next page names the game again, "Re the 'dark-blue' allusion, left hanging," and explains the etymology of a Veen ancestral name that Van likens to that of Proust's aristocrats: "his favorite purple passage remained the one concerning the name 'Guermantes,' with whose hue his adjacent ultramarine merged in the prism of his mind, pleasantly teasing Van's artistic vanity" (*Ada*, 9).

The last page of this brief but demanding first chapter also hints that Van will become a writer, and includes the first editing note by a much older Ada: "Hue or who? Awkward. Reword! (marginal note in Ada Veen's late hand)." In seven pages, we have learned that *Ada* is a meta-novel, penned by Van and edited by Ada, and that they are still together at a much later point in time. If we only knew what to look for, the entire novel has been summed up and the plot resolved. The first chapter thus parodies and yet obscurely grants the exposition and heavy-handed foreshadowing that we might expect from a family novel—Russian, English, or French.

ECHOES OF *ONEGIN*

The *fabula*, motifs, and meta-literary concerns of *Onegin* haunt *Ada*, but so do larger patterns, such as a complex temporal structure taken partly from *Onegin* and partly from the added stratum of Nabokov's own *Commentary* notes.[22] The story proper, with overt references to *Onegin*, begins in the second chapter and with Van and Ada's parents. Demon Veen seduces Marina in the middle of her performance as Tatiana in a travestied stage version of *Evgenii Onegin*, a "trashy ephemeron (an American play based by some pretentious hack on a famous Russian romance)" (*Ada*, 10). Demon "proceeded to possess her between two scenes (Chapter Three and Four of the martyred novel)." The description of the play is as fantastic:

> In the first of these [scenes] she had undressed in graceful silhouette behind a semitransparent screen, reappeared in a flimsy and fetching nightgown, and spent the rest of the wretched scene discussing a local squire, Baron d'O., with an old nurse in Eskimo boots. Upon the infinitely wise countrywoman's suggestion, she goose-penned, from the edge of her bed, on a side table with cabriole legs, a love letter and took five minutes to reread it in a languorous but loud voice for nobody's benefit in particular.

Even before the old Eskimo had shuffled off with the message, Demon Veen had left his pink velvet chair and proceeded to win the wager . . . [Marina] had ample time, too, to change for the next scene, which started with a longish intermezzo staged by a ballet company whose services Scotty had engaged, bringing the Russians all the way in two sleeping cars from Belokonsk, Western Estoty. In a splendid orchard several merry young gardeners wearing for some reason the garb of Georgian tribesmen were popping raspberries into their mouths, while several equally implausible servant girls in sharovars (somebody had goofed—the word "samovars' may have got garbled in the agent's aerocable) were busy plucking marshmallows and peanuts from the branches of fruit trees . . . (*Ada*, 11)

Onegin is never named but is readily recognizable, as is the adaptation that Nabokov seems to have in mind: Tchaikovsky's opera has the same structural breakdown as this American "trashy ephemeron."[23]

The hero and heroine of *Ada* are thus conceived—almost literally—out of *Onegin*, but from another twisted adaptation. The seduction takes place during an intermission, an interval where one kind of time interrupts another. Demon recognizes the peculiar poetry of the moment, "so struck was he by the wonder of that brief abyss of absolute reality between two bogus fulgurations of fabricated life" (*Ada*, 12). Reality takes place in such intermissions throughout *Ada*, and this scene has more allegorical significance than is apparent at first glance. The erotic interlude even serves as a tongue-in-cheek introduction to "Veen's Time," the most significant contribution to philosophy made by Demon's future son.

But the *fabula* of *Onegin* refuses to be confined to the stage and overflows into all other parts of the novel. Demon races home and makes it back to the theater in time "to fetch his new mistress in his jingling sleigh" (*Ada*, 12), a structural tactic familiar from Nabokov's analysis of the pursuit theme in Pushkin. Spectacular duels, snowy landscapes, and dangerous card games follow. A rival materializes out of the same source: Baron d'Onsky, a conflation of Onegin and Lensky. Characters and plots often come across as if garbled by aerocable, as does so much of Antiterra.[24]

Then again, Van is the author of this pseudo-memoir. He reinvents the world in the process of remembering it, without question fictionalizing the portion that precedes his birth. A good deal is imaginatively reenacted, as Ada alerts us in an early marginal note: "(Van, I trust your taste and your talent but are we *quite sure* we should keep reverting so *zestfully* to that wicked world which after all may have existed only oneirologically, Van? Marginal jotting in Ada's 1965 hand; crossed out lightly in her latest one)" (*Ada*, 15). Van must have invented the fanciful pseudonym for his father's anonymous rival, and he repeats the same trick throughout: when he cannot remember the name of the Irish maid that was briefly his father's mistress, he glides from calling her "the Irish rose" to simply Rose, now her given name. (Joyce was a master at this game: we recall the quaking "Quaker" librarian, or the mysterious brown-coated mourner identified by the papers as Mr. M'Intosh in *Ulysses*.) Here the unknown art dealer, rival, and duelist is significant only for his role in Marina and Demon's Pushkin-inspired love story, so Van conveniently blurs fact and fiction.

Once the *Onegin* fabula enters the novel, it spreads and mutates like a virus—or like a fairy tale; for stories also evolve over time and space. The story retains its links to its original context and yet is emancipated from Pushkin's text.[25] As Demon whisks Marina away, "the last-act ballet of Caucasian generals and metamorphosed Cinderellas had come to a sudden close, and Baron d'O., now in black tails and white gloves, was kneeling in the middle of an empty stage, holding the glass slipper that his fickle lady had left him when eluding his belated advances" (*Ada*, 12). In the *Onegin Commentary*, Nabokov had identified a fairy tale motif in Tatiana Larina's transformation from country maiden to St. Petersburg beauty, and here he underscores the resemblance. As he liked to point out in his lectures on literature, great novels are always fairy tales. Van and Ada's story also escapes to find a life outside of Van's memoir, in the competing narratives offered by Mme Larivière's pulp romance about incestuous siblings; in the even worse film adaptation of her novel; in Kim Beauharnais's blackmailing photo album; and in the legends spread through the Ardis countryside by the Cinderella-like maid Blanche.

These fairy tales and floating stories influence our expectations and often lead to the wrong conclusions. Poor Blanche never finds her prince, instead marrying a local peasant and giving birth to a child disfigured by venereal disease. Larivière's novel, the resulting film, and all the Ardis legends fail to mention that the third and far more likeable Veen sibling Lucette, forever excluded from Van and Ada's solipsistic love, commits suicide. Stories repeat, but the future is not predetermined, and narratives must evolve. Clichés are actually dangerous: both readers and characters misidentify patterns and are led astray by stories that turn out to be mortal after all.

Nabokov's variations on romantic themes are sometimes tragic, but more often comic and sly. Demon duels Marina's other lover D'Onsky, but he fails to either die or dispatch his man with Onegin's ease. He only wounds the humiliated Baron in the groin, and his rival comically survives, marries, and eventually perishes from alleged medical complications. Once more, in the Demon-D'Onsky duel, it is not quite clear who plays the part of Onegin and who is Lensky, since the Baron's name conflates both characters. Pushkin used doubles to great effect: the narrator and Onegin, Onegin and Lensky, Tatiana and Olga, Tatiana and the Muse. Nabokov seems to merge and differently redivide his own somewhat similar characters. Van is both the protagonist and narrator of this romantic tale; dark and light Ada and Lucette mimic the Larin sisters; and the twins Aqua and Marina simply confuse us. We seek to identify one sister as the Tatiana figure, but both and neither one fits. In each generation, some grotesque version of *Onegin* infects the plotline; and so Demon not only flirts with, but marries Marina's sister.

Chiasmic reversals of desire between Demon and Marina, unlike Onegin and Tatiana's chaste and star-crossed longing, fuel a cycle of betrayal and deception that dooms both generations of Veens. Pushkin's story was seen as a parable of restraint, but Demon, "not *quite* a gentleman in amorous matters" (*Ada*, 10), uses the fact that Marina "had been in love with him since their last dance on New Year's Eve" (*Ada*, 11) to seduce her in minutes and win a wager. Their dance echoes Onegin's flirtation with Olga, which was meant to prove to Lensky how quickly one turns a vain girl's head. Marrying Aqua, Demon dallies with the wrong sister but also espouses an unstable ghost of Tatiana, whose fascination with the other world and attempts at divination end in tragedy. Demon and Aqua's marriage proves even worse than the anguished wedlock that Onegin foresaw for himself and Tatiana. Walter "Red" Veen, who provides Marina with financial and social stability, plays the part of a cuckolded Prince N. (as Nabokov translated the title of Tatiana's husband in *Onegin*), although another character with that title also appears as Demon's "orchestra-seat neighbor" and the duped loser of his libertine bet.

Forty pages in, another variation on the *Onegin* theme opens *Ada*'s central narrative, this time as Van and Ada's love story. A cynical young aristocrat self-modeled on books moves to the country and encounters two sisters, the older dark-haired and bookish, the younger fair and natural. Sounding very much like the worried mother Larina, Marina describes her elder daughter as plain compared to the younger's healthy glow. Pale Ada could easily be Tatiana's great-granddaughter: the fact that her mother had been cast as Tatiana underscores the family resemblances. Both Marina and Ada resemble imitations, or reflections of the "real" Tatiana: Van, parting with Ada for the first time in the Ardis woods, tells her that she looks like "the young soprano Maria Kuznetsova in the letter scene of Tschchaikow's opera *Onegin and Olga*" (*Ada*, 158).

But that also is the wrong sister, we protest, and suspect a trap. We initially identify Ada as the Tatiana-figure and dismiss the less interesting sister, but it is Lucette who writes Van the excruciating confessional love letter. It is to Lucette that Van quotes Onegin's most famous lines: "I love you with a brother's love and maybe still more tenderly" (*Ada*, 481). The lines are given exactly as Nabokov translates them in his *Eugene Onegin*, missing only the line break. With uncharacteristic restraint Van refuses to share Lucette's letter with his readers: "In the fall of 1891 she had sent him from California a

rambling, indecent, crazy, almost savage declaration of love in a ten-page letter, which shall not be discussed in this memoir" (*Ada*, 366). Tatiana's chaste
love letter was written in French and given over rather callously to the narrator, who preserved the original and rewrote it in Russian. Likewise, Van
tantalizingly withholds the original and retells the content in his own words.
At some point in the novel, the reader is tempted to assume that Lucette is
the real heroine, and that Van will recognize and fall in love with the girl he
once ignored; but not so. Lucette goes the way of Anna Karenina instead.[26]

Simultaneously drawing our attention to these parallels and leading us
further astray, Van also has a near-romance with another Tatiana while recu-
perating from his own duel. In an aside of no more than a page, his romantic
injury seems to conjure this "Tatiana, a remarkably pretty and proud young
nurse, with black hair and diaphanous skin (some of her attitudes and gestures, and that harmony between neck and eyes which is the special, scarcely
yet investigated secret of feminine grace fantastically and agonizingly reminded him of Ada" (*Ada*, 312). But this Tatiana's story remains within the
parentheses. For once the expected seduction leads nowhere, and the girl
vanishes as rapidly as she entered the novel. She too pens Van "a charming and melancholy letter in red ink on pink paper, but other emotions and
events had intervened, and he never met her again)" (*Ada*, 312).

There is much, much more. *"Tak ty zhenat"* ("So you are married,"
Onegin's words to Prince N.), Van quotes in Russian to Greg Erminin, another rival who might have married Ada: "Might have replied 'Ada Veen,'
had Mr. Vinelander not been a quicker suitor" (454), Van reflects. When he
misidentifies yet another man as Ada's husband, his first thought is of Tchaikovsky's libretto: "The next outstretched hand belonged to a handsome, tall,
remarkably substantial and cordial nobleman who could be none other than
the Prince Gremin of the preposterous libretto" (*Ada*, 511). Van persistently
sees his romance, and perhaps all of his romances, in the light of his beloved
Pushkin.[27]

Priscilla Meyer has called *Lolita* a disguised rewriting of *Onegin*: ultimately,
it is possible to read nearly every Nabokov novel in this way.[28] My own
interest is to show deep structural affinities, pattern repetition in narrative
strategies and in parodic style, and similar struggles with cultural capital and
canon formation, as well as infection by plot. Just as my previous chapters
have found to be true of Pushkin's and Nabokov's *Onegin*, foreign plots
haunt *Ada*, some in central roles and others reading as virtuoso throwaways.
Chilean filmmaker and theorist Raúl Ruiz (best known for his adaptation of
Proust's *À la recherche du temps perdu*) uses the term "immortal story" for
fabulae that recur across cultures and ages, story lines he often uses in multiple variations and echoes within the same film.[29] Leland de la Durantaye,

describing the echoing *fabulae* in Nabokov's works, turns to a different medium and calls the technique counterpoint.[30] These ghostly doubles provide depth, historical melancholy, and suggestive cross-cultural echoes; in Nabokov's late novel, stories are shown to repeat across generations and languages, and characters only live by following or adapting the patterns set by other characters. What seemed in Pushkin an appropriative modernism of underdevelopment, in the late twentieth century reads as additionally inspired by the overwhelming noise of time and by the infinite pressure of cultural inheritance.

Onegin and *Ada* are both, in a sense, about the transmission of literary narratives. A multiplicity of stories competes inside of each novel, which nonetheless aspires to be a single meta-story. It would be deeply unsatisfying to read only about Onegin and Tatiana, skipping over the narrator's meta-literary digressions, just as it would be unsatisfying to read Nabokov's novel only for Ada and Van's affair. Instead we suspect that there is crucial meaning in the throwaways and allusions. In both novels, the central story starts late, is interrupted by constant digressions, and is repeated and echoed by endless grotesque variants. Summarized, the *fabula* never quite seems to match the text before us. These self-conscious stories are not about one person or couple, but about many at once: stories overlap, resemble each other, and seem to merge into universal stories that recur across cultures and eras. How then do we maintain the illusion of a single hero or heroine (the Onegin and Ada of the eponymous novels) or even of a single author? The texts offer what seem a synchronic portrayal of literary evolution—including its failures, monsters, and here the stillborn products of literary incest.

In Pascale Casanova's world republic of letters, languages and literatures have their own borders and capital. In *Ada*, the world of letters *is* the real world: Nabokov's beloved nations, languages, and cultural eras form a magical federation. Many readers suspect that only in such an otherworld of letters could a displaced Russian émigré and self-fashioned European intellectual like Vladimir Nabokov be entirely in his element. Moreover, cultural capital *is* capital—*Ada*'s intellectuals inherit the riches of the world not only figuratively but literally: the intellectual aristocracy, in Nabokov's world, is also the financial elite. Historical tragedy and injustice are righted along the way: Russian poets have been safely transplanted to new shores, and that New World is itself more interesting and diverse. African American descent brings automatic prestige in Nabokov's state, because it is a sign that you come from the first families of the great African explorers who discovered the continent. Young Van's exchanges with Demon include the slang phrase, rather incongruous in Nabokov: "That's very black of you, Dad" (*Ada*, 241). But then again, these characters are Pushkin's descendants after all, and on Antiterra African American and Russian aristocratic culture meet quite naturally.[31]

Nabokov began appropriating Pushkin for his own fiction as early as 1919. He wrote an ending to Pushkin's unfinished *Rusalka* at the age of twenty. Even then, the young author realized that the power of the piece lay in its fragmentation, and tried to preserve a tantalizing incompleteness while adding something of his own style. Much later, Nabokov had hoped to reuse that scene for the second part of *The Gift*, his most ambitious Russian-language novel. This volume was to be about Zina's death, and Nabokov thought once again "to complete an unfinished Pushkin work as a means to a second ending-that-is-not-an-ending," the counterpart to the Onegin stanza at the close of the first book.[32]

Nabokov rewrites Pushkin throughout his oeuvre, using texts that he loves as a springboard for his own work, and returning again and again to the scene of the crime. Ironically, the common complaint of early critics was Nabokov's un-Russianness:

> While Russian émigré critics (those inside Russia were to mention Nabokov first in connection with the reports about the filming of *Lolita*) disagreed about the merits of Nabokov's work, many of them did agree on one point: they kept referring to his "un-Russianness," to his lack of ties with Russian literature and its traditions. At the same time some of them made a point of establishing his dependence on contemporary European literature and spoke of the influence of such different writers as Proust.[33]

Nabokov's best response to such critiques was to show that there was no lack of ties between the Russian tradition and contemporary European literature.

PUSHKIN'S RIVALS AND INTERPENETRATING TRADITIONS

Nabokov's efforts to transplant the Russian literary tradition to new soil do more than invent a Russo-American New World. In keeping with his research and his cultural-ambassadorial agenda in *Eugene Onegin*, Nabokov insisted that the Russian canon was always richly interwoven with English and French literary sources, as well as the other way around (and especially in the generations subsequent to Pushkin). *Ada*'s romantic roots reach beyond *Onegin* down to Pushkin's illustrious precursors, similarly working with and against earlier Russian, French, and English texts. Pushkin focused his energies on the authors from whom he most wanted to learn: as Nabokov argued in his *Commentary*, the two most marked Western sources in *Onegin* are Byron and Chateaubriand. While *Ada*'s allusions seem to lead in all directions, it too leans on Byron and Chateaubriand, emphasizing the roots shared with Pushkin throughout and insisting on an interpenetrating and international genealogy for the poetic novel, the genre that *Ada* seeks to reconsider and update.

The strange genealogy works as follows. The main story is born of Pushkin's *Onegin*, whose characters and lines haunt *Ada* at its most poignant moments. Demon most resembles Lermontov's character, inspired by Pushkin's 1823 poem "The Demon," but painted over with symbolist poetry and Mikhail Vrubel's demons, and throbbing with a generous infusion of Milton and Byron.[34] The Veen family tree includes a Dolly, but Demon also mentions an aunt Kitty who married the banker Bolenski (Lensky?) "after divorcing that dreadful old wencher Lyovka Tolstoy, the writer" (*Ada*, 240). Ada hints at Byron's daughter and sister; but see also Byron's character Adah, sister and wife to the unhappy protagonist of his *Cain*. Ada Veen is also the photographic negative of *Bleak House*'s pretty Ada, an angelic blonde who marries her good-for-nothing cousin.[35] Lucette's final swan dive off a transatlantic liner crosses Ophelia with Anna Karenina and Emma Bovary, but compare also Lucile de Chateaubriand, and Shakespeare's Ophelia. There is a Joycean grandpa Dedelus, whose Irish blood sharpens the Veen girls' lovely profile. The ancient noble names of Van's ancestors shade into Proust's Guermantes. Chekhov is inescapable and mostly linked to the theater diva Marina—and this list does not even begin to include the most important poets (Baudelaire, Rimbaud, Marvell, and Blok) or the paintings and films that co-haunt the work. Finally, the lush gardens of Antiterra or Demonia borrow from the Eden of *Paradise Lost*, in Chateaubriand's translation, and crossed with the wild romantic America of his novels.

I focus on the most prevalent sources to sketch a flight map through *Ada*'s allusions. Despite the incest, hybrids, and anachronism, a pattern can be made to emerge from the carpet. There is a linked repetition of Russian, English, and French great triads, creating a framework for all other borrowings. The pattern is set by the initial group Chateaubriand-Byron-Pushkin: the Russian imitates and then devours his French and English rivals. The next generation offers Flaubert-Dickens-Tolstoy; and the last important layer is Proust-Joyce—and Nabokov himself.

In the *Onegin Commentary*, Nabokov used Byron to illustrate the heights and pitfalls of romanticism, and often to show where Pushkin improved on his precursor. But even Pushkin only went so far, leaving plenty of enabling gaps for his heirs. Nabokov writes that from certain passages in *Onegin*, it is

> an easy mule's ride to the desolate Byronic scene—up to the boulders above timberline or down to the sea cliffs where the surf boomed . . . the moonlit ruins remained as noble and blurry as the "passions" inspired by incest in ancient plays . . . only in a few snowscape stylizations did Pushkin switch (in the

established text) from the generalized Arcadian vista to the specific description. (*Commentary*, 3:290)

Is this critical passage not another springboard for that early glimpse of *Ada*,
the first paragraph that came to Nabokov's mind?

Likewise, Nabokov's summaries of Chateaubriand's *Atala* and *René* for
the *Onegin* project translate into still more material for *Ada*. Both of Chateaubriand's novels imagine a fantastic New World: "In the wilds of Louisiana, under a sassafras tree, René, a French expatriate . . . tells the story of his
romantic past." We can find in Nabokov's gloss of *René* the same language
that Ada and Van will so freely borrow:

> [René] contemplates suicide, but Amelie comes and saves him . . . A subtle
> perfume of incest permeates their relationship: *"cher et trop cher René . . ."*
>
> She leaves him for a convent. In her passionate letter to him there is *"je ne
> sais quoi de si triste et de si tendre, que tout mon Coeur se fondait."* After a
> wonderful visit to the country estate where they had lived, and a description
> of her consecration (at which she admits her "criminal passion"), Rene sets
> out for America. (*Commentary*, 3:100)[36]

The theme of incest blends elements from Byron and Chateaubriand's
lives with their most beloved works: Byron had a troubling relationship with
his half-sister Augusta Leigh, scandalizing both British society and his wife,
who firmly believed that his little niece was also his daughter. This did not
prevent Byron from naming his legal daughter Augusta Ada, after his sister.
Chateaubriand in turn immortalized incestuous love in *René*; and the exact
nature of *his* relationship with beloved younger sister Lucille remains a subject of historical dispute.

While Nabokov's *Onegin* pushed to establish Pushkin's international
importance, it also dedicated a good deal of paper to describing and building
an international canon. Thus one of the subtler agendas of Nabokov's *Onegin* was to restore Chateaubriand to his rightful status. If an interpenetrating
French, English, and Russian canon emerges behind the scenes in Nabokov's *Onegin*, in *Ada* it takes the foreground. In 1969 Nabokov attempts to
write a novel that will openly draw on as well as parody and slyly update the
best works of this transnational canon.

In keeping, *Ada* is riddled with Chateaubriandic, Byronic, and mixed
Chateaubyronic signposts. Ada and Van are in on the joke from the start:
Van very quickly becomes Ada's *"cher, trop cher René"* (*Ada*, 131). The pre-
cocious readers find justification in their favorite masterpieces, sharing a
copy of Chateaubriand before they become lovers: "Van, lying prone behind
Ada, lifted his eyes from his book (Ada's copy of *Atala*)."[37] *Atala* hints at

the somewhat excusable incest of these little "natives," but it also offers another fantasy America. As Nabokov pointed out in his notes to *Onegin*, Chateaubriand's Europeanized noble savages endure trials and adventures in a wildly improbable but deliciously exotic Louisiana. Chateaubriand presumably teaches the Veens "how to love" all too well, but he also helps Nabokov imaginatively map and claim the landscapes of his New World.[38]

The French author even crops up as a breed of mosquito, *Culex chateaubriandi*, whose bite and resulting itch are a metaphor for incestuous desire.[39] Chateaubriand's mosquito brings to a breaking point "the excruciating itch that local children experienced in midsummer" (*Ada*, 106). Drawing more attention to this peculiar Latin name, Ada reports that the first bottler of the mosquito "was not related to the great poet" but then quotes Baudelaire instead.[40] This very literary mosquito is "characterized by an insatiable and reckless appetite for Ada's and Ardelia's, Lucette's and Lucile's (multiplied by the itch) blood" (*Ada*, 106): the quick slip shades Lucette's name into that of Chateaubriand's sister. Finally, in the last reunion between the surviving Veens, the same insect reinspires aging Van's lust for aging Ada: "Pensively, youngly, voluptuously, she was scratching her thigh at the rise of the right buttock: Ladore's pink signature on vellum at mosquito dusk" (*Ada*, 562). The lyrical counterpart to *Culex chateaubriandi* is Chateaubriand's poem "Romance à Hélène," whose verses also "plague" *Ada* and provide Van with ample opportunity for parodic, multilingual play.[41]

Van's name was Juan in the earliest drafts of *Ada*, but Van Veen still retains echoes of Don Juan. Ada teasingly calls him *le beau ténébreux* (*Ada*, 503), an archetype that Darkbloom's notes gloss as "wrapt in Byronic gloom" (*Ada*, 604). Demon has a taste for "Lord Byron's Hock," a dish that he says "redeems Our Lady's Tears" (255).[42] Marina's talented and doomed brother Ivan, who died young of tuberculosis, wears a *bayronka* shirt in her framed photograph. Van and Ada even resume their affair for the second-to-last time near the Swiss "Château de Byron (or 'She Yawns Castle')" (*Ada*, 522).[43] These seemingly incidental references continually cast the Veens in darkly romantic and seductively demonic shades.

Nabokov especially likes to cross-reference Byron and Chateaubriand, as the name of the Swiss chateau fortuitously suggests. Just as in the *Onegin Commentary* he combined the two authors to evoke the intermingled French and English romantic strains of a "novel in the Chateaubyronic genre," so he resurrects and parodies that genre here. Except, of course, he infuses the mixture with Pushkin (alas, Pushkin's name does not lend itself so readily to hybridization as "Chateaubyron"; or perhaps Nabokov means to keep him separate to grant the Russian romantic pride of place).

Chateaubriand and Byron are so central to Van and Ada's own story that the Veens even recognize each other by a mixed Chateaubyronic code.

Ada plays a minor role in an odd film, *Don Juan's Last Fling*, which evidently takes its inspiration from Byron's *Don Juan* as well as from Pushkin's 1830 short tragedy, *The Stone Guest*.[44] Ada's beauty achieves a lethal apotheosis in the film, but Van seems to expect her even before she appears on screen. He knows instantly who the actress billed as "Theresa Zegris" must be, for the Zegris were the rival family to the Abencerrages, celebrated in Chateaubriand's 1826 *Les Aventures du dernier Abencerage*. This is a stage name that only Ada would choose; as if proving the mysterious convergence of their minds, Van publishes his first novel *Letters from Terra* under a pseudonym and "under the imprint of two bogus houses, 'Abencerage' in Manhattan and 'Zegris' in London." Ada tells him years later that, had she seen a copy, she would have recognized "Chateaubriand's *lapochka* and hence your little paw, *at once*" (*Ada*, 342).

Nabokov thus uses Chateaubriand and Byron in *Ada* as indexes to incest, and to a romantic discourse about demonic passions. Nabokov precisely locates the roots of *Ada*—sources that the novel will manipulate to new and remarkable ends—in the same soil as those of Pushkin's *Onegin*. He makes use not only of the same key texts, but of the very technique of subversive, innovative appropriation that he had learned from his studies of *Onegin*. What Pushkin's *Onegin* does with Byron and Chateaubriand, Nabokov's *Ada* tries to repeat with the same two authors, before updating the agon to include the great novelists of the later nineteenth and twentieth century.

Pushkin did not look to Byron and Chateaubriand out of mere playful allusiveness: as we have seen, his *Onegin* is riddled with competitive anxiety over the backward state of Russian literature. *Ada* updates the struggle accordingly. The pattern is that the Russian latecomer outdoes the English and French; the twist or novelty is that *Ada* is not in Russian. In 1969 and in the most ambitious moment of his career, Nabokov attempts to revive, expand, and drastically reinvent a translated Russian literary tradition with the potential to surpass Joyce and Proust.

But let us turn briefly to the middle generation of Russian, English, and French novelists, and once more to *Ada*'s famous opening line. Part 1 explicitly begins and ends with Tolstoy, crossed with Flaubert, and somewhat more subtly touched with Dickens. Lucette's suicide recalls that of Anna Karenina and of Emma Bovary; Van's "sentimental education" progresses far more rapidly than that of Flaubert's Frédéric Moreau; Ardis Hall, as a grand old manor in which relatives inevitably fall in love, reads as an X-rated, hallucinogenic *Bleak House*. In Dickens's novel, blonde Ada marries her cousin Richard in secret, and the heroine Esther very nearly marries her guardian (and suspected natural father) John Jarndyce.

88

The final one-line chapter ending part 1, "When in early September Van Veen left Manhattan for Lute, he was pregnant" (*Ada*, 325), has prompted flurries of critical recognition and has been read alternately as a parody of Tolstoy or of Flaubert.[45] Nabokov's own voice weighed in to insist on Tolstoy: in the Darkbloom notes, in the interviews, in *Strong Opinions*, and in later fiction, Nabokov responded to critics and "corrected" their misinterpretations, as if sufficient reading guidelines were not already coded into the novel. Even a small pun such as "horsepittle" warrants a clarifying comment: it is "borrowed from a passage in Dickens' *Bleak House*. Poor Jo's pun, not a poor Joycean one" (*Ada*, 592).

It is tempting to read part 1 of *Ada* in a Tolstoyan light. If the initial group I have identified—Pushkin, Chateaubriand, and Byron—may be credited with the birth of the poetic novel in Nabokov's literary history, the next major layer, that composed of Tolstoy, Flaubert, and Dickens, and in fact the golden age of the novel, reflects and provokes the previous and subsequent generations. But we will slight this generation necessarily, as did Nabokov himself. He had hoped one day to give *Anna Karenina* a *Eugene Onegin*-esque treatment, but abandoned the project. The early Tolstoy chapter of the *Lectures on Russian Literature* is the closest thing we have, and in it we see a less polished but familiar project along the lines of Nabokov's *Onegin*: Nabokov compares Tolstoy to Flaubert and to other contemporaries, and examines his debt to Pushkin.

The pattern that I have teased out does not mean to ignore other textual presences, but to create a framework for making sense of the most persistent. The task is to trace Nabokov's complicated literary bloodlines; I focus on the beginning and end of that genealogy, the former to set the pattern, and the latter to see its dramatic return with Nabokov's own novel in a starring role. Timelines, like family trees, occasionally reverse direction or collapse in on themselves. As Borges writes in his essay on Kafka, literary influence works in both directions.

Nabokov had no interest in fitting into someone else's anthology of Russian writers, but provided his own transnational genealogy in the parodic family trees of *Ada*. Examined, Nabokov's genealogy reveals an implied trajectory for the Russian romantic/modernist novel, extending from Pushkin to culminate unexpectedly in a late twentieth-century hybrid, written mostly in English and after fifty years of emigration. *Ada* is Nabokov's final act of alchemy with the Russian canon—and at the same time, completely out of place in any national literary tradition. Effectively, he tried to infect our world with Antiterra: to rescue his Russian tradition by translating and annexing it to a hybrid, if English-dominant, canon. Nabokov sought not only to escape his own marginalization, but through his creative output and life-long aesthetic propaganda campaign, to push for the reconfiguration of an international cultural playing field—conjuring in the minds of many readers an alluring vision of a transnational Antiterra.

All of Nabokov's great names are writers and artists that he admired without or with little hesitation: this is the "right" side in the culture wars (or recurring dialectic) of the twentieth century. Nabokov's list reflects the camp of the individual aesthetic producer—a camp that stands for conscious effort, aestheticism, and continuity with great traditions. The countermovement stands for subconscious creativity, climate of thought, and questions of individual authorial intent: such is the literature of social engagement, collectives, and of the avant-garde. Nabokov wastes no opportunity to let us know which side of that cultural cold war he is on.[46] In the *Onegin Commentary* he writes, "Old Larin had a high rank in the Army and was a gentleman; his wife, Pauline Larin, may have been—for all we know—née Princess Shcherbastki, paternal grandaunt of Tolstoy's Dolly Oblonski. Soviet commentators miss these fine points" (2:228).

And yet, for all that Nabokov reads as an ambassador for autonomy, on the opposite end on the spectrum from the recurring avant-gardes (and perhaps dialectically linked to the arts of engagement, following Peter Bürger), his purportedly utopian world republic of letters coincides with dystopia: Antiterra is Demonia.[47]

NABOKOV'S READERS: WE, RONALD ORANGER

Ada self-consciously aspires to break free from time and place, and to reach the status of an international classic. To do so, it imagines a transnational canon and an ever-expanding English as the international language—a vision that is, in the end, not unlike Steiner's in *After Babel*. Nabokov's canon resembles that of many Russian and other displaced intellectuals: it includes by necessity the Western classics to which they hope to lay claim, and by birth, their national literature. But a striking aspect of the "Nabokov phenomenon" is the role played by critics and scholars in acknowledging, building, and expanding the once-marginal émigré's vision to make that canon not his alone.

As an especially savvy producer of his own biographical legend, with insider knowledge of the workings of academia and public intellectual forums alike, Nabokov carefully trained not only the Nabokovian reader, but also the Nabokovian critic.[48] He may not always treat his creation charitably, but the bumbling editor Ronald Oranger has the first and final word in *Ada*: from the opening reassurance that, "with the exception of Mr. and Mrs. Ronald Oranger, a few incidental figures, and some non-American citizens, all the persons mentioned by name in this book are dead," to the editing and censoring decisions.

In the 1960s, Nabokov was writing after the rise of critical theory. He not only read but also personally responded to and painstakingly evaluated the work of his critics in *Strong Opinions*, name by name and point by point. He developed relationships with his admirers, rewarding some with privileged access and bitterly denouncing others. Nabokov understood too the university classroom and the syllabus as important sites of canon formation; hence the *Lectures on Literature* and *Lectures on Russian Literature*. And sooner or later, he knew it would all be in Oranger's hands, if under the eagle-eyed gaze of the Nabokov estate.

My conjecture is that allusions in *Ada* are an integral part of the enticing trap. While teasing "allusion-hunters," Nabokov well knew that literary scholars are trained to do precisely that.[49] By loosely burying, or leaving out in the open so many enticing references, he effectively seduces his critics into drawing and redrawing Nabokov's canon. The very difficulty of *Ada* could be catnip for generations of readers, trained by American New Critics or Russian formalists alike to privilege difficulty itself. To make the pleasure of discovery even more tempting, as Eric Naiman has shown us, *Ada*'s hermeneutics are perverse.[50] It is little wonder that we take the bait.

Nabokov's most dedicated readers return time and again to the vexed questions of his precursors, allusions, and parodic style. The sheer density of Nabokov's allusions can easily lead into a quagmire, the mad pursuit of reminiscence against which even he warned in the introduction to *Eugene Onegin*. How has the critical discourse explained a practice so central to Nabokov's poetics, but extreme even among modernists?[51] While I cannot hope to provide even a partial flight map of scholarship on the topic, I will touch on a selection of works influential to this study as an illuminating and indicative sample set.

Maria Virolainen uses the allusions to Pushkin in *Ada* to explain the significance of Nabokov's autonomous artistic discourse.[52] Virolainen acknowledges that *Ada* cites other Russian novels as much if not more than *Onegin*; however, she maintains that *Onegin* holds pride of place. (Similarly, D. Barton Johnson argues that despite the fact that there are more direct references to Tolstoy and *Anna Karenina* in the novel, *Onegin* nonetheless must be the more important source text: the Tolstoy "line of indirection is a snare for the unwary.")[53]

Virolainen points out that in Pushkin's work, the difference between the poetic and the prosaic word amounted to diglossia: poetic discourse markedly belonged to a separate world. *Onegin* instantly signals its artificiality through verse form, rhyme, and meter. After the Golden Age, the distinction between reality and artistic discourse elided. The great nineteenth-century Russian novels yearned to make the novel an extension of life; the symbolists in turn made life an extension of poetry. Virolainen suggests that Nabokov separates the two once more in *Ada*, returning to this forgotten aspect of Pushkin's cultural era. In place of the chasm between poetry and prose that made *Onegin* possible, he introduces actual diglossia in *Ada* for the same effect:

> It is no coincidence that *Ada* is a Russian novel written outside of the boundaries of the Russian language. While it is far from Nabokov's first English-language novel, it is however an emphatically *Russian* English-language novel, with Russian heroes and continual appeals to the Russian novelistic tradition.[54]

Virolainen focuses on the Russian tradition, leaving aside Nabokov's synchronic relationships and, as she notes, the complicating presence of French. Her reading suggests an analogy between Van's childhood and *Onegin* as the fountainhead of Russian literature, and casts *Ada* as Nabokov's last Russian novel, although it is neither in Russian nor actually his last.

Nabokov draws attention to the artifice of prose through the use of complex allusions and counterpoint, tightly controlled and signifying structure, as well as virtuoso multilinguistic play. Many critics distinguish between an all-pervasive state of intertextuality, true of any text, and a technique of allusion or parody.[55] Annapaola Cancogni outlines the fundamental assumptions of an allusive technique:

> It establishes (1) an established literary tradition as source of value; (2) the audience as sharing that tradition with the poet; (3) an echo of familiar yet distinctive and meaningful elements; and (4) a fusion of that echo with elements in the new context . . . it requires a close poet-audience relationship, a social emphasis on literature, a community of knowledge, and a prizing of literary tradition.[56]

These requirements, at odds with Nabokov's disinterested reputation, suggest that the difficult style pulls at least some readers closer in.

A second set of distinctions qualifies which allusions are integral to the novel's meaning. If some allusions determine or affect the plot and overall interpretation, others contribute locally to the sheer pleasure of puzzle, recognition, and intricate pun. Taking up the erotic metaphor, Carl Proffer even writes:

> The allusion may be a mere fleeting detail which the initiated reader uses briefly like a passing harlot. It is no great loss if one does not realize that the "elongated Persty grapes" described on page 251 are taken from a little known lyric by Pushkin. But *Ada cannot be read intelligently* if the clusters

of allusions to works by Lermontov, Tolstoy, Pushkin, and Chekhov remain beyond the consciousness of the reader.[57]

Like details in a realist text, allusions in the modernist novel fall into categories of major or minor significance, though such categorization remains open to interpretation.

The essence of Proffer's and Alfred Appel Jr.'s similar stances in such exegetic works as *Keys to Lolita* and *The Annotated Lolita* is that Nabokov's repeated allusions create an "involuted," overtly artistic texture which warns the reader "to seek no reality" beyond that of art.[58] The position echoes a number of diverse twentieth-century artistic and critical practices, from Joyce to Bertolt Brecht. (Appel declares parody to be the key to Nabokov, but seems to have Joyce equally in mind: "Like Joyce, Nabokov has shown how parody may inform a high literary art.")[59]

Proffer began the preliminary work of annotating *Ada*, an exegesis that finds its apotheosis in Brian Boyd's multiauthor hypertext *AdaOnline* (as well as in the free-form Kinbotean world of the Nabokov electronic discussion list). In his monograph, *Nabokov's Ada: The Place of Consciousness*, Boyd suggests an ethically charged reading. He argues that the layer of artifice establishes a moral and intellectual difference between Nabokov's narrators (Humbert Humbert, V.V., or Van Veen) and the omniscient author. Boyd considers *Ada* to be Nabokov's most moral novel: its allusions teach the reader to look below the surface, and to pay attention to ethical as well as aesthetic details.[60] Following a trail of allusions, the reader discovers that Lucette's story is the hidden counterpoint to Van and Ada's narcissistic love, and the novel's moral center.

Pekka Tammi in turn examines Nabokov's allusions in the light of Kiril Taranovsky's school of Mandelstam studies. Taranovsky underscores the unintelligibility of Mandelstam's poems when viewed alone. Calling Mandelstam a "poet of cryptic messages," he argues that the "motivating context" in a given poem is provided "by *other literary texts*, and such motivating texts may be denoted by the term *subtext*."[61] Tammi applies the Taranovsky method to Nabokov, suggesting terms like "reading in three dimensions,"[62] which demands "the activation of not just a single source (say, a novel by Dostoevsky), but a compound of multiple subtexts within a single textual unit, demanding precisely that we lift out the text, cube-like, from its immediate background, examine it from diverse intertextual angles, and search out the heterogeneous literary sources."[63] The pre-texts may be arbitrarily joined; at other times the combination creates the impression of a "*genetic* (causal) connection." For example, in *Lolita*, Nabokov

operates with a multitude of allusions to Prosper Mérimée's *Carmen* (1847). But, as [Nabokov] himself has been careful to point out elsewhere (in *EO*

3:155–156), Mérimée's novella is, at least in part, modeled on Pushkin's narrative poem *Tsygany* (1824), and an "inexact and limp" prose version of the poem (re-titled *Les Bohémiens*) was actually produced by Mérimée in 1852. . . . In the following passage the causal chain [T1:] *Lolita* → [T2:] *Carmen* → [T3:] *Tsygany* is laid bare.[64]

In *The Mirage in the Mirror: Nabokov's Ada and Its French Pre-Texts*, Cancogni finds that Nabokov's fiction

> turns towards its own literary past, in the name of a literature that refuses to be the alleged mimetic transcription of some presumably universal outer reality and instead, drawing from the unlimited resources of language and imagination that this new freedom opens up, creates a new reality with its own rules, its own systems, and its own referential background.[65]

Adding French subtexts missed by many Anglo- and Russophone critics, Cancogni traces the "springboard of parody" phrase to find that V. Knight borrowed the "famous Flaubertian expression" from an 1877 letter to Turgenev: *"La Réalité, selon moi, ne doit être qu'un tremplin."*[66] (This nod to the Flaubert-Turgenev correspondence again suggests that Nabokov takes every opportunity to draw attention to, or forge, deep cultural connections between literary Russia and western Europe at the crucial moments in the history of the novel.)

Cancogni concludes that Nabokov belongs in the ranks of the great modernists, with Proust and Joyce:

> Unlike the work of most of his contemporaries, whose innovation all too often rests on an alleged break with previous literature and all too seldom soars beyond the level of the experiment, Nabokov's fiction is tautly rooted within a literary tradition and, in this respect, bears greater affinity to that of the so-called "modernists" (and particularly Joyce and Proust) . . . than to that of any of his contemporaries (including Borges).[67]

Michael Wood in "Nabokov's Late Fiction" also draws an explicit comparison between late Nabokov and the modernist monuments of Joyce and Proust. Wood notices that Nabokov's last three novels contain glimpses of a reality "located outside the fiction, rather as Joyce's Molly Bloom suddenly and surprisingly turns out to know her author's name, and as the narrator of Proust's *À la Recherche du temps perdu* allows us to wonder on a couple of occasions whether he is or isn't called Marcel."[68] Ontological walls slip, for many of Nabokov's protagonists peer across the divide of death in the later period Wood terms Nabokov's interview with posterity.

As even this brief summary shows, many critics view Nabokov's allusions as a modernist technique carried to the extreme. Through divergent readings, they conclude that (1) Nabokov's allusions are conscious and overt; (2) Nabokov engages with literary tradition in a manner parodic but not destructive (anti-avant-garde); (3) his highly allusive style is like that of Joyce and Proust; and (4) the density of the allusions forces readers to remain aware of the artifice of the art. Sympathetic readers of *Ada* especially argue that there is more than meets the eye in the texture of its prose, and that beyond the pleasurable literary games, Nabokov insists on the ethics of close reading. Many, if not most, follow Nabokov's own dictum against reductive historicism.

Recently, a number of monographs and articles have reread Nabokov's works against the critical grain, making important interventions and questioning the prevalent ahistoricism of Nabokoviana.[69] Moving beyond the dichotomies of formalism and historicism, it seems high time to build from multiple strands of criticism and to foster emancipatory possibilities rather than interpretive antagonisms. The missing link between the individual text, the authorial oeuvre, and social context or totality is mediation in its many forms (genre, discourse, medium). In "The Genesis of the Media Concept," John Guillory reminds us that this was what Benjamin and Adorno argued over in 1938, prompted by Adorno's rejection of Benjamin's essay on Charles Baudelaire:

> In the section of the work to which Adorno objected most strongly, Benjamin drew a connection between the imposition of a wine tax on the citizens of Paris in the years 1849 and 1850 and the composition of Baudelaire's poems thematizing wine and intoxication. The larger movement of Benjamin's argument can be bracketed in order to consider Adorno's vehement response: "Let me express myself in as simple and Hegelian manner as possible. Unless I am very much mistaken, your dialectic is lacking in one thing: mediation."[70]

We cannot miss the mediation in *Ada*, a novel about style, a pilgrimage into the novel form, and an exploration of the escapist fantasies of artistic immortality. Even old Van has doubts at the end of his memoir:

> Demonian reality dwindles to a casual illusion. Actually, we had passed through all that. Politicians, dubbed Old Felt and Uncle Joe in forgotten comics, had really existed. Tropical countries meant, not only Wild Nature Reserves but famine, and death, and ignorance, and shamans, and agents from distant Atomsk. Our world *was*, in fact, mid-twentieth-century. Terra convalesced after enduring the rack and the stake, the bullies and beasts that Germany inevitably generates when fulfilling her dreams of glory. Russian peasants and poets had not

been transported to Estotiland, and the Barren Grounds, ages ago—they were dying, at this very moment, in the slave camps of Tartary. (*Ada*, 582)[71]

Undercurrents of historical tragedy always lurk behind *Ada*'s wistful world. If Pushkin found Russia and Russian literature to be out of fashion and behind, Nabokov believed his had been struck down in full bloom, doubly murdered in translation and in Stalin's labor camps. In both cases, vast reserves of self-irony provide the keys to escape—from provincialism and marginalization, if never from history.

Both *Onegin* and *Ada* are about their own overt struggles with the dream of literary immortality, about aspirations to break free from the vagaries of fashion. To join an international list of great writers and artists means to win autonomy and a life beyond the local context. Yet both novel in verse and poetic novel remain as much of their time as they are determinedly innovative or retrospective: respectively, the two texts bracket the perceived start of a powerful movement in Russian literature, and the end, or transfiguration, of that movement as perpetuated for half a century in émigré culture. Nabokov's was the last generation to have little to no contact at all with Soviet culture, making *Ada* something like the last novel of imperial Russia. Like *Onegin*, *Ada* marks a temporal border and a sea change.

Ada in Pursuit of Proust and Joyce

> Truth will begin only when the writer takes two
> different objects, establishes their relationship,
> and encloses them in the necessary rings of
> his style (art), or even when, like life itself,
> comparing similar qualities in two sensations,
> he makes their essential nature stand out
> clearly by joining them in a metaphor in order
> to remove them from the contingencies (the
> accidents) of time, and links them together by
> means of timeless words.
> —Marcel Proust, *À la recherche du temps perdu*,
> 1913–1927

> I just don't know what an "anti-novel" is
> specifically. Every original novel is "anti-"
> because it does not resemble the genre of its
> predecessor.
> —Vladimir Nabokov, *Strong Opinions*, 1973

GAMES OF LIGHT AND SHADE

In 1973 the philologist J. E. Rivers met with Nabokov in Switzerland. He had written in advance to say that he would like to talk about Marcel Proust: when Nabokov and Vera came to meet him, Nabokov was carrying a copy of *Pale Fire* marked with one of his famous index cards. "Perhaps you have read this little book of mine, *Pale Fire*," Nabokov said modestly, and explained that the marked passage remained the best summary of his views on Proust. In that passage, Kinbote indirectly reprimands Sybil via an evaluation of Proust:

"Speaking of novels," I said, "you remember we decided once, you, your husband and I, that Proust's rough masterpiece was a huge, ghoulish fairy tale, an asparagus dream, totally unconnected with any possible people in any historical France, a sexual *travestissement* and a colossal farce, the vocabulary of

97

genius and its poetry, but no more, impossibly rude hostesses, please let me speak, and even ruder guests, mechanical Dostoevskian rows and Tolstoian nuances of snobbishness repeated and expanded to an insufferable length, adorable seascapes, melting avenues, no, do not interrupt me, light and shade effects rivaling those of the greatest English poets, a flora of metaphors, described—by Cocteau, I think—as 'a mirage of suspended gardens,' and, I have not yet finished, an absurd, rubber-and-wire romance between a blond young blackguard (the fictitious Marcel), and an improbable *jeune fille* who has a pasted-on bosom, Vronski's (and Lyovin's) thick neck, and a cupid's buttocks for cheeks; but—and now let me finish sweetly—we were wrong, Sybil, we were wrong in denying our little *beau tenebreux* the capacity of evoking 'human interest': it is there, it is there—maybe a rather eighteenth-centuryish, or even seventeenth-centuryish, brand, but it is there."[1]

For his most eloquently phrased evaluation of Proust, Nabokov turns to a passage from one of his later novels. The embedded commentary works beautifully in the context of *Pale Fire*, not only as an overly ingenious retort to Sybil for excluding Kinbote from a party. The quick summary of *À la recherche* harmonizes with *Pale Fire*'s motifs of artistic risk, social exclusion, homosexuality, and memories of lost grandeur. Nabokov's half-admiring and half-devastating pastiche of Proust seems an integral internal echo of his own ghoulish fairy tale. It offers readers a common cultural background with Kinbote/Botkin and an insight into the building blocks of his delusional world: the traumatized Russian immigrant reimagines himself and his past through luridly literary eyes. In a wonderful example of what René Girard calls "mimetic desire," Kinbote casts himself as a glamorous aristocrat, a misplaced Baron de Charlus among the mid-century American plebeians.[2] Nabokov acknowledged a counterpoint structure to his most complex novels, *Pale Fire* and *Ada*: in one manifestation of this technique, an earlier fairy tale begins to feel like a prescient echo of Nabokov's own.

Ada is exponentially more riddled with literary appraisals than is *Pale Fire*. As in the passage above, which discovers Dostoevsky and Tolstoy hidden in Proust, the embedded commentaries run together. Part 1 of *Ada* especially, as many readers realize, presents a parodic history of the novel, transfiguring literary monuments into a super-saturated backdrop for the Veens' erotic adventures. The story of the Venus villas, floramors built by unrelated Veens, reads as one of many built-in parallels to the main narrative. Eric Veen's grandfather, an Antiterran Hugh Hefner, erects pretentious brothels ranging in style "from dodo to dada, from Low Gothic to Hoch Modern. In his parodies of paradise he even permitted himself, just a few times, to express the rectilinear chaos of Cubism (with 'abstract' cast in 'concrete')," drawing inspiration from "Vulner's paperback *History of English*

Architecture" (350). This range of pastiches in architecture, bent to erotic purposes, sounds suspiciously similar to what *Ada* does with literary styles.

Nabokov's favorite literature coexists on anachronistic Antiterra; his parodies fold and overlap in time. Van and Ada's childhood takes place in late nineteenth-century Demonia, but the little Veens are already familiar with Proust, Joyce, Hollywood films, and commercial flights. The romantic plot and physics-fiction conceit of *Ada* are at least in part an excuse for Nabokov's most dazzling games with literature. The Veen incest suggests allegorical implications for literary inbreeding, and the magic of Ardis derives from the glory years of the novel form, remembered in a dreamy anachronistic jumble and yet another paradise lost. Nabokov claims to detest allegory but loves to literalize a metaphor, or to allow images to hover between the allegoric and episodic. From the earliest interviews, he described the *Texture of Time* as the most difficult thing he ever wrote, and as a text that brought metaphors to life.

My earlier chapters argue for Pushkin's centrality as the Russian fountainhead of Nabokov's canon, and that *Ada* continues the Pushkin/Byron/Chateaubriand triads and appropriations explored in *Eugene Onegin*, in novel form. Throughout, Nabokov seeks to internationalize Russian literature by annexing it to a transnational canon. The pattern traced thus far helps to chart *Ada*'s allusions when they turn to the twentieth century: Nabokov updates the agon, learning from Pushkin's example how to borrow from the French- and English-language modernists.

Nabokov turns to Joyce and Proust as the last poetic novelists to produce works on the level of their illustrious nineteenth-century precursors, the torchbearers of a sensibility to which contemporary poets had far less claim. For Nabokov, the greatest poetry of the twentieth century was to be found in Proust's sinewy sentences and in Joyce's multivalent puns. In the *Lectures on Literature*, Nabokov called À *la recherche* "the greatest novel of the first half of our century" (139). By the publication of *Strong Opinions* it had been unseated by *Ulysses*, but these two were clearly the contenders for first place. As he wrote in the *Lectures*, there are many "talents" in the twentieth century, but "geniuses" only three or four: Proust, Joyce, and Kafka. While Kafka lingers behind certain atypical Nabokov novels such as *Bend Sinister* and *Invitation to a Beheading*, there is no comparison with the number of allusions, parodies, and embedded commentaries on Proust and Joyce to be found throughout Nabokov's work.[3]

In one of the many lists (implicit syllabi) of *Strong Opinions*, Nabokov recounts: "In Western Europe, between the ages of 20 and 40, my favorites were Housman, Rupert Brooke, Norman Douglas, Bergson, Joyce, Proust, and Pushkin . . . by now [these] are probably beyond change as far as I am concerned" (*Strong Opinions*, 43). The first three belong to the Cambridge of his early twenties and seem a feint against the English modernist poets, but the latter four form the gist of my study. Again, *Ada* seems qualitatively different from Nabokov's other novels, the novel in which he overtly tangles with *Ulysses* and *À la recherche* as never before. His readings—expository in the *Lectures on Literature* and literary in *Ada*—mingle Proust and Joyce with the Russian novel, continuing to break down the borders of national canons and to create precursors for Nabokov's own practice.

LECTURES ON PROUST AND JOYCE

While he may have later preferred his fictionalized ruminations on literature, the most accessible treatment of Proust and Joyce in Nabokov's published work is found in the *Lectures on Literature*. Nabokov's *Lectures* share with his *Commentary* to *Eugene Onegin* a tone of evaluative exegesis: Nabokov tries to parse when Proust and Joyce are at their best and when they slip, as well as the distinctive stylistic, thematic, and compositional traits that comprise their respective signatures. He systematically highlights their most brilliant innovations and lamentable overindulgences—all the key points of substance and style that speak to or against his own work. The *Lectures* thus give us an opportunity to reread Proust and Joyce with Nabokov, to catch the peculiarities that he finds most worthy of admiration or of censure, or simply the most memorable. They reveal something about their subjects, but far more about Nabokov's tastes.

According to the *Lectures*, the first half of *À la recherche* (the portion revised during Proust's lifetime) forms the greatest novel of the early twentieth century. Nabokov's broadly stroked analysis promises to focus on the first tome, but ranges over the monumental text. Nabokov focuses on Proust's interest in the visual arts and vividly visual verbal descriptions—as well as on time, memory, the philosophy of recall at which Marcel arrives, and its relation to literature. The novel is a "treasure hunt where the treasure is time and the hiding place the past" (*LL*, 207).

Nabokov begins by explaining that Proust's ideas about time and memory are inspired by Bergson's philosophy of time:

> In his youth Proust had studied the philosophy of Henri Bergson. Proust's fundamental ideas regarding the flow of time concern the constant evolution of personality in terms of duration, the unsuspected riches of our subliminal minds which we can retrieve only by an act of intuition, of memory, of involuntary associations; also the subordination of mere reason to the genius of inner inspiration and the consideration of art as the only reality in the world; these Proustian ideas are colored editions of the Bergsonian thought.[4]

However, Nabokov seems to conflate Bergson with Proust, even stating in one interview that he had been a great admirer of Bergson's novels in his youth (Bergson never wrote novels).[5] Foster suggests that the formula, Proust is Bergson in colored edition, may give "the impression that Proust is secondary to Bergson," but considering the centrality of the verbal image for Proust, Bergson, and Nabokov, the formula rather makes Bergson "the precursor, in mere black and white, for Proust's more vivid achievement."[6]

Proust's prose style manifests his philosophy of time through compound metaphors and hybrids combining metaphor with simile; the expanded sentence; and seamlessly merged dialogue, narrative digressions and meditations, and extended visual descriptions. Even without the recognizable philosophy outlined above, a few sentences alone would allow us to identify Proust's signature. (Needless to say, Nabokov does not delve into the socioeconomic dimensions of Proust's work. If the inhabitants of this dreamy world "happen to be what the gazettes call society people men and ladies of leisure, the wealthy unemployed," it is because the only professions Proust cares to show in action are artistic and scholarly: "Proust's prismatic people have no jobs: their job is to amuse the author" [*Lectures on Literature*, 208].)

Painting and the visual arts are central to Proust's novel, but his text depends on visual imagination throughout. Nabokov sums up the work as a series of exquisitely curated images. The whole of *À la recherche* is "but an extended comparison revolving on the words, *as if*—" (*Lectures on Literature*, 208). (In part 4 of *Ada*, Van will end his *Texture of Time* treatise with a similar broken comparison, "it is like—" [*Ada* 563].) Nabokov summarizes: "The key to the problem of reestablishing the past turns out to be the key of art. The treasure hunt comes to a happy end in a cave full of music, in a temple rich with stained glass" (*Lectures on Literature*, 208).

Color is key to this stained glass temple, where the very name of Guermantes "emerges from the inner colors of the church" (*Lectures on Literature*, 227). Proust was another synaesthete, Nabokov leaps to point out. Words, bloodlines, and memories all have a particular tint: Gilberte's name is "like a cloud passing over, sheds for Marcel 'a marvelous little band of light, of the colour of heliotrope,' and then with an inner simile it turns the lawn to a magic carpet" (*Lectures on Literature*, 241, nota bene the magic carpet). *À la recherche* is shot through with

> a mauve color, the violet tint that runs the whole book, the very color of time. This rosy-purple mauve, a pinkish lilac, a violet flush, is linked in European literature with a certain sophistication of the artistic temperament. It is the color of an orchid, *Cattleya labiata* . . . It adorns Swann's lovemaking in a famous but not very convincing scene. From this mauve to the delicate pink

of hawthorns in the Combray chapters there are all kinds of shadings within Proust's flushed prism. (*Lectures on Literature*, 241)

The entire novel emerges from the magic lantern of the opening pages, and is peppered with the play of light and shadow. Proust's light and shade effects in prose, as Nabokov has Kinbote repeat years later, rival those of the greatest English poets.

Thus are the Edenic moments captured in this otherwise melancholy monument. Nabokov draws attention to the children's games in the Bois de Boulogne and how perfectly Proust manipulates readers' imaginations to create a four-dimensional memory: in one long sentence Nabokov finds what he calls "space-time in parentheses, the content of which should be noted for this bright bit of lawn and bit of time in the girls' afternoon, with the shuttlecock beating time" (*Lectures on Literature*, 241). The passage, and Nabokov's description of it here, foreshadows Ada's light and shade games in Ardis as well as Lolita's tennis. Such passages do something to the reader's sense of time, creating an image so memorable and precise that it seems to capture a moment otherwise never shared.

Nabokov stresses Swann's peculiarity of falling in love with young mistresses for their resemblance to figures in Old Master paintings, a fancy quirk he passes on to Albinus in *Laughter in the Dark*, Humbert in *Lolita*, and all the artistic Veens.[7] Proust's narrator shares the proclivity, for "Swann sets the pattern, and the narrator follows it" (*Lectures on Literature*, 239). The first incarnation is nearly always the truest, more bright and beautiful than what follows: every particle of Proust's world seems to long for some earlier idyllic time. Everything returns but loses color in subsequent iterations, and the narrator seems condemned to play out grayer versions of Swann's love.

In the last book of *À la recherche*, Marcel arrives simultaneously at an understanding of time and of art. Simple memory, the act of visualizing something in retrospect, does not re-create the past: more is involved; and the inner meaning must be sought. Only art has the ability "'to rediscover, grasp again and lay before us that reality from which we live so far removed . . . that reality which there is grave danger we might die without ever having known and yet which is simply our life, life as it really is, life disclosed at last and made clear'" (*Lectures on Literature*, 248). Nabokov quotes at length one of Proust's loveliest passages:

> If, at least, there were granted me time enough to complete my work, I would not fail to stamp it with the seal of that Time the understanding of which was this day so forcibly impressing itself upon me, and I would therein describe men—even should that give them the semblance of monstrous creatures—as occupying in Time a place far more considerable than the so restricted one

allotted them in space, a place, on the contrary, extending boundlessly, since, giant-like, reaching far back into the years, they touch simultaneously epochs of their lives—with countless intervening days between—so widely separated from one another in Time. (*Lectures on Literature*, 249)

Nabokov emphasizes the not-quite perfect identity between the text and metatext described in *À la recherche*, as well as between the author and authorial stand-in: "The book that the narrator in Proust's book is supposed to write is still a book-within-the-book and is not quite *In Search of Lost Time*—just as the narrator is not quite Proust." This above marks the close of *À la recherche*, but might just as easily stand at the end of Nabokov's *Speak, Memory* and of *Ada*.

Nabokov pays Proust his biggest compliment in the appended early essay "The Art of Literature and Common Sense," where he describes artistic inspiration in terms that shade from perfectly Proustian to recognizably Nabokovian:

The inspiration of genius adds a third ingredient: it is the past and the present *and* the future (your book) that come together in a sudden flash; thus the entire circle of time is perceived, which is another way of saying that time ceases to exist. It is a combined sensation of having the whole universe entering you and of yourself wholly dissolving in the universe surrounding you. It is the prison wall of the ego suddenly crumbling away with the nonego rushing in from the outside to save the prisoner—who is already dancing in the open. (*Lectures on Literature*, 378)

What begins as Marcel's insight ends with Nabokov's own distinctive and defiantly joyous imagery; but the passage implies that Nabokov's very notion of artistic insight is deeply colored by Proust.

Between the *Lectures on Literature* and the *Pale Fire* pastiche, Nabokov soured slightly on his French precursor. To his students in the 1950s, he insisted on the magic of this "enormous and yet singularly light and translucid" work. But his later fiction betrays impatience with nuances of snobbery taken to "insufferable lengths," ludicrous erotic obsessions, and the wild improbabilities of what was, in his final analysis, a rough and unedited masterpiece. By 1962 and the short pastiche included in *Pale Fire*, Nabokov was already more critical; by 1969 and *Ada*, he believed he could do better.

Ulysses closes Nabokov's canon of great fairy tales in the *Lectures*. Nabokov's fascination with Proust seems to correspond with his European years, but he increasingly considered Joyce's masterpiece, that impossibly "rich book with a vocabulary of about thirty thousand words" (*Lectures on Literature*, 285), the summit of twentieth-century literature. Nabokov reads Joyce with an eye to his parodies and stylistic pyrotechnics, including the much-lauded stream of consciousness technique, and to his complex structures and counterpoint. If Proust hunts for the treasure of time through metaphors and the sheer duration of his prose, Joyce captures a multirhythmic, palimpsestic present with all its moving parts.[8]

While he begins, ends, and intersperses this lecture with some of his most admiring remarks on literature, Nabokov insists that not one of his authors achieves perfection consistently. To bring out the diamonds, there is much to clean away—not to mention, in the exegetic paper trail that Joyce has amassed:

> *Ulysses* is a splendid and permanent structure, but it has been slightly over-rated by the kind of critic who is more interested in ideas and generalities and human aspects than in the work of art itself. I must especially warn against seeing in Leopold Bloom's humdrum wanderings and minor adventures on a summer day in Dublin a close parody of the *Odyssey* . . . . That there is a very vague and very general Homeric echo of the theme of wanderings in Bloom's case is obvious, as the title of the novel suggests, and there are a number of classical allusions among the many other allusions in the course of the book; but it would be a complete waste of time to look for close parallels in every character and every scene of the book. There is nothing more tedious than a protracted and sustained allegory based on a well-worn myth; and after the work had appeared in parts, Joyce promptly deleted the pseudo-Homeric titles of his chapters when he saw what scholarly and pseudoscholarly bores were up to. (*Lectures on Literature*, 287–88)

En passant, Nabokov inserts a short sermon on how not to read, and attributes to Joyce the very Nabokovian move of doctoring his manuscript against the misreadings of bores.

As in the lecture on Proust, Nabokov chooses to focus on Joyce's signature style and his treatment of time, the backbone of the modernist poetic novel.[9] The secret of *Ulysses* lies in the interaction of prose style and temporal structure; in place of Proust's painterly vision, Joyce offers ironic verbal techniques and virtuoso parodies, the only sincere way that this author is able to conjure the past.

Joyce's style in *Ulysses* may be divided into his own prose style; the "incomplete, rapid broken wording rendering the so-called stream of consciousness"; and various parodies of literature, pulp fiction, journalese, and other forms of writing (*Lectures on Literature*, 289–90). Nabokov has unreserved admiration only for Joyce's original voice. Stream of consciousness "exaggerates the verbal side of thought" at the expense of imagery, and the parodies are a mixed blessing. Rapidly switching between styles allows Joyce to introduce unexpected lyrical strains, but as quickly descends "to all sorts of verbal tricks, to puns, transposition of words, verbal echoes, monstrous twinning of verbs, or the imitation of sounds" (*Lectures on Literature*, 290). The sheer weight of these unmotivated special effects, alongside the local allusions and foreign expressions, can introduce "needless obscurity."

> There is no special reason why . . . one chapter should be told straight, another through a stream-of-consciousness gurgle, a third through the prism of parody. There is no special reason, but it may be argued that this constant shift of the viewpoint conveys a more varied knowledge, fresh vivid glimpses from this or that side. If you have ever tried to stand and bend your head so as to look back between your knees, with your face turned upside down, you will see the world in a totally different light. Try it on the beach: it is very funny to see people walking when you look at them upside down. They seem to be, with each step, disengaging their feet from the glue of gravitation, without losing their dignity. Well, this trick of changing the vista, of changing the prism and the viewpoint, can be compared to Joyce's new literary technique, to the kind of new twist through which you see a greener grass, a fresher world. (*Lectures on Literature*, 288–89)

This description converges with formalist notions of estrangement, but also foreshadows Van Veen's acrobatic stunts: Nabokov's narrator in *Ada* not only imitates Joyce in style and obscurity, but takes the metaphor of turning upside down literally.

What Nabokov admires the most in *Ulysses* is the counterpoint technique, from the synchronized group scenes to "one of the greatest passages in all literature," when Bloom brings Molly her breakfast. Joyce intercuts their dialogue with Bloom's inner thoughts, rife with divergent language and discourse. Elsewhere Joyce manipulates banter about the horse Throwaway, the casual phrase "throw it away," and the throwaway Elijah pamphlet: the phrase, like the pamphlet, crops up recurrently and lends a complex rhythm to the novel. The blind piano tuner with his tapping stick is another agent of time, synchronizing events in the chapter. Bloom helps him "cross the street in an eastward direction, about two o'clock" (*Lectures on Literature*, 334); the musical tapping sound of his passage serves as the blind youth's leitmotif and pulls together several key scenes. Through such verbal magic, Joyce conjures the entire buzzing Dublin machine with all its moving parts.[10]

A passing cloud offers another synchronizing agent. Nabokov quotes and explicates in between sentences of Joyce: "'A cloud began to cover the sun wholly slowly wholly. Grey. Far.' . . . Stephen saw the same cloud before breakfast: 'A cloud began to cover the sun slowly, shadowing the bay in deeper green. It lay behind him, a bowl of bitter waters'" (*Lectures on Literature*, 304). In the first instance Bloom with his singsong vocabulary thinks of advertising posters and the East; in the second, Stephen's loftier mind returns to the bowl of green bile at his dying mother's side, for the "great mother" sea reminds him of his culpability and of his simultaneous rejection of God and humanity.

Nabokov reads *Ulysses* too in temporal terms: the hopeless past, the ridiculous and tragic present, and the pathetic future. If there is no past without the creative intervention of the present in Proust, in Joyce the present is infected by the past. History weighs us down even stylistically, and only a self-ironizing intelligence can grasp for autonomy under the immense pressure of accumulated cultural debris: hence the parodies and pastiches of *Ulysses*. When Nabokov analyzes the Gerty McDowell passage in Episode 13, he comes up with a veritable manifesto for modernist aesthetics:

> When we say cliché, stereotype, trite pseudoelegant phrase, and so on, we simply mean, among other things, that when used for the first time in literature the phrase was original and had a vivid meaning. In fact, it became hackneyed because its meaning was at first vivid and neat, and attractive, and so the phrase was used over and over again until it became a stereotype, a cliché. We can thus define clichés as bits of dead prose and of rotting poetry . . . Now what Joyce does here is to cause some of that dead and rotten stuff to reveal here and there its live source, its primary freshness. Here and there the poetry is still alive. (*Lectures on Literature*, 346)

When Joyce has the readers realize alongside Bloom that Gerty is hopelessly lame, "the very clichés of her thought acquire something real—pathos, pity, compassion—out of the dead formulas which he parodies." This is Joyce, and parody, at the very best.

At other times Nabokov finds Joyce's technique less revolutionary and overly ornamental. At such moments the reader understands the slip from *Ulysses* to the "grotesque, inflated, broken, mimicking, and punning style of the author's next and last novel, *Finnegans Wake* (1939), one of the greatest failures in literature" (*Lectures on Literature*, 349). Likewise, Nabokov has reservations about Joyce's stream of consciousness device, his most unduly famous technical innovation:

> First, the device is not more "realistic" or more "scientific" than any other. . . . the stream of consciousness is a stylistic convention because obviously we do not think continuously in words—we think also in images; but the switch from words to images can be recorded in direct words only if description is eliminated as it is here. Another thing: some of our reflections come and go,

others stay; they stop as it were, amorphous and sluggish, and it takes some time for the flowing thoughts and thoughtlets to run around those rocks of thought. (*Lectures on Literature*, 363)

And anyway, Nabokov stresses, Tolstoy had done it better in *Anna Karenina*.

Nabokov misses in such passages the visual imagination so prevalent in Proust. Yet when Joyce permits himself to write in his own voice, his descriptions of Dublin and the light and shade effects of his imagery do not suffer the comparison. Joyce's scalpel wit allows none of the emotional overindulgence or purple prose that overwhelms the second half of Proust's enormous novel. When Joyce is overindulgent, it is with pun and irony.

The most peculiarly Nabokovian moment in the lecture on *Ulysses* is his idiosyncratic claim about the identity of the mysterious Macintosh, or M'Intosh:

Do we know who he is? I think we do. The clue comes in chapter 4 of part two, the scene at the library. Stephen is discussing Shakespeare and affirms that Shakespeare himself is present in his, Shakespeare's, works. Shakespeare, he says, tensely: "He has hidden his own name, a fair name, William, in his plays, a super here, a clown there, as a painter of old Italy set his face in a dark corner of his canvas . . ." and this is exactly what Joyce has done—setting his face in a dark corner of this canvas. The Man in the Brown Macintosh who passes through the dream of the book is no other than the author himself. Bloom glimpses his maker! (*Lectures on Literature*, 319–20)[11]

Leland de la Durantaye notes, "no other Joyce scholar that I know of has contended [that] before or since."[12] Authorial visits of this kind are far more typical of Nabokov, who again reads backward, finding traces of his own style in his Irish precursor.

Curiously, Nabokov adds rather prudishly, "Joyce with all his genius has a perverse leaning towards the disgusting" (*Lectures on Literature*, 342). Does the following passage tell us something about Nabokov's reading of the "perverse" modernists, or about his own characters?

In the sexual department Bloom is, if not on the verge of insanity, at least a good clinical example of extreme sexual preoccupation and perversity with all kinds of curious complications. His case is strictly heterosexual, of course— not homosexual as most of the ladies and gentlemen are in Proust. . . . but within the wide limits of Bloom's love for the opposite sex he indulges in acts and dreams that are definitely subnormal in the zoological, evolutional sense. I shall not bore you with a list of his curious desires, but this I will say: in Bloom's mind and in Joyce's book the theme of sex is continually mixed and intertwined with the theme of the latrine. God knows I have no objection to so-called frankness in novels. On the contrary, we have too little of it, and what there is has become in its turn conventional and trite. . . . But I do object to the following: Bloom is supposed to be a rather ordinary citizen. Now it is not true that the mind of the ordinary citizen continuously dwells on physiological things. I object to the continuously, not to the disgusting. (*Lectures on Literature*, 287)

This is hardly the response that we might expect from the author of *Lolita* and *Ada*, but Nabokov finds the obsessive sexual jealousy and "deviance" in Proust and Joyce silly. His own characters parody modernism's overemphasis on the sexual oddity.[13]

Despite Nabokov's frequent insistence on the originality of genius, the *Lectures* often offer the following lines of descent:

A master of Flaubert's artistic power manages to transform what he has conceived as a sordid world inhabited by frauds and philistines and mediocrities and brutes and wayward ladies into one of the most perfect pieces of poetical fiction known, and this he achieves by bringing all the parts into harmony, by the inner force of style, by all such devices of form as the counterpoint of transition from one theme to another, of foreshadowing and echoes. Without Flaubert there would have been no Marcel Proust in France, no James Joyce in Ireland. Chekhov in Russia would not have been quite Chekhov. So much for Flaubert's literary influence. (*Lectures on Literature*, 147)

Artistic talent transforms everything into poetry: its alchemy uses style and formal structure, counterpoint, complexity, and echo. Flaubert's example allows for the existence of such literary heirs as Proust and Joyce. Then Nabokov catches himself and ironizes such "influence-chasing."

Yet Nabokov cannot hold back from genealogies. Describing Flaubert's bravura set piece, in which Rodolphe seduces Emma at a country fair and one banal horror counterpoints another, he claims that this "wonderful chapter" had "an enormous influence on James Joyce; and I do not think that, despite superficial innovations, Joyce has gone any further than Flaubert" (*Lectures on Literature*, 160). In another lecture, Nabokov conjures Proust studying Flaubert's prose style: "Proust says somewhere that Flaubert's mastery of time, of flowing time, is expressed by his use of the imperfect, of the *imparfait* . . . . to express the continuity of time" (*Lectures on Literature*, 173). After quoting from a wonderful moonlit scene in *À la recherche* he exclaims that Proust "had a precursor" in Tolstoy (*Lectures on Literature*, 220; e.g., the scene in which Prince Andrei listens to Natasha singing by moonlight).

Just as in the *Commentary* to *Eugene Onegin*, Nabokov invents his tradition in the annotated syllabus of the *Lectures on Literature*. He compiles and authorizes these lists and evaluations as his final word in the selected (and amended) interviews in *Strong Opinions*. In one, Nabokov gives his top four novels of the twentieth century as Joyce's *Ulysses*, Kafka's *Trial*, Bely's *Petersburg*, and the first half of Proust's *À la recherche du temps perdu*. Bely, I suspect, serves as a Russian placeholder for Nabokov himself.[14] The modernist poets meanwhile are unequivocally dismissed: "I was never exposed in the twenties and thirties, as so many of my coevals have been, to the poetry of the not quite first-rate Eliot and of definitely second-rate Pound," Nabokov writes. "I read them late in the season, 1945, in the guest room of an American friend's house, and not only remained completely indifferent to them, but could not understand why anybody should bother about them" (*Strong Opinions*, 43; he evidently has Wilson in mind). In a letter to Wilson, Nabokov berated: "How could you even *mention* that Eliot in the same sentence as P. and J.?"

PROUST AND COLORED MEMORY IN *ADA*

Proust appears in *Ada* through direct reference, hidden allusion, stylistic parody, and embedded analysis: en masse, we find an enormous, layered Proustian presence in substance and in style. Proust serves as a secret language between the Veen children, and between the characters and readers as well: his readers identify one another quickly. (In the *Lectures* Nabokov spoke of a "Joycean reader," for "every new type of writer evolves a new type of reader; every genius produces a legion of young insomniacs" [*Lectures on Literature*, 316].) If we share with Van and Ada much of their favorite art and culture, are we drawn into sympathy, or even made complicit with them? Shared literature provides a common language, idiosyncratic and yet potentially more international than English, French, or Russian: Shakespeare, for example, has been translated into over eighty languages.

Proust offers another road into *Ada*: the Proustian reader finds much to recognize and compare. These echoes may well be traps for the influence hunter; having seen what the scholarly bores were up to with his previous work, Nabokov delivers a novel so full of "influence" and "family romance" as to drive the comparativist or psychoanalyst mad. And yet the quiddity of the novel lies in the texture of these layered allusions, challenging the reader to unravel its skeins at the same time as it declares the task to be impossible.

The Veens, with their exotic aristocratic past, glamorous opulence, and unrelenting awareness of who is and is not of their set, read as exaggerated Russified Guermantes. In *Ada* too the only professions we see in action are artistic and scholarly. (If the Veens share something with the *Speak, Memory* Nabokovs, it is because the characters of that memoir too are suspiciously Proustian.)[15] Nabokov keeps the connection explicit and colorful:

> A former viceroy of Estoty, Prince Ivan Temnosiniy, father of the children's great-great-grandmother, Princess Sofia Zemski (1755–1809), and a direct descendant of the Yaroslav rulers of pre-Tartar times, had a millennium-old name that meant in Russian "dark blue." While happening to be immune to the sumptuous thrills of genealogic awareness, and indifferent to the fact that oafs attribute both the aloofness and the fervor to snobbishness, Van could not help feeling esthetically moved by the velvet background he was always able to distinguish as a comforting, omnipresent summer sky through the black foliage of the family tree. In later years he had never been able to re-read Proust (as he had never been able to enjoy again the perfumed gum of Turkish paste) without a roll-wave of surfeit and a rasp of gravelly heartburn; yet his favorite purple passage remained the one concerning the name "Guermantes," with whose hue his adjacent ultramarine merged in the prism of his mind, pleasantly teasing Van's artistic vanity.
>
> Hue or who? Awkward. Reword! (marginal note in Ada Veen's late hand). (*Ada*, 9)

Van's Proustianisms in this early paragraph range from overt reference to intonation. The Guermantes are mentioned by name; Proust's color-memory is translated and transposed into the Russian Temnosiniy; there is even an early hint of Van's Bergsonian/Proustian philosophy of time. However, there is also assessment, critique, and parody. Van's enjoyment of Proust is conditional in later years; this passage itself is a purple pastiche likely to cause heartburn; and an older Ada attempts to reign in his colorful vagueness. We are only on page nine, but it is already evident that *Ada* is the "most steeped in Proust" of all Nabokov's novels.[16]

The earlier generation of Veens swarms with Swann-like art dealers: Demon collects "old masters and young mistresses," while his cousin Daniel "Red" Veen deals art professionally (*Ada*, 4). Both recognize masterpieces in the living world around them, although the less dashing Dan falls for fakes and goes mad under the influence of Hieronymus Bosch.[17] Likewise both Demon and Baron D'Onsky recognize Marina in "an unknown product of Parmigianino's tender art." The sketch, a nonexistent composite of several Parmigianino sketches, which resembles his "Adam" more than "Eve":[18]

> showed a naked girl with a peach-like apple cupped in her half-raised hand sitting sideways on a convolvulus-garlanded support, and had for its discoverer the additional appeal of recalling Marina when, run out of a hotel bath-

room by the phone, and perched on the arm of a chair, she muffled the receiver while asking her lover something that he could not make out because the bath's voice drowned out her whisper. (*Ada*, 12–13)

No Proustian reader can fail to recall that Swann falls in love with Odette for her resemblance to Botticelli's blondes, a weakness that Nabokov already borrowed for Humbert, who finds tear-streaked Lolita Botticelli-pink, and for Albinus, who falls for fake old masters and cheap Margot. Men's fashions on Antiterra mimic closely those of *À la recherche*: like Swann, Demon sports a mustache and a monocle. Cancogni notes that even Demon's "means of transportation throughout the first period of courtship is a most evocative swan-sleigh."[19]

In the next generation, the wunderkinder Van and Ada recognize each other by their reading, and their favorite literature provides them with the language to live and later write their lives. At first, snobbish little Ada tells Van: "Our reading lists do not match" (*Ada*, 53). But they do, the children soon discover. Their mutual favorites are Joyce and Proust: "Did he like elms? Did he know Joyce's poem about the two washwomen? He did, indeed" (54); "At ten or earlier the child had read—as Van had—*Les Malheurs de Swann*" (55).[20]

See also Ada's "shadow and shine" games in the Eden of Ardis:

> The shadows of leaves on the sand were variously interrupted by roundlets of live light. The player chose his roundlet—the best, the brightest he could find—and firmly outlined it with the point of his stick; whereupon the yellow round light would appear to grow convex like the brimming surface of some golden dye. Then the player delicately scooped out the earth with his stick or fingers within the roundlet. The level of that gleaming *infusion de tilleul* would magically sink in its goblet of earth and finally dwindle to one precious drop. (*Ada*, 51–52)[21]

The infusion recalls Marcel's famous madeleine with lime tea, which prompts involuntary recall in *À la recherche*. Ada's strange and lovely games are thus explicitly linked with Proust's art and memory even in these early chapters. Proust functions as an index to what is most real, artistic, memorable, and beautiful. However, just as Ada and Lucette compete for Tatiana's role, so too do both little Ada and little Lucette resemble Gilberte in the Combray gardens. Which is the right little girl? Nabokov's parallels are carefully imperfect: associations slip, fold, and collapse.

Just when we expect Proust to signify the real and the beautiful, he is knocked off the pedestal with obscene mockery. Mlle Larivière remembers Van as a "*bambin angélique* who adored *à neuf ans*—the precious dear!—

Gilberte Swann *et la Lesbie de Catulle.*" Van adds, "and who had learned, all by himself, to release the adoration as soon as the kerosene lamp had left the mobile bedroom in his black nurse's fist" (*Ada*, 66). Virile little Van is a far cry from neurosthenic Marcel. Equally precocious Ada is fond of "the noble larva of the Cattleya Hawkmoth (mauve shades of Monsieur Proust), a seven-inch-long colossus, flesh colored, with turquoise arabesques, rearing its hyacinth head in a stiff 'Sphinxian' attitude" (56). Paragraphs later "the Odettian Sphinx had turned, bless him, into an elephantoid mummy with a comically encased trunk of the guermantoid type" (56–57). In the *Lectures* Nabokov found Swann and Odette's erotic code, *"faire Cattleya"* for lovemaking, to be silly and unconvincing. Here he indulges in a naturalist's revenge.

What are readers to make of all this? Rivers writes, "Sometimes Nabokov pays homage to Proust; sometimes he quarrels with him; sometimes he makes fun of him; but always he is aware of him."[22] Boyd observes: "In place of Proust's meditative languor and torpid narrative speed, Nabokov hurtles the action along at a preposterous pace . . . the breakneck narrative of Demon's and Marina's affair takes only six pages." If Swann and Odette's love affair has moments of redemption that Marcel and Albertine's lacks, in *Ada* the brevity and meaninglessness of Demon's affair with Marina "contrasts sharply with the extraordinary durability—over eighty years!—of Van's and Ada's love."[23] Many critics notice an inversion: if in Proust each generation is a feeble imitation of the previous one, in Nabokov things ameliorate. For all the irony of its first sentence, *Ada* really does seem to hold that only happy families are worth the ink. Yet a good deal of anguish, jealousy, betrayal, and death must take place before two very plump, middle-aged Veens settle down to enjoy their remaining forty plus years in twenty-odd pages.

Part 1 borrows heavily from Pushkin and Tolstoy, but is at the same time profoundly indebted to Proust. At the end of this section Van loses Ardis forever. His Marcel-like sexual jealousy is underscored by Ada's very literary lesbian adventures. (Vanda, possibly Ada's first lover, sounds suspiciously like a double of Vivian Darkbloom—an authorial joke on Van.) Nabokov also inserts a passage of literary criticism already familiar to us from the *Lectures* and from *Pale Fire*:

> Our professor of French literature maintains that there is a grave philosophical, and hence artistic, flaw in the entire treatment of the Marcel and Albertine affair. It makes sense if the good reader *knows* that the narrator is a pansy, and that the good fat cheeks of Albertine are the good fat buttocks of Albert. It makes none if the reader cannot be supposed, and should not be required, to know *anything* about this or any other author's sexual habits in order to enjoy to the last drop a work of art. My teacher contends that if the

reader knows nothing about Proust's perversion, the detailed description of a heterosexual male jealously watchful of a homosexual female is preposterous because a normal man would be only amused, tickled pink in fact, by his girl's frolics with a female partner. The professor concludes that a novel which can be appreciated only by *quelque petite blanchisseuse* who has examined the author's dirty linen is, artistically, a failure. (*Ada*, 168–69)

The professor is of course another double of Vladimir Nabokov, borrowed from his *Lecture* notes but rendered a good deal more Veenish.

In truth Van is jealous of Ada's affairs regardless of gender; but while his anguish is familiar from the earlier literature, the Veens' middle-aged happiness is not. The Veens seem to arrive at a triumphant if dearly bought redemption. They are allowed to reunite only after Lucette, Marina, Demon, and Andrey Vinelander have all died; after Ada has failed as a film star and Van has retired from the public eye; after they have lost physical beauty, health, sexual drive, and even their physical similarity; and when both are confirmed childless.

We must remember that young Van and Ada, as well as their parents, live and speak Proust because such is the style of old narrating Van. After Van's indecent above-quoted monologue to Cordula and Ada, the latter mutters, "But *you*'ve had too much Marcel." The narration, and not the young protagonist, responds to the critique by changing style: "Our damp trio found a nice corner table and with sighs of banal relief undid their raincoats. He hoped Ada would discard her heavy-seas hat but she did not, because she had cut her hair because of dreadful migraines, because she did not want him to see her in the role of a moribund Romeo. (On fait *son grand Joyce* after doing one's *petit Proust*. In Ada's lovely hand)" (*Ada*, 169). As is so often the case in *Ada*, Joyce immediately follows Proust. The two are organically linked for an author seeking to find a style adequate to his subject and century. Hundreds of pages later, in the Bergson-laced treatise on time, Van is still struggling with Proust's influence. He warns himself: "beware . . . of the marcel wave of fashionable art, avoid the Proustian bed" (541).

I will turn to a lengthy and markedly Proustian passage for vivid examples of the characteristic ways that Nabokov manipulates Proust's presence in his text. Nabokov borrows his precursor's style, embellishes and expands on it, and uses it to enchant and snare his reader. We recognize family resemblances and enjoy catching allusions, but are never comfortably sure about the extent—and intent—of the parody. Does a grand Proustian style exonerate these characters, or damn them further? Many readers ask the same question of Nabokov himself. This passage presents a troubling meta-literary moment and describes a troubling scene, one of the sadder tableaux of the novel: Marina, Demon, and their two biological children dine together, but deceits run between them like fault lines.[24] The reunited family masquerades as something else, yet this may have been the closest to happiness that the Veens will ever come. Here is a gruesome family portrait—the parents who know nothing, and the children everything:

> It was a black hot humid night in mid-July, 1888, at Ardis, in Ladore county, let us not forget, let us never forget, with a family of four seated around an oval dinner table, bright with flowers and crystal—not a scene in a play, as might have seemed—nay, *must* have seemed—to a spectator (with a camera or a program) placed in the velvet pit of the garden. Sixteen years had elapsed from the end of Marina's three-year affair with Demon. Intermissions of various length—a break of two months in the spring of 1870, another, of almost four, in the middle of 1871—had at the time only increased the tenderness and the torture. Her singularly coarsened features, her attire, that sequin-spangled dress, the glittering net over her strawberry-blond dyed hair, her red sunburnt chest and melodramatic make-up, with too much ochre and maroon in it, did not even vaguely remind the man, who had loved her more keenly than any other woman in his philanderings, of the dash, the glamour, the lyricism of Marina Durmanov's beauty. It aggrieved him—that complete collapse of the past, the dispersal of its itinerant court and music-makers, the logical impossibility to relate the dubious reality of the present to the unquestionable one of remembrance. Even these hors-d'oeuvres on the *zakusochnïy stol* of Ardis Manor and its painted dining room did not link up with their *petits soupers*, although, God knows, the triple staple to start with was always much the same. . . .
>
> Demon popped into his mouth a last morsel of black bread with elastic samlet, gulped down a last pony of vodka and took his place at the table with Marina facing him across its oblong length, beyond the great bronze bowl with carved-looking Calville apples and elongated Persty grapes. . . . [He] tried to *realize* (in the rare full sense of the word), tried to *possess* the reality of a fact by forcing it into the sensuous center, that here was a woman whom he had intolerably loved, who had loved him hysterically and skittishly, who insisted they make love on rugs and cushions laid on the floor ("as respectable people do in the Tigris-Euphrates valley"), who would woosh down fluffy slopes on a bobsleigh a fortnight after parturition, or arrive by the Orient Express with five trunks, Dack's grandsire, and a maid, to Dr. Stella Ospenko's *ospedale* where he was recovering from a scratch received in a sword duel (and still visible as a white weal under his eighth rib after a lapse of nearly seventeen years). How strange that when one met after a long separation a chum or fat aunt whom one had been fond of as a child the unimpaired human warmth of the friendship was rediscovered at once, but with an old mistress this never happened—

the human part of one's affection seemed to be swept away with the dust of the inhuman passion, in a wholesale operation of demolishment. . . .

Marina, essentially a dummy in human disguise, experienced no such qualms, lacking as she did that *third sight* (individual, magically detailed imagination) which many otherwise ordinary and conformant people may also possess, but without which memory (even that of a profound "thinker" or technician of genius) is, let us face it, a stereotype or a tear-sheet. . . . "poor old" Demon (all her pillow mates being retired with that title) appeared before her like a harmless ghost, in the foyers of theaters "between mirror and fan," or in the drawing rooms of common friends, or once in Lincoln Park, indicating an indigo-buttocked ape with his cane and not saluting her, according to the rules of the *beau monde*, because he was with a courtesan. Somewhere, further back, much further back, safely transformed by her screen-corrupted mind into a stale melodrama was her three-year-long period of hectically spaced love-meetings with Demon, *A Torrid Affair* (the title of her only cinema hit), passion in *palaces*, the palms and larches, his Utter Devotion, his impossible temper, separations, reconciliations, Blue Trains, tears, treachery, terror, an insane sister's threats, helpless, no doubt, but leaving their tiger-marks on the drapery of dreams, especially when dampness and dark affect one with fever. And the shadow of retribution on the backwall (with ridiculous legal innuendos). All this was mere scenery, easily packed, labeled "Hell" and freighted away; and only very infrequently some reminder would come—say, in the trick-work close-up of two left hands belonging to different sexes—doing what? Marina could no longer recall (though only *four* years had elapsed!)—playing *à quatre mains?*—no, neither took piano lessons—casting bunny-shadows on a wall?—closer, warmer, but still wrong; measuring something? But what? Climbing a tree? The polished trunk of a tree? But where, when? Someday, she mused, one's past must be put in order. Retouched, retaken. Certain "wipes" and "inserts" will have to be made in the picture; certain telltale abrasions in the emulsion will have to be corrected; "dissolves" in the sequence discreetly combined with the trimming out of unwanted, embarrassing "footage," and definite guarantees obtained; yes, someday—before death with its clap-stick closes the scene.

Tonight she contented herself with the automatic ceremony of giving him what she remembered, more or less correctly, when planning the menu, as being his favorite food—*zelyonïya shchi*, a velvety green sorrel-and-spinach soup, containing slippery hard-boiled eggs and served with finger-burning, irresistibly soft, meat-filled or carrot-filled or cabbage-filled *pirozhki*—peer-rush-KEY, thus pronounced, thus celebrated here, for ever and ever. After that, she had decided, there would be bread-crumbed sander (*sudak*) with boiled potatoes, hazel-hen (*ryabchiki*) and that special asparagus (*bezukhanka*) which does not produce Proust's After-effect, as cookbooks say. (*Ada*, 250–54)

The passage hums with Proust from beginning to end, adding Russian and other cultural allusions as ever-present cultural counterpoint.[25] The flower and crystal-laden setting conjures an Old Master backdrop, viewed through the Swann-like eyes of an artistic connoisseur. The exaggeratedly novelistic opening sentence, replete with unnecessary information and markers of space and time (in mid-July, 1888, at Ardis, in Ladore) alerts us that a significant literary passage is afoot. The first person plural is Proustian and Flaubertian; the momentarily frozen scene limns a verbal painting, a prose poem, and an attempt to capture lost time.

The scene is thus described through the self-conscious lenses of litera-ture and art. We read it as a markedly literary passage in prose; we imagine a painting; and it *"must* have seemed" (note the repetition and emphasis) like a scene in a play. Kim Beauharnais must be peeping outside with a camera and not a program, but "the velvet pit of the garden" recalls the start of Demon and Marina's affair during the travestied *Onegin* play. The synopsis of their romance—sixteen years ago, three years in length, with intermissions—recalls also that first theatrical intermission. Once more reality masquerades as art, or else art as reality. Just as in *À la recherche*, the narrator of *Ada* must have recourse to all the other arts to master his own.

For the rereader, time flows backward as well as forward: Marina's dyed hair and coarsened features resemble the older Ada. Van and Ada overcome the shock of physical aging, but Demon experiences "that complete collapse of the past," when human affection for an old lover vanishes with "the dust of the inhuman passion." How similarly Marcel mourns the collapse of his memories, his past selves, and the vanished house of Combray; how exagger-atedly Proustian too is Demon's ardor—an inhuman or inhumane passion. The only real emotion on Demonia, ardor is defined through the agonies of longing, jealousy, and loss. The narrator of *À la recherche* similarly confesses that, aside from jealousy, he has not known love; aside from erotic longing, he has felt little real emotion for others.[26]

Marina herself is a re-mastered Odette to Demon's Swann. (The "Lin-coln Park" courtesan evokes Odette again, in an American incarnation and marginalized according to the beau monde's special code.) Demon grasps the bitter magic of the moment, and attempts to conjure the past through the opulent meal.[27] But Marina, the cinema automaton, finds a shortcut in montage: her love affair has been safely remade into stale melodrama, sans the troubling details. By the rules of *Ada*, precise and vivid memories make us human; Marina's children judge their "automaton" mother harshly for forgetting. The best Marina can do is to locate the *à quatre mains* image on a polished tree trunk, but the Nabokov-trained reader recognizes the omi-nous and erotically charged banister leading to the scene of many incestuous trysts. Yet there is something Proustian about Marina's cinematic memory as well: all memories are inevitably "Retouched, retaken." The evocative abrasions, emulsions, dissolves, retrospective edits, and final clap-stick of Marina's movie cannot be entirely dismissed.

All of this seems quite serious and melancholy. Yet various oddities pepper this grand passage, with its painterly surfeit and anguished musings on time and memory. Nabokov translates Proust's lavish feasts into amusingly mixed high- and low-register Russian fare: in place of Françoise's sculptural constructions in *À la recherche*, we have *shchi* with boiled potatoes and cabbage pirozhki. The "elongated Persty grapes," a seemingly gratuitous Pushkin allusion, add to the sense that this Proustian pastiche is infected thoroughly with Russian food, words, and literary tradition. The resulting cultural synthesis is colored by Nabokov's brand of humor, ending with a self-conscious and comical flourish: special *bezukhanka* asparagus that does not produce "Proust's After-effect." We slide seamlessly from homage to Proust at his most philosophical and profound to an arch pastiche of his memorably laughable moments.

Excluded from the family portrait described above, Kim Beauharnais lurks outside as the spectator "with a camera or a program" of the opening sentence. This imagined or reconstructed spectator enables the entire scene: it is to him that the family dinner must have seemed like a scene in a play, which is how Van goes on to describe it. Without an imagined audience and without readers, Van and Ada's elaborate history does not quite work. The Veens alternately encourage voyeurs and violently defend their privacy.

The offhand way in which Van describes blinding Beauharnais strikes many readers as one of the book's crueler moments, outside of the scenes with Lucette. (Blindness and cruelty are linked in several key passages, including a description of one of Van's psychiatric patients, and in Van and Ada's flippant exchange about Blanche's blind child: "Love is blind," they quip.)[28] Even more pointed is Van's choice of weapon: he blinds Kim with an alpenstock. As an index to Van's violence, it resembles the engraved walking stick in *Despair* that dooms Hermann and betrays his intellectual mediocrity; but here the tool works simultaneously as a specific allusion. In the later volumes of *À la recherche*, Proust mentions that, for a season or two, alpenstocks were all the rage in the Faubourg Saint-Germain. Proust's modish stick finds its way into Van's hands, who grimly uses it to blind his blackmailer.[29] The social cruelties of Proust's feverishly class-conscious world translate into physical violence in Antiterra, in one of the novel's many moments of sudden uncomfortable dissonance with its modernist precursors.

To give the screw another turn, his propensity to lurk near windows or behind bushes, just as the hero and heroine engage in their amorous pursuits, makes the peeping Kim Beauharnais a parody of Proust's narrator.[30]

In the *Lectures*, Nabokov repeatedly mocked Marcel's fortuitous placement just outside conveniently open windows in one scene after another. Passing Mlle Vinteuil's window, Marcel happens to witness her lesbian relationship: "The whole scene," lectures Nabokov, "is a little lame . . . with the eavesdropping business enhancing its awkwardness" (*Lectures on Literature*, 232). Gossipy old Aunt Leonie serves as a built-in self-parody, a grotesque shadow "of Marcel himself in his capacity of sick author spinning his web and catching up into that web the life buzzing around him" (*Lectures on Literature*, 228). Most outrageous of all, in another early passage we find Marcel "eavesdropping" on his aunt's dreams. Nabokov comments, "Eavesdropping is, of course, one of the oldest literary devices, but here the author goes to the limits of the device" (*Lectures on Literature*, 230). Nabokov thus takes a tired literary device and forces it into the open, simultaneously exposing readers and certain authors as incurable eavesdroppers and voyeurs.[31] When Van blinds Kim, the moment shows brutality on the level of character and plot, but on a meta-literary level it serves as Nabokov's retort to Proust's eavesdropping device and jab at Proust himself.

The final grotesque incarnation of Proust in *Ada* is in drag, as the French governess Mme Larivière. Her amalgam of literary pretensions blends Guy de Maupassant (Larivière thinks "that in some former Hindooish state she was a boulevardier in Paris; and writes accordingly" [*Ada*, 53]) with the eighteenth-century lady writer of English amatory pulp Delarivier Manley; perhaps George Sand; but also Proust. An increasingly famous writer throughout *Ada* and in unrequited love with Marina, the governess shows a marked preference for Proust's purple tones. Just as little Ada's memory-games feature the occasional "mauve tower" (*Ada*, 150), the governess also appears clad entirely in mauve.[32] Blending together mostly inferior influences with occasional gems, this authoress seems a talentless turn-of-the-century French double of Nabokov himself. Has Nabokov moved past his earlier infatuation with Proust, marking his evolution with *Ada*'s parodies?

We might close with Proust's own words on the subject of influence and cleansing pastiche from "À propos du style de Flaubert":

> *Aussi pour ce qui concerne l'intoxication flaubertienne, je na saurais trop re-*
> *commander aux écrivains la vertu purgative, exorcisante, du pastiche. Quand*
> *on vient de finir un livre, non seulement on voudrait continuer à vivre avec*
> *ses personnages, avec Mme de Beauseant, avec Frederic Moreau, mais encore*
> *notre voix interieure qui a été disciplinée pendant toute la durée de la lecture*
> *à suivre le rhythme d'un Balzac, d'un Flaubert, voudrait continuer à parler*
> *comme eux. Il faut la laisser faire un moment, laisser la pedale prolonger le*
> *son, c'est-à-dire faire un pastiche volontaire, pour pouvoir après cela, redeve-*
> *nir original, ne pas faire toute sa vie du pastiche involontaire.*[33]

The intonations of earlier generations haunt us: Proust haunts Nabokov and Flaubert haunts Proust, who teaches his heirs to free themselves through conscious pastiche. *Ada* simultaneously celebrates her many ghosts and performs an elaborate exorcism.

JOYCE AND LANGUAGE GAMES IN *ADA*

What did Nabokov learn from Joyce? According to most of his interviews, nothing. But in one he responded far more modestly: "Oh, yes, let people compare me to Joyce by all means, but my English is patball to Joyce's champion game" (*Strong Opinions*, 56). One notes that his narrators, even Van Veen, are never entirely native speakers of English. There is humility and arrogance, competition and deference in his attitude toward his precursors: often the contradictory responses blend beyond recognition. However, when Nabokov needs an example of twentieth-century literary genius, he turns to Joyce. Grumbling about how generously the word "genius" gets passed around in English, he continues, "Genius still means to me, in my Russian fastidiousness and pride of phrase, a unique, dazzling gift, the genius of James Joyce, not the talent of Henry James" (*Strong Opinions*, 147).

The blood of the Irish genius runs in the veins of the Veens, crossbred with closely related literary giants. Even in early descriptions of the novel then in progress, Nabokov insisted on the ancestry of his characters: "Both my female creatures have Irish and Russian blood. One girl lasts 700 pages, dying young; her sister stays with me till the happy ending, when 95 candles burn in a birthday cake the size of a manhole lid" (*Strong Opinions*, 116). The finished novel explicitly plants a Grandfather Dedalus Veen, whose Irish blood shapes the Veen profile. Through plot points and stylistic inspiration, Joyce is as much of a presence in *Ada* as is Proust; the overtly comic and verbally explosive *Ada* is even more indebted to *Ulysses* than to *À la recherche*.

Like *Ulysses*, Ada devours high and low styles. Nabokov never merely shows us a landscape, but instead offers a composite of literary landscapes parodying eighteenth-, nineteenth-, and twentieth-century culture, such as a bar scene seen through the eyes of Blok, Toulouse-Lautrec, Lautreamont, and modern *New Yorker* advertisements.[34] His narrator Van mimics various other Joycean tricks, such as that of deriving names from metonymic characteristics. Inner monologue and the stream of consciousness technique are put to brilliant use at emotionally strained moments, always with a self-conscious nod to the master, as well as to the master's master in Nabokov's reading, Tolstoy.

To turn once more to the early passage about the Veen ancestry, we find that besides the Guermantes link it also contains other allusions. Van refers to the sea as "his dark-blue great grandmother" (*Ada*, 8): literally he means Princess Sofia Temnosiniy, but the epithet also harks back to the most famous opening chapter of twentieth-century fiction. Buck Mulligan, showing off in the first pages of *Ulysses*, asks: "Isn't the sea what Algy calls it: a grey sweet mother? The snotgreen sea. The scrotumtightening sea. *Epi oinopa pontoon.*"[35] The green-gray Irish sea, the wine-dark Greek sea, the "mother and lover of men" metamorphoses into a Veen great-grandmother. The Veens come from water like Venus, their goddess and planet. Greek mythology combines with Old Testament stories, for they are also Adam and Eve: born of Aqua or Marina (whose joined names form another shade of blue) and chased from the garden. All is color and sensuality and shades of literary allusion: the Veens' dark blue claims a space in the rainbow between Proust's purple and Joyce's Irish green.

Even Demon and Marina's affair, analyzed thus far through Pushkinian and Proustian lenses, points also to Joyce. Boyd recalls that in Episode 4 of *Ulysses*, "Bloom associates Molly with a picture of the *Bath of the Nymph* over their bed, just after the novel's first mention of Blazes Boylan . . . The *Bath of the Nymph* develops into a motif" linked with Molly's infidelity.[36] In *Ada*, Marina becomes a nymph called from her bath, cradling the phone in a beautiful Parmigianino gesture. Marina's betrayal is discovered through a series of recognized gestures and paintings: Demon reasons at first that "such nymphs were really very much alike . . . the similarities of young bodies of water are but murmurs of natural innocence and double-talk mirrors, that's my hat, his is older, but we have the same London hatter" (*Ada*, 13). However, the resemblance between his girl and that of his rival art-connoisseur is more than that of all young beauty. Just so, Nabokov's literary allusions point to a particular character, a unique scene, and specific works of art.

When in the next generation of Veens, Van in turn is overcome with sexual jealousy, his obsession with predecessors also has in it something of Bloom. Jealousy, stylistic excess, and perversion link the two modernists in Nabokov's mind. Ever suspicious of his century's prurient interest in either latrine or "mauve" sexuality, Nabokov picks up on this aspect of the modernist revolution in art, and returns it too in parodic form. Van's constant, morbid sexuality especially reeks of Bloom when it heads in the direction of the toilet. Before important events in his life, Van informs us that he has "structurally perfect [stools]" (*Ada*, 309–10, 389); as an impotent old man, he enjoys "*le plaisir anglais*" (571) of urinating into his bathwater.

Grandfather Dedalus Veen is mentioned outright at several magic moments, for example when Van learns to walk on his hands:

What pleasure (thus in the MS.). The pleasure of suddenly discovering the right knack of topsy-turvy locomotion was rather like learning to man, after

many a painful and ignominious fall, those delightful gliders called Magicar-
pets (or "jikkers") that were given a boy on his twelfth birthday in the adven-
turous days before the Great Reaction—and then what a breathtaking long
neural caress when one became airborne for the first time and managed to
skim over a haystack, a tree, a burn, a barn, while Grandfather Dedalus Veen,
running with upturned face, flourished a flag and fell into the horsepond.
(*Ada*, 81–82)

This passage is additionally marked by the Joycean "Questions for study and
discussion" at the end: "1. Did *both* palms leave the ground?"[37] The flight of
the magic carpet, like hand-walking, literalizes a metaphor for literary levita-
tion or acrobatics. These physical powers are kin to Van's later spectacular
abilities with words.[38]

It was the standing of a metaphor on its head not for the sake of the trick's difficulty, but in order to perceive an ascending waterfall or a sunrise in reverse:
a triumph, in a sense, over the ardis of time. Thus the rapture young Mas-
codagama derived from overcoming gravity was akin to that of artistic reve-
lation in the sense utterly and naturally unknown to the innocents of critical
appraisal, the social-scene commentators, the moralists, the idea-mongers
and so forth. Van on the stage was performing organically what his figures of
speech were to perform later in life—acrobatic wonders that had never been
expected from them and which frightened children. (*Ada*,184–85)

In just these terms Nabokov described Joyce's frequent and unmotivated
changes of style in *Ulysses*: viewing the world upside down conveys "a more
varied knowledge, fresh glimpses" and a means to see "greener grass, a
fresher world" (*Lectures on Literature*, 289).

We have already noted Nabokov's multivalent and multilingual puns,
as well as his reaction to critics calling *Ada* "the same fish fried in an inferior Joycepan."[39] *Ada*'s style-shifts and alternations between pyrotechnics
and relative flatness have also been called Joycean. One example is painterly
and drug-induced. Demon shows up in Manhattan under the influence of a
"dragon drug": a veritable talking palette of Boschian imagery at first, he discovers Van and Ada's affair and abruptly crashes. The prose style, the entire
world, and the painting quietly worked on by a butcher-aproned artist across
the way all turn gray. Joyce used such shifts in style frequently and dramatically; but Nabokov motivates his own style shifts, often with a comical or
attention-grabbing plot device.

Similarly, in the set piece of Van, Ada, and Cordula's chaperoned
school date, after Van delivers his wild Proustian pastiche and is warned by
Ada against "too much Marcel," he shifts styles to evoke Joyce: "On fait *son*

grand Joyce after doing one's *petit Proust*" (*Ada*, 169). The bleak railway station, the tearoom, the heavy rain garb and other vaguely nautical elements all borrow from the drabber landscape of *Ulysses*, but surely Nabokov also means to draw our attention to the repeated "becauses," "our damp trio," and other limp turns of phrase. Such moments are typical of Joyce's parodies of genre literature and journalese conventions: Nabokov parodies the master parodying.

Nabokov introduces another important technique at the breakfast table: little Ada is prone to monologue about "a dream, a natural history wonder, a special belletristic device—Paul Bourget's '*monologue intérieur*' borrowed from old Leo" (*Ada*, 61). Presumably in response to critical readings, Darkbloom's note clarifies this reference, pointedly excluding Joyce: "the so-called 'stream-of-consciousness' device, used by Leo Tolstoy (in describing, for instance, Anna's last impressions whilst her carriage rolls through the streets of Moscow)" (*Ada*, 593).[40] The stream of consciousness device, when it occurs in *Ada*, inevitably blends Russian and Irish sources; but Nabokov was incensed at the negative comparisons with Joyce that his ambitious novel had elicited.

The same early scene includes another joke on translation turning "flowers into bloomers" (*Ada*, 64), much commented on by critics. Van confronts nationalist Mlle Larivière with "atrocious bloomers in French translations from the English" as well as the other way around (*Ada*, 270). The word "bloomer" contains a subsidiary echo of *Ulysses*: Leopold Bloom uses the pseudonym Henry Flower for a clandestine but cheap epistolary romance.[41] Stranger occasional references crop up throughout: for example, "Van returned to the still-throbbing jolls-joyce" (*Ada*, 473). Equally offhand, a James Jones delivers Van some Very Private Letters: the name is "a formula whose complete lack of connotation made an ideal pseudonym despite its happening to be his real name" (*Ada*, 330). Is this another Irish shadow or a feint? As car or messenger, Joyce serves as a means of transport—not inappropriate in a book about cultural transmission.

Clearly, Joyce casts a wide shadow over *Ada*, providing Nabokov's novel with both material and the stylistic means. *Ada*'s stylistic excesses out-Joyce Joyce. Yet Nabokov was careful to express reservations even about *Ulysses*, and considered *Finnegans Wake* one of the great failures of the twentieth century. Why then would he try to match it with *Ada*?[42]

For many readers, *Ada* marks the same crossed boundary in Nabokov's fiction as did Joyce's last novel. They suspect that Nabokov, like Joyce, ceased to care about reception. Durantaye writes, "Writers haughtily unconcerned for who will follow the densities and intricacies of their work were not rare in the twentieth century. One need only think of the dense arcana of Pound and Eliot, both of whom Nabokov detested, or the kaleidoscopic allusiveness of Joyce, whom Nabokov adored."[43] He recounts James Mercanton's visit to Joyce that "found him and Stuart Gilbert at work on the then *Work-in-Progress* (which became *Finnegans Wake*), 'gleefully' inserting words taken from a Samoyed dictionary so as to make it more 'obscure.'"[44] Nabokov plays close to this edge, pushing the bounds but then beating a hasty retreat to lushly seductive narrative.

A closer look at two highly charged passages in *Ada* will illustrate Nabokov's complicated relationship with Joyce's literary techniques. In the first and shorter scene, Van flees Ardis forever:

> "The express does not stop at Torfyanka, does it, Trofim?"
>
> "I'll take you five versts across the bog," said Trofim, "the nearest is Volosyanka."
>
> His vulgar Russian word for Maidenhair; a whistle stop; train probably crowded.
>
> Maidenhair. Idiot! Percy boy might have been buried by now! Maidenhair. Thus named because of the huge spreading Chinese tree at the end of the platform. Once, vaguely, confused with the Venus'-hair fern. She walked to the end of the platform in Tolstoy's novel. First exponent of the inner monologue, later exploited by the French and the Irish. *N'est vert, n'est vert, n'est vert. L'arbre aux quarante écus d'or*, at least in the fall. Never, never shall I hear again her "botanical" voice fall at *biloba*, "sorry, my Latin is showing." *Ginkgo*, gingko, ink, inkog. Known also as Salisbury's adiantofolia, Ada's infolio, poor *Salisburia*: sunk; poor Stream of Consciousness, *marée noire* by now. Who wants Ardis Hall!
>
> "*Barin, a barin*," said Trofim, turning his blond-bearded face to his passenger.
>
> "*Da?*"
>
> "*Dazhe skvoz' kozhanïy fartuk ne stal-bï ya trogat' etu frantsuzskuyu devku.*"
>
> *Bárin*: master. *Dázhe skvoz' kózhanïy fártuk*: even through a leathern apron. *Ne stal-bï ya trógat'*: I would not think of touching. *Étu*: this (that). *Frantsúzskuyu*: French (adj., accus.). *Dévku*: wench. *Úzhas, otcháyanie*: horror, despair. *Zhálost'*: pity. *Kóncheno, zagázheno, rastérzano*: finished, fouled, torn to shreds. (*Ada*, 299–300)

The dialogue with Trofim prompts and intercuts with Van's inner monologue, a stream of consciousness with brief incomplete sentences, three languages, and the fragmented logic of disturbed emotions grasping at verbal straws: for example, "the skipping stones of consciousness" (*Lectures on Literature*). This being *Ada*, Van's internal monologue jumps straight to literature and to its own stylistic precedents: "She walked to the end of platform in Tolstoy's novel." Van's associations skip from Maidenhair, Venus hair, love, his own misery, self-conscious stream of consciousness, literary precedents, to trains. Van despairs enough to contemplate suicide, and yet is sufficiently composed to remember that Tolstoy used the technique of inner monologue long before the French and Joyce made it famous. In this passage, Van's agonized inner monologue is also about the very device of inner monologue, without dampening the local emotional impact.

Flaubert also joins the mix: that final trio of words echoes *L'Éducation sentimentale*, translated (and transfigured, like the *n'est vert n'est vert* variant on *King Lear*'s "Never, never, never, never, never") into Russian and then English.[45] The Russian coachman would not touch the diseased French girl, but he means the wrong girl and the wrong disease, besides which he will go on to marry Blanche himself.[46] Flaubert's style passes into Russian (Tolstoy) and then English, just as Tolstoy's inner monologue passes the other direction into French and English literature. Cultural cross-fertilization on the level of story and action is suggested by Van's determination to duel the neighboring country squire, followed by more Russian dialogue. Yet the Irish seems dominant: the very ability to retell one's intense emotional experiences through a filter of ironic models is mostly Joyce in method if not in content (which merges all three cultures). Anna Karenina's inner monologue offers little comic relief. But in *Ada*, as in *Ulysses*, patches of sincerity shine through the shades of parody, through earlier and absorbed literary styles.

More prolonged and brilliant still is the scene of Lucette's suicide, an echo of the previous passage, and for many readers the heart of the novel. On a transatlantic ocean liner and after one final attempt to win Van, Lucette does what Van only contemplated, joining the ranks of Anna and Emma Bovary.

> She drank a "Cossack pony" of Klass vodka—hateful, vulgar, but potent stuff; had another; and was hardly able to down a third because her head had started to swim like hell. Swim like hell from sharks, Tobakovich!
>
> She had no purse with her. She almost fell from her convex ridiculous seat as she fumbled in her shirt pocket for a stray bank note.
>
> "Beddydee," said Toby the barman with a fatherly smile, which she mistook for a leer. "Bedtime, miss," he repeated and patted her ungloved hand.
>
> Lucette recoiled and forced herself to retort distinctly and haughtily:
>
> "Mr. Veen, my cousin, will pay you tomorrow and bash your false teeth in."
>
> Six, seven—no, more than that, about ten steps up. *Dix marches.* Legs and arms. *Dimanche. Déjeuner sur l'herbe. Tout le monde pue. Ma belle-mère avale son râtelier. Sa petite chienne,* after too much exercise, gulps twice and quietly vomits, a pink pudding onto the picnic *nappe. Après quoi* she waddles off. These steps are something.

While dragging herself up she had to hang onto the rail. Her twisted progress was that of a cripple. Once on the open deck she felt the solid impact of the black night, and the mobility of the accidental home she was about to leave.

Although Lucette had never died before—no, *dived* before, Violet—from such a height, in such a disorder of shadows and snaking reflections, she went with hardly a splash through the wave that humped to welcome her. That perfect end was spoiled by her instinctively surfacing in an immediate sweep— instead of surrendering under water to her drugged lassitude as she had planned to do on her last night ashore if it ever did come to this. The silly girl had not rehearsed the technique of suicide as, say, free-fall parachutists do every day in the element of another chapter. Owing to the tumultuous swell and her not being sure which way to peer through the spray and the darkness and her own tentaclinging hair—t,a,c,l—she could not make out the lights of the liner, an easily imagined many-eyed bulk mightily receding in heartless triumph. Now I've lost my next note.

Got it.

The sky was also heartless and dark, and her body, her head, and particularly those damned thirsty trousers, felt clogged with Oceanus Nox, n,o,x. At every slap and splash of cold wild salt, she heaved with anise-flavored nausea and there was an increasing number, okay, or numbness, in her neck and arms. As she began losing track of herself, she thought it proper to inform a series of receding Lucettes—telling them to pass it on and on in a trick-crystal regression—that what death amounted to was only a more complete assortment of the infinite fractions of solitude.

She did not see her whole life flash before her as we all were afraid she might have done; the red rubber of a favorite doll remained safely decomposed among the myosotes of an unanalyzable brook; but she did see a few odds and ends as she swam like a dilettante Tobakoff in a circle of brief panic and merciful torpor. She saw a pair of new vair-furred bedroom slippers, which Brigitte had forgotten to pack; she saw Van wiping his mouth before answering, and then, still withholding the answer, throwing his napkin on the table as they both got up; and she saw a girl with long black hair quickly bend in passing to clap her hands over a dackel in a half-torn wreath.

A brilliantly illumined motorboat was launched from the not-too-distant ship with Van and the swimming coach and the oilskin-hooded Toby among the would-be saviors; but by that time a lot of sea had rolled by and Lucette was too tired to wait. Then the night was filled with the rattle of an old but still strong helicopter. Its diligent beam could spot only the dark head of Van, who, having been propelled out of the boat when it shied from its own sudden shadow, kept bobbing and bawling the drowned girl's name in the black, foam-veined, complicated waters. (*Ada*, 493–95)

This passage, the novel's climax, is Nabokov's most moving virtuoso display. Lucette downs her cheap Russian vodka, incarnates simultaneously Emma, Anna, and Ophelia, and feels herself to be a cheap parody of all. We move seamlessly from vivid visual description—Lucette's last swan dive, "she went with hardly a splash through the wave that humped to welcome her"—to free indirect discourse: "Her head started to swim like hell" must be Lucette's words. And then we are entirely inside her head: "Swim like hell from the sharks" is inner monologue, lines retold from a remembered anecdote.

Lucette, we realize, is even more literary, artistic, and ironic than Van on her way to death. Her inner monologue is verbal and visual (recalling her art history classes and love for Édouard Manet's *Déjeuner sur l'herbe*); for all claims that "she did not see her whole life flash before her as we were all afraid she might," the combination of images and fragments (Van withholding his answer; Ada unnamed) betrays a lonely, intelligent, bewildered life. But just then, we are reminded once more that it must be Van who invents for her these final words and thoughts. He pays Lucette the belated compliment of recognizing her posthumously as a kindred spirit—or perhaps Nabokov prompts him.

Stylistically, Lucette's inner monologue varies from the model of *Ulysses* to that of *Anna Karenina*. From the shortest fragments like "Legs and arms" and "These steps are something" and the French puns (*dix marches, dimanche*), Nabokov switches back to description: "While dragging herself up she had to hang onto the rail. Her twisted progress was that of a cripple." Nabokov argued in the *Lectures* that Joyce overemphasized the verbal: we think in images as well as in words. Descriptions in literature have the advantage of conveying both, and in fact can feel more natural than an exaggerated stream of consciousness. Here as never before, Nabokov shows us what he means: we are in Lucette's tormented head, and then we see her on the deck, over the rail, diving from "such a height," going in with hardly a splash and cruelly resurfacing. (Anna almost stands up after her leap between the wheels.) If Joyce leans heavily on verbal texture at the expense of visual substance, in this passage Nabokov gives us both.

He then does something even more spectacular, building from Joyce once more. This passage is rife with narrative interruptions, increasingly painful in tone. Lucette had "never died before—no, *dived* before, Violet," old man Van corrects his typist. He stops to spell "tentaclinging," and then again "Nox," presumably to distinguish from the last name of his pretty secretary. Just as Lucette is horribly sinking, he fumbles the narration entirely: "Now I've lost my next note. Got it." Just as we feel most in the moment, totally enthralled by the recounted past, the narrating present interrupts, interferes, makes itself felt, chokes with age and with grief. Old Van still attempts to joke with his secretary, even as he conjures a vision of Lucette fighting to remain ironic in her last moments.

Nabokov beats Joyce at his own game by experimenting simultaneously with two layers of narrative: he gives us two counterpointed monologues and inner states. We see the illustrated thoughts of the dying girl, and hear the old man's interrupted narration. The presence of Violet, the typewriter, Van's reshuffled notes, his presumable emotional state all force us to visualize this other layer simultaneously: old Van is still not quite able to narrate this one unspeakable event, but tries to concentrate on details and force himself through, echoing the anguish of the dying girl. A film is able to do this quite simply by means of delineated flashbacks, but Nabokov employs no such ready-made markers to differentiate between temporal levels. The Nabokov-trained reader must follow the cues and catch both temporal layers—and distinguish the narrator from the author besides.

Nabokov tries to shake the ornamentalism of *Finnegans Wake* by motivating his verbal acrobatics through the narrative, and keeping such dense passages in *Ada* highly emotionally fraught. If Nabokov succeeds, the reader is too enchanted by Lucette, the darkly romantic Veen world, and Nabokov's pyrotechnics to balk at meta-literary strategies. The magic and the reward should occur on two levels: the seduction of the plot, and the intellectual and aesthetic pleasure of recognizing the craftsman's mastery.

In the last sentence, Van shouts the dead girl's name in the "black, foam-veined, complicated waters." We return to the old grandmother sea, and to the moral culpability that so often goes hand in hand with great freedom. Their dark-blue element catches up to the Veens. After Lucette, the others will go fairly quickly: in book-space, if not narrative time, Marina and Demon die one after another, until only our sterile couple is left. The sea has turned as black as death: when it kills Lucette it is a material substance, visualizable by means of detail ("foam-veined"), light and shade, and still something we can only understand abstractly, literarily as "complicated."

THE MODERNIST AGON

Nabokov was highly sensitive to comparisons with Proust and Joyce, especially when incautious critics suggested influence (implying a derivative art practice) rather than conscious mimicry (e.g., total mastery). "My sense of places is Nabokovian rather than Proustian," he snapped at Simona Morini in a 1972 interview for *Vogue* (*Strong Opinions*, 197). Or in response to the question, what had he learned from Joyce:

> James Joyce has not influenced me in any manner whatsoever. My first brief contact with *Ulysses* was around 1920 at Cambridge University, when a friend, Peter Mrozovski, who had brought a copy from Paris, chanced to read

to me, as he stomped up and down my digs, one or two spicy passages from Molly's monologue, which, *entre nous soit dit*, is the weakest chapter in the book. Only fifteen years later, when I was already well formed as a writer and reluctant to learn or unlearn anything, I read *Ulysses* and liked it enormously. I am indifferent to *Finnegans Wake* as I am to all regional literature written in dialect—even if it be the dialect of genius. (*Strong Opinions*, 102–3, 1966 interview with Herbert Gold)

Appel called Nabokov's attention to a series of echoes, beginning with Flaubert's fingernail fetish in *Madame Bovary*, made famous by Joyce's demand that the artist remain "behind or beyond or above his handiwork, invisible, refined out of existence, indifferent, paring his fingernails," and seemingly alluded to in *Pale Fire*'s lines, "I stand before the window and I pare / My fingernails" (lines 185–86). The interviewer was his former student and friend, and the traced allusion specific and clever; but Nabokov would have none of it: "Neither Kinbote nor Shade, nor their maker, is answering Joyce in *Pale Fire*. Actually, I never liked *A Portrait of the Artist as a Young Man*. I find it a feeble and garrulous book. The phrase you quote is an unpleasant coincidence" (*Strong Opinions*, 70–71).[47]

Yet in *Ada*, through the mask of Van Veen, Nabokov very visibly indulges his grand Joyce after his petit Proust. He appropriates from the French- and English-language modernists aspects of technique, signature style, as well as familiar themes and motifs. *Ada* merges Proust and Joyce, transplanted onto Antiterra and crossed with the Russian literary tradition. If Pushkin's *Onegin* was a novel in the Chateaubyronic genre, *Ada* belongs to a category defined by Marcel Joyce or James Proust.

Nabokov uses Proust's "art of memory" to resurrect the cultural past, and Joyce's technique of shifting parodic styles to show a scene as it might have been written by Pushkin, Chateaubriand, Byron, Dickens, Flaubert, Tolstoy—and Proust and Joyce themselves. Literature flows across linguistic borders: Proust and Joyce are carriers of a transnational tradition of unchecked imagination, masterful craftsmanship, innovation, and creative risk. Nabokov reads Joyce and Proust to be as much the spiritual heirs of Pushkin and Tolstoy as of French- and English-language writers. Pushkin's humor, lightness and speed, and inexhaustible talent for parody find full expression in the adopted Irish grandson; Proust's visual imagination and profound treatment of memory resembles the descriptive precision and temporal complexity of the greatest Russian classics.

If Russian literature had missed the opportunity to respond fully to the modernist challenge, Nabokov takes it up and accelerates it in *Ada*. In the process, he addresses what bothered him even in the work of his favorites. He considered only the edited half of Proust's *À la recherche* a masterpiece:

Ada parodies Proust by hinting that old Van similarly dies while editing part 1: "I am weak. I write badly. I may die tonight. My magic carpet no longer skims over crown canopies and gaping nestlings, and her rarest orchids. Insert" (*Ada*, 221). Old Ada may have finished part 1 for him: Darkbloom notes that the final one-sentence paragraph "imitates, in significant brevity of intonation (as if spoken by an outside voice), a famous Tolstoyan ending, with Van in the role of Kitty Lyovin" (*Ada*, 601).[48] By the final paragraphs of the novel both Veens must be dead, for the concluding blurb, in its utter lack of sympathy or subtlety (Lucette's death "one of the highlights of this delightful book"?), drips with Nabokov's sarcasm.[49] The point, of course, is that Van dies before editing his book, but Nabokov does not: *his* novel, unlike Van's or Proust's, is perfectly edited.[50]

Significantly, the incestuous lovers Van and Ada Veen, heirs to the greatest literary traditions in the world, die childless.[51] The motif of inbreeding forms one of the central paradoxes of the novel: since Antiterran chronology reads as a double- or triple-exposure, the great writers of the nineteenth and twentieth centuries coexist in the Veen library and exchange secrets of the trade with Van. The pages of *Ada* are a veritable Olympus for literary immortals, or a Garden of Eden built on great books and erotic freedom. But the Veens' incest and sterility take on looming allegorical significance for the inbreeding of literary masterpieces: crossing related outliers sometimes yields woollier and woollier sheep, and sometimes a sterile and legless lamb. The great love story of *Ada* may well end with the death of the novel.[52]

Is *Ada* a burlesque, where Van falls into the traps of imitating Proust and Joyce? It is small wonder that readers are left divided, unsure of which "author" to trust. *Ada* explores the aesthetic codes of modernism even as it seems their ultimate incarnation, with all the narcissism, desire for novelty and shock value, voyeuristic sexuality, and stylistic indulgences of its heritage. The romantic legacy personified by Demon Veen is simultaneously adored and condemned by his demon-blooded children; similarly, using the subsequent generation of Veens as straw-novelists and modernists (the Lenskys and Onegins to his authorial persona), Nabokov celebrates and exorcises his favorite literature. As Nabokov wrote in *Strong Opinions*, every original novel is an anti-novel, because it opens a genre different from that of its precursors. Nabokov's very mastery of modernist motifs and methods suggests it is time to move on.

Once he successfully broke out of the provincialism of national discourse, Nabokov faced the same problem as had Samuel Beckett: how to write novels after Joyce and Proust? Critics as different as Pascale Casanova and Harold Bloom see Beckett as the terminal point for one powerful trajectory of neo-romantic culture. Beckett, to escape his cultural baggage, abandoned Dublin for Paris and began writing in French. Divorced from his native English, he could strive for a literature as abstract and hence as international and autonomous as possible. Specifically, he attempted to break free from the confines of national tradition by paring down his literariness to find a bare new idiom all his own. Beckett found inspiration in abstract painting, and sought to reproduce its effects in prose. Nabokov, who has the opposite tastes in visual art, seeks a radically different exit out of the shadows of the literary past. If Beckett moved forward by subtracting, Nabokov innovates by adding. Nabokov's densely allusive and exaggeratedly literary prose outpaces the modernists, reflecting back on their practices and on the status of the novel in the late twentieth century.

If we read Nabokov's most provocative narrators—V.V. in *Pnin*, Humbert in *Lolita*, Kinbote (or Shade) in *Pale Fire*, and Van and Ada Veen in *Ada, or Ardor*—as producers of borderline or purple prose, how do the books that contain them convince us of their quality? How do texts purportedly by problematic, pretentious, derivative, and even hysterical writers, by virtue of their implicit framing, register as good novels? Nabokov's escalating experiments with form reveal an eminent desire to push the boundaries of the novel form, to detonate its borders and limitations. Read in this way, his experiments with graphomaniacal narrators begin to approach conceptualism.[53]

Frederic Jameson has read Nabokov as a misplaced modernist, spinning out "unseasonable forms" from the lofty and isolated perch of Swiss retreat.[54] But perhaps we can reconsider *Ada* as not only the last in a series—the conclusive entry in the last triad of modernist monuments—but as the forerunner of emergent forms. Just as a new canon of French, English, and Russian novels seems completed and confirmed, the structure shakes once more. By maintaining the distance between Nabokov and Van Veen, the text deconstructs its own triumphalist claims, questioning the self-declared genius of the internal author(s) with arch romantic irony at every turn.

Bergson and *The Texture of Time*

> I once premeditated making a study of Kafka's
> precursors. At first I had considered him to be
> as singular as the phoenix of rhetorical praise;
> after frequenting his pages a bit, I came to think
> I could recognize his voice, or his practices, in
> texts from diverse literatures and periods . . .
>   The first is Zeno's paradox against
> movement. A moving object at A (declares
> Aristotle) cannot reach point B, because it
> must first cover half the distance between
> the two, and before that, half of the half, and
> before that, half of the half of the half, and
> so on to infinity; the form of this illustrious
> problem is, exactly, that of *The Castle*; and the
> moving body and the arrow and Achilles are
> the first Kafkian characters in literature.
>   . . . In each of these texts we find Kafka's
> idiosyncrasy to a greater or lesser degree, but
> if Kafka had never written a line, we would not
> perceive this quality; in other words, it would
> not exist. . . . In the critics' vocabulary, the word
> "precursor" is indispensable, but it should be
> cleansed of all connotation of polemics or rivalry.
> The fact is that every writer *creates* his own
> precursors. His work modifies our conception of
> the past, as it will modify the future.
> —Jorge Luis Borges, "Kafka and his Precur-
> sors," 1951

ADA AS ZENO'S PARADOX

One of the oddities of *Ada*, remarked on by many readers, is its structure: the
sizeable novel begins with an enormous first section and then appears to lose

steam from there. However, the breakdown into five parts of receding size is hardly accidental. All of *Ada* appears to be structured as an immense allusion to Zeno's paradox.[1] Part 1 (323 pages) is approximately half the total novel, part 2 (118 pages) is close to one fourth, part 3 (84 pages) about one eighth, part 4 (31 pages) one sixteenth, and part 5 (22 pages) not far from a brief thirty-secondth. Even the "Notes by Vivian Darkbloom" in subsequent editions fit the pattern of diminishing returns, taking up only sixteen pages in the regressive sequence—proving that the pattern is Nabokov's and not Van's.

The Eleatic philosopher's most famous paradox is alternately illustrated by Achilles's race with the tortoise, or by the arrow that never reaches its goal.[2] The crux of the paradox is that the arrow always remains halfway between its previous position and the target. The Greek word for arrow is Ardis, the name of the Veen estate, as Van points out during an early game of Flavita (Scrabble on Antiterra). He toys with the name throughout. Darkbloom's notes remind us that "ardis: arrow" (*Ada*, 655), glossing Van's reference to the "the ardis of Time" (*Ada*, 538). Ardis Hall is a New World Eden, paradise lost, a romantic manor built from novels, and the setting for Van's first two liaisons with Ada. When they reunite, he jokes that the only arrow that always remains in flight is one that reaches its goal; when he first considers writing a memoir about their life and love, the title that he proposes (and that resurfaces in *Look at the Harlequins!*) is *Ardis*.

Ada's seductive plot is the ardis-arrow, flying toward or reaching its target—death—depending on whether one accepts Van Veen's philosophical and artistic conclusions. Once we grasp this structural play, Van's arrows and ardises fall into place. While critics have noticed that there is something odd about *Ada*'s structure, many attribute the way that the action speeds up to Nabokov's lack of interest in or control over his text.[3] (In this, *Ada*'s harshest reviews resemble those of Pushkin's *Onegin* a century and a half earlier.) But on the contrary, few works exhibit a similar degree of control.[4] The entire novel forms an immense compositional allusion to Zeno, and through Zeno's paradox, to the philosophy of Henri Bergson.

In this chapter I study *Ada* in the context of its suggestive working title and part 4 of the finished novel, *The Texture of Time*. Where does Van Veen's philosophy come from, and does it inform the style and structure of the novel? What is the texture of time, and how does it relate to Nabokov's ambitions for a transnational literary canon?

VAN VEEN, BERGSONIAN

Van (crossly): "I don't understand the first word . . . What's that? *L'adorée?* Wait a second" (to Lucette). "Please, stay where you are." (Lucette whispers a French child-word with two "p"s.). "Okay" (pointing toward the corridor). "Sorry, Polly. Well, is it *l'adorée*? No? Give me the context. Ah—*la durée. La durée* is not . . . sin on what? Synonymous with duration. Aha. Sorry again, I must stopper that orgiastic soda. Hold the line." . . .

"*La durée* . . . For goodness sake, come in without knocking . . . No, Polly, knocking does not concern you—it's my little cousin. All right. *La durée* is not synonymous with duration, being saturated—yes, as in Saturday—with that particular philosopher's thought. What's wrong now? You don't know if it's *dorée* or *durée*? D, U, R. I thought you knew French. Oh, I see. So long.

"My typist, a trivial but always available blonde, could not make out *durée* in my quite legible hand because, she says, she knows French, but not scientific French."

"Actually," observed Lucette, wiping the long envelope which a drop of soda had stained, "Bergson is only for very young people or very unhappy people, such as this available *rousse.*"

"Spotting Bergson," said the assistant lecher, "rates a B minus *dans ton petit cas*, hardly more." (*Ada*, 376–77)

As far as his scholarly work is concerned, Van is shamelessly derivative of Bergson. The strange scene above marks his first encounter with the adult Lucette. Her sudden beauty distracts Van and the reader both: for the latter it triggers expectations of an *Onegin*-like reversal in desire and a new direction for the plot. But Nabokov uses the moment to plant the information that Van has become a doctor of philosophy (an assistant professor as well as lecher) and a specialist on Bergson.

Van and Lucette's flirtatious dialogue finds an intriguing counterpoint in his phone conversation: Van rebukes his typist for fumbling the word *durée*, which cannot be translated simply as "duration" since Van refers specifically to Bergson's term. The two interactions interpenetrate, making it difficult to place which is the main conversation and which the intermission. Overtly theatrical, the scene includes stage directions; in *Ada*, such accumulating self-conscious markers usually signal an important passage. Subtly, this scene foreshadows Lucette's watery death. Eavesdropping Lucette catches the philosophical reference that Polly missed, tries to impress Van, and simultaneously warns him that she is very unhappy.

When dictating the story of her suicide many decades later, Van will spell things out similarly ("Nox, N-O-X") to another blonde typist. The two passages reflect one another and bookend a love affair that never took place. The beloved older sister (*l'adorée*—the homonym rings with Ada's name) haunts all of Lucette's interactions with Van, who has not yet guessed the origins of the letter amid the spilled soda. Different layers of the past endure into the narrative present, even as he mentions offhand or offstage Bergson's famous notion of *durée*. Water powers much of the machinery of Antiterra and of *Ada*, perhaps even Polly's polliphone, performing magical (Demonian) functions closely linked to language. The mysterious ability of water to record sounds, or of carpets to levitate, reads as a metaphor for language and literature. In this scene love, death, and Bergson all blend in the fluid medium of Nabokov's novel.

When Van retires from academia, he delivers three farewell lectures "on Mr. Bergson's Time at a great university." Bergson's own public lectures were famous events, but this stylized description may borrow from Nabokov's Cornell fantasies:

> I was a little late for the first (dealing with the Past) and observed with a not-unpleasant thrill, as if arriving at my own funeral, the brilliantly lighted windows of Counterstone Hall and the small figure of a Japanese student who, being also late, overtook me at a wild scurry, and disappeared in the doorway long before I reached its semicircular steps. At the second lecture—the one on the Present—during the five seconds of silence and "inward attention" which I requested from the audience in order to provide an illustration for the point I, or rather the speaking jewel in my waistcoat pocket, was about to make regarding the true perception of time, the behemoth snores of a white-bearded sleeper filled the house—which, of course, collapsed. At the third and last lecture, on the Future ("Sham Time"), after working perfectly for a few minutes, my secretly recorded voice underwent an obscure mechanical disaster, and I preferred simulating a heart attack and being carried out into the night forever (insofar as lecturing was concerned) to trying to decipher and sort out the batch of crumpled notes in pale pencil which poor speakers are obsessed with in familiar dreams (attributed by Dr. Froid of Signy-Mondieu-Mondieu to the dreamer's having read in infancy his adulterous parents' love letters). (*Ada*, 548–49)

Each lecture is marked by an incident illustrative of the points Van intends to prove. He is late for the past but witnesses it like a ghost attending his own funeral (the past is still with us); the real present unexpectedly interrupts his illustrative intermission through unplanned snores and laughter; and the future, only one of many possible projections based on the past and present, is as fake as his cardiac arrest. Van's lectures suggest that he is not only a scholar of Bergson but also his heir; by his nineties, Veen's Time will be popularly "termed in one breath, one breeze, with 'Bergson's Duration'" (*Ada*, 579). As we shall see, Bergson also offers Nabokov a far more enticing model for the workings of the mind than does Freud, here "Dr. Froid."

But Nabokov finally explains Veen's Time only in part 4, the inset philosophical treatise that tantalizingly postpones the denouement of Van and Ada's great love for thirty more pages. After accumulating hints about the nature of Van's work, we see an excerpted selection or a rephrased summary of his wildly successful *The Texture of Time*—for Nabokov lends Van *Ada*'s early working title. A philosophical work and not fiction wins Van fame: his earlier novels toil in relative obscurity, with the exception of *Letters from Terra*, which benefited from the notoriety of French director Victor Vitry's racy and "totally unauthorized" film adaptation.[5]

The Texture of Time chapter serves to prove that Van is a philosopher, but what is his philosophy? The crucial characteristics of Veen's Time include the following concepts, all borrowed directly from Bergson and very thinly disguised: (1) an attempt to separate time conceptually from metaphors of space; (2) a differentiation between perceived time and "real" time; and (3) the accessibility and duration of the past into the present. These ideas are explored overtly in part 4 but more subtly permeate the whole novel. The notion of duration provides the clue to *Ada*'s content, style, and structure, for Van's memoir illustrates and applies Bergson's philosophy of time.

First as a philosopher and then as a poet, Van tries to grasp the nature of "Pure Time, Perceptual Time, Tangible Time, Time free of content, context, and running commentary" (*Ada*, 539). However, the final target of Van's attacks throughout the novel is teleological, irreversible time, or as Van calls it, "the ardis of Time" (*Ada*, 538). Life infects philosophy, philosophy life. As Nabokov described the project early on, "I have to devise an essay, a scholarly-looking essay on time and then gradually turn it into the story I have in mind. The metaphors start to live."[6]

Most readers approach Van's treatise as if it were Nabokov's own, inserted into *Ada* unadultered. Nabokov litters interviews and occasional pieces with contradictory clues: for example, "My conception of the texture of time somewhat resembles its image in Part Four of *Ada*" (*Strong Opinions*, 184). He calls memory and imagination "negations" of time, and when asked whether memories helped to "combat time or offer any clue to its mysteries," Nabokov quotes from *Ada*: "Physiologically the sense of Time is a sense of continuous becoming. . . . Philosophically, on the other hand, Time is but memory in the making." He interrupts himself to differentiate his own ideas from those of his invented scholar: "This is Van speaking, Van Veen, the charming villain of my book. I have not decided yet if I agree with him in all his views on the texture of time. I suspect I don't" (*Strong Opinions*, 142–43).[7]

Indeed, the structure of the novel is one of the strongest indicators of the difference between Van Veen and his author. Van hopes to postpone death and the end of his memoir indefinitely. (If the Veen story could continue to be told in shorter and shorter chapters, perhaps this sleight of hand would work.) But life—or novels—cannot quite be so subdivided. At some definite point in time, the Veens die, doomed despite Van's florid eloquence.

According to *Ada*'s central conceit, Van composes the story of his life, dictates it to Violet, and edits much of the first part with Ada's help. But like Proust with *À la recherche*, Van dies before completing his project and leaves a "rough masterpiece" behind, with elements in place that demonstrate his loss of control. The ultimate mastermind remains Nabokov, who stages every false layer and clever, signifying structure of the entire monumental illusion.

BERGSON'S *DURÉE*

It is difficult today to imagine the popularity of Henri Bergson's thought in the early twentieth century. Bergson's hugely influential (and Nobel Prize–winning) philosophy sparked and shaped international modernisms from Paris to St. Petersburg.[8] His seminal writings about the duration of the past into the present (*la durée*), our illusory and habitual perceptions of the world around us, and the preeminence of the subjective and creative mind, were central to the symbolists, to Joyce and Proust, to the Anglo-American modernist poets, and to the Russian modernists alike.

Bergson's emphasis on intuition, on the individual subjective experience, and on the role of figurative language, which serves simultaneously as a conduit to and as the glass panel separating us from truth, all marked a radical paradigm shift. Bergson captured the zeitgeist of the creative classes, and his ideas continued to be disseminated in the years after World War I. Isaiah Berlin describes what Bergson's lectures were like:

> In Paris the servants of rich ladies used to come to the lectures in the hall in which Bergson spoke; they came an hour before and attended the lecture of, let us say, some Professor of Assyrian archaeology; he and others were very surprised to find the entire lecture hall so full of odd-looking people very unlike academics. No sooner was the lecture over than the audience rose to its feet and made room for the smart ladies who crowded in to hear Professor Bergson.[9]

In the late 1930s and after World War II, Bergson faded from view, to be rediscovered decades later through the interventions of Jacques Derrida and Gilles Deleuze.[10]

Bergson's most visible heritage remains the literature of modernism, which derived from his work the authority to openly privilege the intuitive over the analytical. The most relevant and enabling theme was the exploration of interiority, "the nature of consciousness, and the operation of memory."[11] I will briefly overview several of Bergson's best-known formulations, with an eye to the phrasing as well as to the substance of his thought. As the comparison will show, Van Veen's philosophy is built with blocks of translated and transfigured Bergson.

Bergson's first major work marked his breakthrough: in *Time and Free Will*, he argued that philosophical models consistently confuse motion, or time, with space. Beginning with the Greeks, he ascribes the paradoxes of the Eleatics to the confusion between time and the space traversed; for "the interval which separates the two points is infinitely divisible," and if time were similarly so, the interval could never be crossed—a summary of Zeno's paradox. But the truth is that "each of Achilles's steps is a simple indivisible act, and that, after a given number of these acts, Achilles will have passed the tortoise."[12] What Zeno's paradox leaves out when reconstructing Achilles's movement is that space alone "can be divided and put together again any way we like." Bergson concludes that models of time fundamentally misillustrate time with metaphors appropriate only to space.

Bergson returned to the subject throughout his long career. In *The Creative Mind* he claimed that metaphysics was born out of Zeno's arguments: "It was Zeno who, by drawing attention to the absurdity of what he called movement and change, led the philosophers—Plato first and foremost—to seek the true and coherent reality in what does not change."[13] Again Bergson stresses that Zeno's arguments never questioned the conviction that one could divide time just as one divides space: "Achilles, they say, will never overtake the tortoise he is pursuing, for when he arrives at the point where the tortoise was the latter will have had time to go further, and so on indefinitely."[14] Bergson argues that Western philosophy arises from the wrong response to the wrong problem, fundamentally misguiding us about the nature of our experiences, and about ourselves.

Conventional metaphors for time partake of this conceptual original sin: time is a river; time is a road. The equal and opposite philosophical or religious reaction seeks the essence of the self in some indivisible abstraction. However, rather than one constant or several divisible selves perceiving fixed objects, we experience self and the world through infinitely shifting impressions. Just as Bergson seeks a different model for time, so he attempts to unify the fluctuating personality through the idea of duration, *la durée*. Later thinkers have called this conceptual breakthrough Bergson's "Copernican revolution"; the notion of duration has found continued relevance in the work of late-twentieth-century philosophers, as in Derrida's interest in the lingering trace.[15]

Bergson writes, "It is the same self which perceives distinct states at first, and which, by afterwards concentrating its attention, will see these states melt into one another like the crystals of a snow-flake when touched for some time with the finger."[16] He replaces the conventional metaphors of everyday speech and of Western philosophy with novel, piled-on imagery that illustrates fluctuation and identity through change. Thus history cannot be "instantaneously unfurled like a fan" but "unfolds itself gradually, as if it occupied a duration like our own. If I want to mix a glass of sugar and water, I must, willy nilly, wait until the sugar melts."[17] The *durée* of an experience, of history, or of the individual personality can only be glimpsed through such imagery as gradually dissolving sugar and melting snowflakes. We must rely on intuition, insight, and poetry to find the figurative language that will best express how we interact with the world.

In *Creative Evolution*, Bergson offers an expanded formulation, turning his attention to how duration may explain the workings of the mind:

> Duration is the continuous progress of the past which gnaws into the future and which swells as it advances. . . . [Memory] is not a faculty of putting away recollections in a drawer, or of inscribing them in a register. There is no register, no drawer; there is not even, properly speaking, a faculty. . . . In reality, the past is preserved by itself, automatically. In its entirety, probably, it follows us at every instant; all that we have felt, thought and willed from our earlier infancy is there, leaning over the present which is about to join it, pressing against the portals of consciousness that would fain leave it outside. The cerebral mechanism is arranged just so as to drive back into the unconscious almost the whole of this past, and to admit beyond the threshold only that which can cast light on the present situation or further the action now being prepared—in short, only that which can give *useful* work. At the most, a few superfluous recollections may succeed in smuggling themselves through the half-open door. These memories, messengers from the unconscious, remind us of what we are dragging behind us unawares. But, even though we may have no distinct idea of it, we feel vaguely that our past remains present to us. What are we, in fact, what is our *character*, if not the condensation of the history that we have lived from our birth—nay, even before our birth, since we bring with us prenatal dispositions? Doubtless we think with only a small part of our past, but it is with our entire past, including the original bent of our soul, that we desire, will, and act.[18]

Bergson's thought offers a rich but radically different understanding of memory and the unconscious than does Freudian psychoanalysis, while similarly stressing the formative power of the past and of hidden memories. Bergson posits that the personality is nothing but the swelling accumulation of experiences, but his model allows for infinite variation and individual difference. In Nabokov-inflected terms, Bergson's model accounts for the unconscious without imposing a universal myth of family romance: for example, "bitter little embryos spying . . . upon the love life of their parents."[19]

Nabokov notoriously held up Freud as the paradigmatic example of criminally reductive thinking.[20] Freud and Bergson were exact contemporaries: both responded to the era's materialism with systems of thought that sought to explain the mystery and richness of subjective experience. Yet to Nabokov, Freud appeared to "unseat man from the center of his own consciousness and hence to undermine the notion of the artist as a creature capable of consciously achieving his aesthetic ends."[21] For Nabokov, a work of art is hardly the product of primal and unconscious forces, but rather the closest we can come to a conscious mastery of lived experience. Bergson offers a rival Gallic school of psychology to that of Freud and his disciples. We might guess that James Joyce disappointed Nabokov not only with stylistic excesses in *Finnegans Wake*, but also with his interest in Carl Jung and the collective unconscious. Nabokov responds to this wrong turn by writing his own alternative monument.

Indeed, Bergson stressed that we can only hope to gain permanent access to the buried past through conscious and arduous work: "We shall never reach the past unless we frankly place ourselves within it. . . . unless we follow and adopt the movement by which it expands into a present image, thus emerging from obscurity into the light of day."[22] We must learn to use and understand memory in a way that harmonizes with its fluctuating and ever-expanding nature. Here Bergson turns to his famous snowball simile: memory carries the past into the present, "continually swelling with the duration which it accumulates: it goes on increasing—rolling upon itself, as a snowball on the snow." While we only notice change when it grows sufficiently substantial to impose a new attitude or direction, "the truth is that we change without ceasing, and that the state [of becoming] itself is nothing but change."[23]

The goal of any meaningful, examined, and well-lived life should be the greatest possible awareness of this continual change, and the farthest-reaching understanding and overview of our past and present:

> An attention to life, sufficiently powerful and sufficiently separated from all practical interest, would thus include in an undivided present the entire past history of the conscious person—not as instantaneity, not like a cluster of simultaneous parts, but as something continually present . . . [such] is the melody which one perceives as indivisible, and which constitutes . . . a perpetual present. . . . a present which endures.
>
> This is not a hypothesis. It happens in exceptional cases that the attention suddenly loses the interest it had in life: immediately, as though by magic, the past once more becomes present. In people who see the threat of sudden death unexpectedly before them, in the mountain climber falling down a precipice, in drowning men, in men being hanged, it seems that a sharp con-

version of the attention can take place—something like a change of orientation of the consciousness which, up until then turned toward the future and absorbed by the necessities of action, suddenly loses all interest in them. That is enough to call to mind a thousand different "forgotten" details and to unroll the whole history of the person before him in a moving panorama.[24]

Bergson's call for a perpetual present, illustrated by the perpetually moving yet unified melodic line, recalls the symbolist motto: *la musique avant toute chose*. The poetry of symbolism seeks to dethrone abstract verbal logic in favor of an intuitive and musical poetics of change and a palimpsestic present.

The above passage harmonizes well with the succession of images at Lucette's death, with Van's convulsive inner monologues at the most fraught moments of his life, and even with Ada's sole film performance, which captures for Van her beauty in all the stages of their love affair. Moreover, as Van and Ada's pseudo-memoir, *Ada* subsumes these examples in an ultimate attempt to erase the border between past and present, and to fully engage with the examined life. Or, to take yet another step back, Nabokov invents these characters and their supposed memoir to engage in an even more grand and subtle game with the reader's experience of literature.

Bergson writes that literature often and quite paradoxically feels "real," and that we experience the novelistic insight as personal disillusionment:

> If some bold novelist, tearing aside the cleverly woven curtain of our conventional ego, shows us under this appearance of logic a fundamental absurdity, under this juxtaposition of simple states an infinite permeation of a thousand different impressions which have already ceased to exist the instant they are named, we commend him for having known us better than we knew ourselves. This is not the case, however, and the very fact that he spreads out our feeling in a homogenous time, and expresses its elements by words, shows that he in his turn is only offering us its shadow: but he has arranged this shadow in such a way as to make us suspect the extraordinary and illogical nature of the object which projects it. . . . Encouraged by him, we have put aside for an instant the veil which we interposed between our consciousness and ourselves.[25]

Disillusionment rests on more manipulations and subjective representations of time, and yet we feel we have been brought "back" into our own presence. The artist is ever an enchanter, but the illusions prompt in us a genuine response.

Years before either his friendship or feud with Nabokov, Edmund Wilson studied the Bergsonian current in the great literary works of the early twentieth century. Wilson's evocative 1931 book *Axel's Castle* predates the critical rigidification of terms such as modernism: Wilson identifies the new and neo-romantic strain as "symbolism" in a very broad sense, largely overlapping if not perfectly coinciding with what today commonly falls under the umbrella category of modernism or European modernism.[26] The new aesthetic tendency and poetic sensibility emerged, very much like those of romanticism a century before, from a subjective revolt against an increasingly mechanized world.[27] If the romantics reflected and inspired a revolution in thought, the symbolists were über-romantics, responding to another revolution, in part spearheaded by Bergson. (The similarities between the two movements, romanticism and symbolism, shed further light on the "My Pushkin" trend in Russian modernism.)

Wilson finds traces of Bergson in the poetics that shaped the new century:

> The assumptions which underlay Symbolism lead us to formulate some such doctrine as the following: Every feeling or sensation we have, every moment of consciousness, is different from every other; and it is, in consequence, impossible to render our sensations as we actually experience them through the conventional and universal language of ordinary literature. Each poet has his unique personality; each of his moments has its special tone, this special combination of elements. And it is the poet's task to find, to invent, the special language which will alone be capable of expressing his personality and feelings. Such a language must make use of symbols: what is so special, so fleeting and so vague cannot be conveyed by direct statement or description, but only by a succession of words, of images, which will serve to suggest it to the reader.[28]

Symbols meant different things to different writers, and the images and descriptions of some poets and poetic prose-writers are more exquisitely detail-oriented than others. Nevertheless, a recognizable if nebulous doctrine underlay much of the new work. The new metaphysics found an especially brilliant embodiment in Proust's prose fiction:

> Proust had been deeply influenced by Bergson, one of the forerunners of the modern anti-mechanists, and this had helped him to develop and apply on an unprecedented scale the metaphysics implicit in Symbolism. . . . for the Symbolist, all that is perceived in any moment of human experience is relative to the person who perceives it, and to the surroundings, the moment, the mood. The world becomes . . . fourth dimensional—with Time as the fourth dimension.[29]

We recall Nabokov's own formulation from the *Lectures on Literature* that Proust was Bergson in an illustrated edition. While Nabokov shied away from general studies of "climate of thought," and defined symbolism far more narrowly and negatively, as marked by self-indulgence and a lack of interest in detail, his understanding of Proust's and even of Joyce's poetics shares a good deal with that of Wilson.

Nabokov often described matter and memory in Bergsonian terms. The best-known line of *Speak, Memory*, "I confess I do not believe in time. I like to fold my magic carpet, after use, in such a way as to superimpose one part of the pattern upon another," sounds very like *Ada*. Magic carpets or "jikkers" literally defy gravity in the late novel, just as Van hopes to defy one-way time through the creative superimpositions of memory and art. In *Strong Opinions*, Nabokov's description of memory essentially repeats Bergson's formulations, adding a patch of color borrowed from Proust:

> The Past is a constant accumulation of images, but our brain is not an ideal organ for constant retrospection and the best we can do is to pick out and try to retain those patches of rainbow light flitting through memory. The act of retention is the act of art, artistic selection, artistic blending, artistic recombination of actual events. The bad memoirist re-touches his past, and the result is a blue-tinted or pink-shaded photograph taken by a stranger to console sentimental bereavement. The good memoirist, on the other hand, does his best to preserve the utmost truth of detail. One of the ways he achieves his intent is to find the right spot on his canvas for placing the right patch of remembered color. (*Strong Opinions*, 186)[30]

The artist chooses carefully the right patch of color and illustrates how selective recombination can alchemically re-create the effect of an organic whole.

Leona Toker writes that Nabokov mentioned Bergson "among the poets and novelists who were his 'top favorites' between the two World Wars," but that "it is not easy to determine whether (or to what extent) Nabokov was actually influenced by Bergson."[31] Toker remarks on the extensive presence of Bergson in Van's *Texture of Time*, but comments: "Paradoxically, the Bergsonian idea of time that Nabokov refers to most explicitly may be the one about which he is most skeptical."[32] Van's treatise borrows freely from Bergson's *Time and Free Will*, but Nabokov seems to have more sympathy with Ada's pragmatic point of view: "We can know the time, we can know a time. We can never know Time" (*Ada*, 563). Toker concludes that Bergson's influence on Nabokov is most evident in the Russian-American author's lingering and "tentative mysticism."

Conversely, Michael Glynn suggests that Nabokov's aesthetic and ethical stances are closer to the anti- or post-symbolist formalist critics and to Bergson, whom he places in a similar category: what interests Glynn is the role of art in shaking the veil of habit or delusion.[33] John Burt Foster acknowledges that there is little "detailed intertextual evidence" regarding Nabokov's early response to Bergson, but argues that during the 1930s, "Nabokov starts to take an interest in portraying fictive philosophers who share key traits with Bergson."[34] The fictional Pierre Delalande and Adam Krug from *Bend Sinister* are forerunners of Van Veen. Krug's philosophy and manner of exposition are even introduced by way of a parodic-sounding simile involving a snowball and a snowman's broom (*Bend Sinister*, 46), an allusion to Bergson's metaphorical illustrations, and even specifically to the famous simile comparing *la durée* with a rolling snowball.[35]

Foster draws attention to *Ada* and to Van's treatise, which proves that he is a philosopher just as the 999-line "Pale Fire" proved John Shade to be a poet. Even more intriguing is the conclusion of Van's essay with the broken phrase: "It is like—." Despite all efforts, philosophical language must use figurative language and spatial metaphors. To end on this note is another concession to Bergson, for the French philosopher found chains of metaphor to be the only possible language for philosophy and for ungraspable concepts such as time. Literary language rather than abstract exactitude shows language at its most vivid and visual: images "direct consciousness to fuller understanding than was possible with conceptual thought."[36] In consequence, and as Benjamin wrote in the 1930s, Bergson defined the nature of lived experience, duration, and memory "in such a way that the reader is bound to conclude that only a poet can be the adequate subject of such an experience."[37]

VEEN'S TIME

Van writes his treatise to purify his notion of time, to examine its very essence and not only its lapse. Or in his words, "I wish to caress Time":

> One can be an amateur of Time, an epicure of duration. I delight sensually in Time, in its stuff and spread, in the fall of its folds, in the very impalpability of its grayish gauze, in the coolness of its continuum. I wish to do something about it; to indulge in a simulacrum of possession. I am aware that all who have tried to reach the charmed castle have got lost in obscurity or have bogged down in Space. I am also aware that Time is a fluid medium for the culture of metaphors. (*Ada*, 537)

Van's principal task seems to be a reductive recapitulation of Bergson's central argument in his first work *Time and Free Will*: the conceptual need to divide time from space. Van, the Bergson specialist, acknowledges his debt: "Space flutters to the ground, but Time remains between thinker and thumb, when Monsieur Bergson uses his scissors" (*Ada*, 542). However, Van means to get even closer to the true essence of time. Laughably, he eroticizes the intellectual feat and casts Time in explicitly feminine terms. Even the "charmed castle" that he casually throws in alludes to Donna Anna's abode in *Don Juan's Last Fling,* and thus again to the goal of sexual possession. For Van, the philosophical pursuit of time is yet another test of virility.

Several passages from Van's dense and difficult essay illustrate the play with both Bergson's philosophy and his method of exposition through accumulated metaphor and simile. Van does not quite succeed in his attempt to go beyond Bergson:[38]

> Why is it so difficult—so degradingly difficult—to bring the notion of Time into mental focus and keep it there for inspection? . . . It is like rummaging with one hand in the glove compartment for the road map—fishing out Montenegro, the Dolomites, paper money, a telegram—everything except the stretch of chaotic country between Ardez and Somethingsoprano, in the dark, in the rain, while trying to take advantage of a red light in the coal black, with the wipers functioning metronomically, chronometrically: the blind finger of space poking and tearing the texture of time. . . .
>
> Lost again. Where was I? Where am I? Mud road. Stopped car. Time is rhythm . . .
>
> If my eye tells me something about Space, my ear tells me something about Time. . . . I can listen to Time only between stresses, for a brief concave moment warily and worriedly, with the growing realization that I am listening not to Time itself but to the blood current coursing through my brain, and thence through the veins of the neck heartward, back to the seat of private throes which have no relation to Time.
>
> The direction of Time, the ardis of Time, one-way Time, here is something that looks useful to me one moment, but dwindles the next to the level of an illusion obscurely related to the mysteries of growth and gravitation. The irreversibility of Time (which is not heading anywhere in the first place) is a very parochial affair: had our organs and orgitrons not been asymmetrical, our view of Time might have been amphitheatric and altogether grand, like ragged night and jagged mountains around a small, twinkling, satisfied hamlet. We are told that if a creature loses its teeth and becomes a bird, the best the latter can do when needing teeth again is to evolve a serrated beak, never the real dentition it once possessed. The scene is Eocene and the actors are fossils. It is an amusing instance of the way nature cheats but it reveals as little relation to essential Time, straight or round, as the fact of my writing from left to right does to the course of my thought. (*Ada,* 537–39)

Van's "culture of metaphors" overflows the petri dish. Bergson's fans and snowballs seem restrained compared to this baroque profusion on the pitfalls of spatial metaphor and simile. Trying to grasp time is like looking for a road map in the dark; the sound of time is one's own troubled circulatory system; one-way time is like gravity; and Van's own philosophical endeavors are like a bird trying to grow teeth. Or in an even more telling formulation, the ardis of time is to real Time as linear writing is to real thought.

Van pulls his primary comparisons from his immediate experience, a one-way drive through space. Even ignoring the distraction of the final target, Ada and perhaps ardor, his language is hopelessly infected with space: "I can put my Past in reverse gear, enjoy this moment of recollection" (*Ada*, 536). He loses his way mentally and literally ("Mud road. Stopped car") and cannot escape thoughts of the road map, the car, his heart, or the twinkling hamlet in the jagged mountains. Not the least distraction is the ever-present possibility of death, which plays counterpoint throughout Van's agitated alpine drive.

When he turns to analyze memory, the accumulation of the past and its persistence into the present, Van takes another crucial kernel of Bergson's philosophy and illustrates mental duration with scenes from his own life, which the reader is by now well-equipped to follow and share:

> The Past, then, is a constant accumulation of images. . . . It is now a generous chaos out of which the genius of total recall, summoned on this summer morning in 1922, can pick anything he pleases: diamonds scattered all over the parquet in 1888; a russet black-hatted beauty at a Parisian bar in 1901; a humid red rose among artificial ones in 1883; the pensive half-smile of a young English governess, in 1880, neatly reclosing her charge's prepuce after the bedtime treat; a little girl, in 1884, licking the breakfast honey off the badly bitten nails of her spread fingers; the same, at thirty-three, confessing, rather late in the day, that she did not like flowers in vases; the awful pain striking him in the side while two children with a basket of mushrooms looked on in the merrily burning pine forest; and the startled quonk of a Belgian car, which he had overtaken and passed yesterday on a blind bend of the alpine highway. (*Ada*, 545–46)

Though Van appears to be in earnest, he can no more help injecting obscene Veen humor and class prejudice into the mix (young governess, prepuce) than he can help exponentially increasing the accumulation of metaphors.

Van insists that Veen's time is about the essence of Time "stopped by me and closely attended to by my tense-willed mind," and not at all an exploration of lost time or time's lapse. However, the larger stakes of his project are precisely a denial of aging, of mortality and death. It would be "idle and evil" to confuse his project with a study of lost time, he raves: "Of course, at fifty years of age, one year seems to pass faster because it is a smaller fraction of my increased stock of existence and also because I am less often bored. . . . But that 'quickening' depends precisely upon one's not being attentive to Time" (*Ada*, 539–40). Van's mental feats will slow the passage of time; or as he responded to a heckler attending his last lecture, who says that I shall die?

The treatise appears to end abruptly with Van's arrival in Mont Roux. He confesses that he has been wounded in the duel with the impostor Space, and notes down the time from every available conventional source: "Today is Monday, July 14, 1922, five-thirteen P.M. by my wrist watch, eleven fifty-two by my car's built-in clock, four-ten by all the timepieces in town. The author is in a confused state of exhilaration, exhaustion, expectancy and panic" (*Ada*, 551). The future cannot be predicted and does not yet exist: all Van knows of fifty-something Ada, after seventeen years of letters and telegrams, is her voice. Aurally, through the medium of music and melody, Van's rejection of the ardis of time seems to work:

> The phone had preserved the very essence, the bright vibration, of her vocal cords, the little "leap" in her larynx, the laugh clinging to the contour of the phrase, as if afraid in girlish glee to slip off the quick words it rode. It was the timbre of their past, as if the past had put through that call, a miraculous connection ("Ardis, one eight eight six"—*comment? Non, non, pas huitante-huit—huitante-six*). Goldenly, youthfully, it bubbled with all the melodious characteristics he knew—or better say recollected, at once, in the sequence they came: that *entrain*, that whelming of quasi-erotic pleasure, that assurance and animation . . .
>
> Would Van come down? She was *neveroyatno golodnaya* (incredibly hungry).
>
> That telephone voice, by resurrecting the past and linking it up with the present, with the darkening slate-blue mountains beyond the lake, with the spangles of the sun wake dancing through the poplar, formed the centerpiece in his deepest perception of tangible time, the glittering "now" that was the only reality of Time's texture. After the glory of the summit there came the difficult descent. (*Ada*, 555–56)

All three of Nabokov's beloved languages are present in this vital passage, which as he told interviewers was another of the early sparks of the novel, calling the rest into being. For one triumphant moment, Van's "deepest perception of tangible time" appears to capture effortlessly the perpetual present. The past has not been lost, the intervening years not wasted, for the glittering "now" is the only reality that matters.

The setup for Van's visual disappointment when the aged lovers meet is positively Proustian. The difficulty of capturing the perpetual present is what prompts the Veens to try and conquer time once more, this time with their memoir.

ANACHRONISTIC *ADA*

If Pushkin's *Onegin* betrays anxieties about not being on time—on levels of plot, literary fashion, or national culture—*Ada* reads as a defiant attack on conventional timeliness. Challenging commonsense notions of time at every step in the search for "real" time, *Ada* celebrates the anachronistic, the triumph of creative human will against Tyrant Time. The Veen timeline collapses in on itself as much as their incestuous family tree. Birth and marriage dates are falsified to hide adultery, betrayal, and incest. *Ada*'s heroes stubbornly do everything at the wrong age and often several times: they fall in love too young and love passionately into their late nineties. Repeated story lines from one generation to the next complicate any linear narrative trajectory: a male Veen inevitably tangles with two sisters; the less-beloved sister commits suicide clad ceremoniously in yellow and maroon; and either Van or uncle Ivan wrestles with insomnia and nightmares in the Ardis hammock. Time may be a spiral or a vicious circle, but it is certainly not a straight line.

The exceptional hero and heroine are defined through temporal terms from the start: they are like no one else, except each other. As children they are extravagantly precocious, untimely in both intellectual and erotic prowess. On one occasion their erudite chatter (doubly at the wrong time in this case, at the breakfast table) garners Marina's complaint: "'When I was your age, Ada, and my brother was *your* age, Van, we talked about croquet and ponies, and puppies, and the last *fete-d'enfants*, and the next picnic, and—oh, millions of nice normal things'" (*Ada*, 65). But Van and Ada were never nice or normal Mlle Larivière says of Ada: "'She was never a baby' . . . 'She could break the back of her pony before she could walk'" (*Ada*, 155). When Van and Ada meet again in 1888, both have changed but by concurrent stages, "so that their brains and senses stayed attuned and were to stay thus always, through all separations. Neither had remained the brash *Wunderkind* of 1884, but in bookish knowledge both surpassed their coevals to an even more absurd extent than in childhood" (*Ada*, 218).

Ada and Van's exceptional status is their best justification for a life of constant transgression on conventional morality. Ada's proud summary of their love, eighty years later, serves as a far edgier blurb than the book's last and evidently non-Veen paragraphs:

> No point would there be, if we left out, for example, the little matter of prodigious individual awareness and young genius, which makes, in some cases, of this or that particular gasp an *unprecedented unrepeatable event* in the continuum of life or at least a thematic anthemia of such events in a work of art, or a denouncer's article. The details that shine through or shade through . . . convey the fact, the fact, the fact—that among those billions of brilliant

couples in one cross section of what you will allow me to call spacetime (for the convenience of reasoning), one couple is a unique super-imperial couple, *sverhimperatorskaya cheta*, in consequence of which (to be inquired into, to be painted, to be denounced, to be put into music, or to the question and death, if the decade has a scorpion tail after all) the particularities of their love-making influence in a special unique way two long lives and a few readers, those pensive reeds, and their pens and mental paintbrushes. . . . the detail is all . . . *that* has to be heard, smelled and seen through the transparency of death and ardent beauty. (*Ada*, 70–71)

Young genius, long lives, and an unprecedented unrepeatable event in spacetime: the super-imperial couple claims the status and ethical exemption of immortals. Not unlike Humbert's defense of nympholepsy on grounds of artistic sensibility and real love, Van and Ada's defense rests on whether they are able to convince readers that their love is a unique event that cannot be judged by mortal standards.

After a grim and lonely adulthood that the novel omits, "real time" resumes. Van and Ada reunite in late middle age and triumphantly refuse to grow old. Overcoming the years and the distance between them, they laugh at a monolingual Englishman breakfasting nearby ("That's not bananas, sir. That's *ananas*, pineapple juice"): "Young Van smiled back at young Ada. Oddly, that little exchange at the next table acted as a kind of delicious release" (*Ada*, 557). The past, they realize, is not lost.

Even in the last brief section of the book, Van remains chronologically defiant: "I, Van Veen, salute you, life, Ada Veen, Dr. Lagosse, Stepan Nootkin, Violet Knox, Ronald Oranger. Today is my ninety-seventh birthday. . . . This Part Five is not meant as an epilogue; it is the true introduction of my ninety-seven percent true, and three percent likely, *Ada or Ardor, a family chronicle*" (*Ada*, 567). Against all probability, the Veens have enjoyed over forty cloudless years together, beating many a happy marriage. At the very end, one or both suffer tremendously: in the last few pages the words "time" and "pain" become interchangeable. By now indistinguishable, the Veens insist that this epilogue is only an introduction, and their novel remains a cry against death. Not unlike Oscar Wilde's Dorian Gray and his ageless portrait, the attractively demonic Van and Ada try to conflate literary with metaphysical immortality by dying into their book: "If our time-racked, flat-lying couple ever intended to die they would die, as it were, *into* the finished book, into Eden or Hades, into the prose of the book or the poetry of its blurb" (*Ada*, 587).[39]

Several paragraphs before the final period, it is clear that the "I" of the book has in fact died in the book. By now both Veens are in Eden or Hades, and Oranger—or someone—has taken over the manuscript. The ardis of time has been hurtling toward its final destination from the beginning of the story; only sleight of logic can keep the arrow and target apart. Nabokov seems to grant Van and Ada's wish to die into their book: the Russian pun on *ad* ("hades"), whether it turns out to be a pagan Hades or Christian Hell, is all too apropos. The moralist may rest assured that the Veens are in eternal flames; the sensualist may imagine a pagan paradise.

But the Veens' untimely lives hardly constitute *Ada*'s only chronological defiance: their entire planet is temporally mad. It is still the nineteenth century on Antiterra or Demonia when the story opens; the twin planets of Terra and Antiterra are off-sync by between fifty years to a century, although the temporal gap shifts continuously. The conceit allows several historical times to coexist and blur together, a parallel to the Veens' collapsed timeline and family tree.

The unexplained L disaster simultaneously causes and curses Terra, makes electricity an obscene word, and drives many of Antiterra's sensitive souls to madness or high art.[40] What hints the Antiterrans have of Terra, a scrambled reflection of our world, only further highlights the chronological disarray:

> If, in Terrestrial spatial terms, the Amerussia of Abraham Milton was split into its components, with tangible water and ice separating the political, rather than poetical, notions of "America" and "Russia," a more complicated and even more preposterous discrepancy arose in regard to time—not only because the history of each part of the amalgam did not quite match the history of each counterpart in its discrete condition, but because a gap of up to a hundred years one way or another existed between the two earths; a gap marked by a bizarre confusion of directional signs at the crossroads of passing time with not *all* the no-longers of one world corresponding to the not-yets of the other. (*Ada*, 18)

In practical terms, the novel is free to conflate duels and fancy sports cars, airplanes and sleighs, phone calls with dramatic horseback arrivals. Antiterra operates according to Veen's time and chronologies elide, though most readers glide past, buoyed by Nabokov's super-saturated prose.[41]

Given Nabokov's earlier novels, we might well wonder if Antiterra exists at all. Not content with solipsistic love and language games, have the Veens invented their own planet of love, Venus or Demonia? One might even conjecture that the Veens' anguish and guilt over Lucette prompts them to invent the L disaster, and that literary Fate bifurcates as a result.[42] Furthermore, by powering a planet with ardor and literature, and by locating the active part of the Veens' young lives in the nineteenth century and skipping over their years together until the very end in the late 1960s, *Ada* tries to cover a hundred years while avoiding the real tragedies of the twentieth century. While glimpses of real history shine as through a distorting mirror, the Veen narrative tries to break free of time. In this reading, Van's Antiterra is Kinbote's Zembla, only far grander in scope: Kinbote invented a kingdom, but Van can run a planet.

Two embedded works of art within *Ada* suggestively reflect the novel's structural and stylistic play with time. The anachronistic conflations that Van favors inevitably capture the duration of the past in the present, using ghosts and echoes (or traces) to create a perpetual present, at least in art. What Van ultimately hopes to do with his memoir is akin to the magic of cinema.

Another mysterious double or authorial stand-in, the brilliant French director Victor Vitry (V.V.), improves on Van's early anonymous novel *Letters from Terra* by taking wild and unauthorized liberties with its temporal backdrop:

> Vitry dated Theresa's visit to Antiterra as taking place in 1940, but 1940 by the Terranean calendar, and about 1890 by ours. The conceit allowed certain pleasing dips into the modes and manners of our past (did you remember that horses wore hats—yes, hats—when heat waves swept Manhattan?) and gave the impression—which physics-fiction literature had much exploited—of the capsulist traveling backward in terms of time. Philosophers asked nasty questions, but were ignored by the wishing-to-be-gulled moviegoers. (*Ada*, 580)

Vitry's conceit is like that of *Ada*, but technically easier to pull off in the medium of film than in linear prose. (Conversely, we might remember Kubrick's 1962 trailer: "How did they ever make a movie of *Lolita*?")

Nabokov's narrator-protagonists often have a peculiar relationship to time, or an exaggerated time-pathology that expresses itself in disturbing erotic obsessions. Humbert's moral and philosophical failure arises from his desire to freeze time. Humbert's nymphets inhabit an enchanted island whose borders are the ages of nine and fourteen (time mapped as space, once more); he fantasizes about retiring with a self-perpetuating breed of lolitas; and even after his alleged redemption, he wishes that the children he hears playing in the distance would "never grow up."[43]

Van Veen's chrono-erotic obsessions are more complicated.[44] On board the transatlantic liner with Lucette, Van accidentally catches Ada's only real film role in *Don Juan's Last Fling*. This film too shares much with *Ada* the novel, and "reads" as a parodic collage of Byron, Pushkin, Mérimée, Cervantes, and Nabokov-masquerading-as-Borges (yet another retort to critics eager to see similarities in their work) by a second brilliant director, Yuzlik. When he recognizes Ada, Van's reaction speaks volumes:

The main picture had now started. . . .

On the way to the remote castle where the difficult lady, widowed by his sword, has finally promised him a long night of love in her chaste and chilly chamber, the aging libertine nurses his potency by spurning the advances of a succession of robust belles. A *gitana* predicts to the gloomy cavalier that before reaching the castle he will have succumbed to the wiles of her sister, Dolores, a dancing girl (lifted from Osberg's novella, as was to be proved in the ensuing lawsuit). She also predicted something to Van, for even before Dolores came out of the circus tent to water Juan's horse, Van knew who she would be.

In the magic rays of the camera, in the controlled delirium of ballerina grace, ten years of her life had glanced off and she was again that slip of a girl *qui n'en porte pas* (as he had jested once to annoy her governess by a fictitious Frenchman's mistranslation): a remembered triviality that intruded upon the chill of his present emotion with the jarring stupidity of an innocent stranger's asking an absorbed voyeur for directions in a labyrinth of mean lanes. . . .

Terrible? Wrong? She was absolutely perfect, and strange, and poignantly familiar. By some stroke of art, by some enchantment of chance, the few brief scenes she was given formed a perfect compendium of her 1884 and 1888 and 1892 looks. . . .

It is no longer another man's Dolores, but a little girl twisting an aquarelle brush in the paint of Van's blood, and Donna Anna's castle is now a bog flower.

The Don rides past three windmills, whirling black against an ominous sunset, and saves her from the miller. . . . She fingers voluptuously the jeweled pommel of his sword, she rubs her firm girl belly against his embroidered tights, and all at once the grimace of a premature spasm writhes across the poor Don's expressive face. . . .

Van, however, did not understand until much later (when he saw—*had* to see; and then see again and again—the entire film, with its melancholy and grotesque ending in Donna Anna's castle) that what seemed an incidental embrace constituted the Stone Cuckold's revenge. (*Ada*, 488–89)

Decades later, Van's treatise on time still draws from *Don Juan's Last Fling* to cast elusive Time as Donna Anna's castle. The aging libertine Van fails in his philosophical conquest as predicted. More immediately, Ada's sole film performance distracts Van from Lucette, seated next to him in full color, and prompts her suicide.

Like Vitry's anachronistic portrayal of Terra, Yuzlik's film serves as a provocative double to *Ada* as a whole. For Van at least, if not for general audiences, the film creates an apotheosis of time, an enchanted moving collage that captures Ada in all the stages of their love affair. The beauty of the past endures and haunts the perpetual present: this must be how a bewildered scholar of Bergson experiences love.

These commercial films deftly achieve what Van will devote his life to re-creating in prose, for film has a different relationship to and existence in time. A director has far more control over the viewer's temporal experience than does an author over his reader; and film has the ability to convey many things at once in composite images, while building a complex narrative in time. It is no accident that Bergson's popularity coincided with the birth of the new medium, which quickly achieved a fetish status in the early twentieth century as the medium best equipped to reflect the modern era. (Another of Bergson's most famous analogies suggested that the intellect operates like the film projector.)[45] Film offered new possibilities for artistic synthesis, but also for an experience of time as change or duration while relying on space and the visual.

Marina filters her memories through the clichéd conventions of film, and longs to edit and clean her past in post-production, to eliminate embarrassing scratches, discrepancies, and unflattering angles. Van condemns Marina's conventional mind but does the same in his prose. He too fills in missing details and embellishes; his memoir draws equally upon cinematic devices and the glamour of the movies. In *Ada*, film comes to stand for memory itself; the materiality of the medium is rife with metaphors for the mind.

Dan Veen's microfilm early in the novel can be dated through "shades of heliocolor":

> A reel box containing what turned out to be (according to Kim, the kitchen boy, as will be understood later) a tremendous stretch of microfilm taken by the globetrotter, with many of its quaint bazaars, painted cherubs and pissing urchins reappearing three times at different points, in different shades of heliocolor . . . most of the film, accompanied by purely factual notes, not always easy to locate—because of the elusive or misleading bookmarks in the several guidebooks scattered around—was run by Dan many times for his bride during their instructive honeymoon in Manhattan. (*Ada*, 6–7)

Decades and hundreds of pages later, Van investigates memory in similar terms: "Does the coloration of a recollected object (or anything else about its visual effect) differ from date to date? Could I tell by its tint if it comes earlier or later, lower or higher, in the stratigraphy of my past? Is there any mental uranium whose dream-delta decay might be used to measure the age of a recollection?" (*Ada*, 545).

A great deal of what the Veens wish to preserve but have not already covered in their memoir ends up on film. Van erects in Lucette's memory "his famous Lucinda Villa, a miniature museum just two stories high, with a still growing collection of microphotographed paintings from all public and private galleries in the world (not excluding Tartary) on one floor and a honeycomb of projection cells on the other" (*Ada*, 336). The other collection donated to the Lucinda Museum consists of the filmed butterflies that Ada, like her author, collects until very late in life: "One would need another book to describe Ada's adventures in Adaland. The films—and the crucified actors (Identification Mounts)—can be seen by arrangement at the Lucinda Museum, 5, Park Lane, Manhattan" (*Ada*, 568). Film offers one way to preserve mortal beauty, and through this function serves as a stand in, or index to memory.

Dmitri Nabokov once described his father's writing as "all there, inside his mind, like film waiting to be developed."[46] Nabokov himself used cinematic metaphors both inside and outside of his fiction. Fascinated by the suggestive power and the subjective montages of film, he leaned on metaphors and representations of film in his novels to find new and poetic ways to interrogate time, memory, and his characters' experience of the world. For certain of Nabokov's protagonists, "particularly Humbert Humbert and Van Veen, film offers a form of refuge, the potential for transformation, the means by which to realize their creative ideals and, most critically, the promise of immortality."[47] Humbert fails to freeze the past, but in *Ada*, films run in Veen's time.

Van's enchanted response to Ada, to their love story, or even to his own novels as "captured" on film, contrasts sharply with his horror at Kim Beauharnais's photo album.[48] Kim's utilitarian photographs arrest time primitively and falsely: Van's violent response is as much of a reaction to bad art as to blackmail. There is something of the vengeful Apollo flaying Marsyas in Van's ritualistic blinding of the false visual artist with Proust's alpenstock—or at least, this is how Van wishes his actions to be read. Yet he nevertheless muses that an early erotic romp with Ada and Lucette might "have been filmed rather entertainingly had snoopy Kim the kitchen photo-fiend possessed the necessary apparatus" (*Ada*, 205). Van too lacks the necessary apparatus: like Humbert Humbert he too has "only words to play with," so he responds to Beauharnais's snapshots with a memoir.[49] But he learns from these entertaining films how to weave together temporal layers, to montage, and to double-expose—only in prose.

Van and Ada's climactic final meeting illustrates the aims and difficulties inherent in Van's ideas about time, and ultimately makes possible *Ada* the book. After the brief euphoria of hearing Ada's lovely youthful telephone voice, Van nearly loses her forever. The "ravage and outrage of age deplored by poets" humiliates both. Conventional time, the utterly ordinary passage of years, looks poised to conquer. As for so many literary lovers, by the time their stars align, it appears to be too late.[50] Van's *Texture of Time* seemed to end with triumphant arrival at Ada's charmed castle, if not quite the castle of Time; now we realize that the essay was only interrupted. Van resumes his work. Their brief and sad encounter was another intermission, a moment of intensely experienced time in the ordinary fabric of life. He sees Ada off and returns to his room alone.

> Had they lived together these seventeen wretched years, they would have been spared the shock and the humiliation; their aging would have been a gradual adjustment, as imperceptible as Time itself. . . .
>
> Let us recapitulate.
>
> Physiologically the sense of Time is a sense of continuous becoming, and if "becoming" has a voice, the latter might be, not unnaturally, a steady vibration; but for Log's sake, let us not confuse Time with Tinnitus, and the seashell hum of duration with the throb of our blood. Philosophically, on the other hand, Time is but memory in the making. In every individual life there goes on from cradle to deathbed the gradual shaping and strengthening of that *backbone of consciousness*, which is the Time of the strong. "To be" means to know one "has been." "Not to be" implies the only "new" kind of (sham) time: the future. I dismiss it. Life, love, libraries, have no future.
>
> Time is anything but the popular triptych: a no-longer existing Past, the durationless point of the Present, and a "not-yet" that may never come. No. There are only two panels. The Past (ever-existing in my mind) and the Present (to which my mind gives duration and, therefore, reality) . . . the Tortoise of the Past will never overtake the Achilles of the future, no matter how we parse distances on our cloudy blackboards. (*Ada*, 558–60)

Van reverses the positions of Achilles and the tortoise, and his logic is clouded by the potent sleeping pill he has just taken, but we can follow the argument familiar from Bergson. The future is but a "hypothetical present" based on our experiences, but hope can do no more about the future than can "our regrets change the Past." Every moment brings an "infinity of branching possibilities." One possible future, so ardently hoped for during Van's alpine drive, vanished over the awkward dinner with Ada. He peers over his balcony to the inviting pavement below. The reader recognizes parallels with Lucette's swan dive; this is the third time that Van has contemplated suicide in the novel; but all is averted. Ada is waiting for Van on the balcony below. Love and the present tense take over, excluding the reader for the next forty years, until the Veens finish *Ada* the book.

The duration of the past into the present; its accessibility through memory and art; and the individual's freedom to choose and shape a wholly novel and unpredictable future are the keys to *Ada*'s aesthetics. Van's and Ada's meta-novel means to bring these principles to literary life.

> Not only in ear-trumpet age—in what Van called their dot-dot-dotage—but even more so in their adolescence (summer, 1888), did they seek a scholarly excitement in establishing the past evolution (summer, 1884) of their love, the initial stages of its revelations, the freak discrepancies in gappy chronographies. . . . They had to rely on oral tradition, on the mutual correction of common memories. "And do you remember, *a tï pomnish', et te souviens-tu*" (invariably with that implied codetta of "and," introducing the bead to be threaded in the torn necklace) became with them, in their intense talks, the standard device for beginning every other sentence. Calendar dates were debated, sequences sifted and shifted, sentimental notes compared, hesitations and resolutions passionately analyzed. (*Ada*, 109)

Nabokov studied closely what he called the Pursuit device in Pushkin's *Onegin*, comparing drafts, revisions and rewritings, and using the painterly term "pentimento" to describe the effects of the verbal artist's temporal layering. On many occasions he noticed an earlier version, or an earlier stylistic choice, shining through the final copy. Nabokov's monumental *Commentary* carefully reinserted these earlier drafts and discarded stanzas. The serial publication of Pushkin's novel over time also created a constant sense of change and growth. Thankfully, Nabokov remarks, Pushkin was methodical about dating his manuscripts.[51]

Ada in turn abounds with fictive temporal layers: the story of the Veens' childhood is prefaced by their parents' romance, and by the initial genealogies and family tree. Many intervals of Van and Ada's separation are left out entirely or briefly retold through subsequent meetings. In the last ten years of his life, Van writes the bulk of the memoir, and then at some point dictates it to his secretary. Then both Veens edit the manuscript, leaving much of the text littered with their last annotations. Finally, Oranger marries Van's secretary and introduces changes of his own, most noticeably and comically in the final section, where he deletes the exact amount of his wife's salary and whatever followed Van's connoisseurial observations: "Violet Knox [now Mrs. Ronald Oranger. Ed.], born in 1940, came to live with us in 1957. She was (and still is—ten years later) an enchanting English blonde with doll eyes, a velvet carnation and a tweed-cupped little rump [. . . . .]" (*Ada*, 576). As a result, *Ada* reads as a forged pentimento, complete with the illusion of many temporal levels. The closer we look, the more we realize that sections, paragraphs, and even individual sentences contain multiple layers of invention and intervention, each with their own chronology.

Critics have noticed and attempted to interpret this complex Nabokovian effect in various ways. Cancogni finds the precision of *Ada*'s timing
one of its most remarkable characteristics. Readers are presented not only
with "the exact temporal frame of the story," ranging through the genealogical information to include "two hundred and sixty-eight years, though only
ninety-seven and ninety-five of these are respectively spanned by its hero
and heroine," but also with the time elapsed during its narration, a decade
spanning from 1957 to 1967 and that includes "several revisions, rewritings,
annotations, and a blurb."[52] Many years of Ada and Van's life together are in
fact thus subtly included in the novel, subsumed by the narration of the early
years, and glimpsed through the edits and parenthetical comments made by
the aging lovers. If early critics of *Ada* initially found the novel structureless,
Cancogni concludes that *Ada* is "all story."[53] A crucial side effect is that it
begins to feel like all present tense. Every temporal layer becomes simultaneously present to the reader. The most significant emotional moments in
Ada, such as Lucette's death, turn out to be also the densest treatments of
narrative time.[54]

Lucette haunts the novel through déjà vus, which further refute linear
narrative progression and introduce a cinematic sense of temporal suspen-
sion. As Boyd notes, Van is haunted from childhood on by the image of a
beautiful redhead in black, drinking alone at a bar. Years later, in their fateful
Paris encounter before the transatlantic cruise, that image finally coalesces
into a flesh-and-blood Lucette. Through another twist in time, Lucette is
also the lady who hands adolescent Van his coach upon first arrival to Ladore: "Suddenly a hackney coach drove up to the platform and a red-haired
lady, carrying her straw hat and laughing at her own haste, made for the
train and just managed to board it before it moved. So Van agreed to use
the means of transportation made available to him by a chance crease in the
texture of time, and seated himself in the old calèche" (*Ada*, 34). Recurring
visions and glimpses of Lucette, echoes of her favorite painters, and of her
vivid colors (red and green; the yellow and maroon of her and Aqua's suicide
garb) all enforce a foreboding sense of eternal return. The Veens' perpetual
present may be simultaneously paradise and the depths of a very subtle hell.

Even the basic building blocks of Nabokov's language bring together
different temporalities through metaphor and simile. In *The Texture of Time*
especially, Van uses recognizable elements from earlier in the novel to form
the key metaphors of his philosophical treatise. For example, Van writes: "If
now, with some poor scraps of teased-out knowledge related to the colored
contents of the Past, we shift our view and regard it simply as a coherent reconstruction of elapsed events . . . we can indulge in an easier game with the
light and shade of its avenues" (*Ada*, 547). The light and shade of time's avenues refer back to Ada's games in Ardis Park.[55] Retrospectively, we realize

that Nabokov lingered over the light and shade games in order to make this particular "memory" stick in the reader's mind. The striking metaphor utilizes light and shade—by now, shorthand indexes to visual beauty—to highlight the aesthetic pursuit of memory in purest terms, and moreover in language, that most fluid medium.

BEYOND BERGSONIAN MODERNISM

The most poignant Bergsonian experiment with time to emerge out of *Ada* is with literary tradition itself. While Van tries to make sense of his life through accumulated personal memories, Nabokov compiles memories of literature. *Ada*'s allusions, in this reading, are the memories of prose fiction itself: the novel form dreams about its own past. When Van first sights Ardis, "the romantic mansion appeared on the gentle eminence of old novels" (*Ada*, 35). His love for Ada repeats the common literary trope of recognition: even at fourteen, love can only be remembered or regained, for it is based on earlier literature. Part 1 of *Ada* especially teems with novelistic signposts: Van and Ada "met in the passage, and would have kissed at some earlier stage of the Novel's Evolution in the History of Literature" (*Ada*, 96); "They had one moment to plan things, it was all, historically speaking, at the dawn of the novel which was still in the hands of parsonage ladies and French academicians, so such moments were precious" (*Ada*, 127). But listen to how Nabokov explains his own strategy: as Van procures for Ada all the hitherto forbidden masterpieces of the Ardis library, we are told that it "promised a long idyll of bibliolatry; it might have become a chapter in one of the old novels on its own shelves; a touch of parody gave its theme the comic relief of life" (*Ada*, 137).

While many Nabokov novels train the reader to be a rereader, *Ada* enforces a strategy for reading in Veen's Time, demanding not only cover-to-cover perusal, but also constant returns to decode the novel's many codes. The reader is compelled to familiarize herself with the work and only then to examine its inner workings: she must read in four dimensions and across multiple imagined media, including the Veens' filmed montages. Marie-Laure Ryan interrogates such hybrid forms in *Narrative across Media*: "The question, 'Is it a narrative?' is even more problematic when the text embodies the artistic intent to both arouse and frustrate narrative desire."[56] Nearly more game than novel, *Ada* pushes the boundaries of narrative to the point of exasperation for many readers.

We are familiar with the conventional illusion of greater realism that comes from depicting dissonance between earlier literature and the characters' own experiences: sentimentally trained Tatiana or young Marcel misunderstand life and love because they have read too many novels, and so Pushkin or Proust seem the more real. However, in Nabokov the technique doubles and triples until it becomes a parody and has the opposite result. Rather than feeling that "thus things really are," the reader concludes, "thus things are in literature, which really is another world." But at that very moment, paradoxically, things are no longer so in literature at all.

Bergson's philosophy affords Nabokov with yet another example of transnational traditions and borrowing across cultural and linguistic borders. But again the distance between narrator and author suggests another layer of meaning: the literary conquest of time is here the subject of the novel. For it is Van Veen who collapses time (and land), applying Bergson's *durée* to literature. A triumphalist reading of the pseudo-memoir finds in it a total conquest of time: a perfect literary genealogy; the immortality of great art, and even of the Veens themselves, vanishing into the pages of their book. But as Nabokov continually reminded his students, Marcel in *À la recherche* is not quite Proust, and Pushkin's lyric persona in *Onegin* is not quite the author. Like Pushkin with his *Onegin*, Nabokov lets his characters play out literary fashions perhaps not so distant from his own recent practice—and leaves them behind.

If Nabokov once saw *À la recherche* as a beautiful illustration of Bergsonian thought, he attempts to outdo and draw attention to that accomplishment in *Ada*. By making Van a parody of Bergson and of the modernist sensibility, Nabokov writes his layer cake and has it too. Bergson's philosophy in *Ada* is not an underlying doctrine, as for Joyce and Proust and the writers and artists of the early twentieth century, but the subject—unexpectedly rehistoricized. In other words, *Ada* is not a late modernist monument at all but a novel about modernism, underscoring thereby the distance between its author and his literary precursors. The closing gesture is there, but Nabokov deconstructs his canon as soon as it is forged. Rather than simply advocating for his own list of great books, in *Ada* Nabokov simultaneously exposes the struggles and stakes of canon formation. To some of his readers—the international writers and artists who continue to find inspiration in his works—this might well be his most important legacy.

World Literature and the Butterfly Man

Все это живописец плавный
передо мною развернул,
и, кажется, совсем недавно
в лицо мне этот ветер дул,
изображенный им в летучих
осенних листьях, зыбких тучах,
и плыл по набережной гул,
во мгле колокола гудели—
собора медные качели . . .

Какой там двор знакомый есть,
какие тумбы! Хорошо бы
туда перешагнуть, пролезть,
там постоять, где спят сугробы
и плотно сложены дрова,
или под аркой, на канале,
где нежно в каменном овале
синеют крепость и Нева.

All this smoothly the painter
in front of me unfolded, and
I had the sense that only lately
this very wind my face had fanned
which he'd depicted by the flying
autumn leaves, by the untidy clouds,
and down the quay a humming flowed,
the bells in the penumbra dinned—
the cathedral's bronzen swings . . .

What a familiar courtyard stands nearby,
what stony posts! If I could only
step across, clamber inside,
stand for a while where snow-banks slumber
and where logs lie, compactly stacked,

or 'neath the arch on the canal,
where on the stony oval, tinted blue,
shimmer fortress and Neva.
—Vladimir Nabokov, 1926, "Ut pictura poesis"

The strange unreality of such an existence in
a foreign land seems to me nowhere more
clearly expressed than in Nabokov's remark,
made in passing, that he had appeared as an
extra in evening dress in several of the films
shot in Berlin at that time, which frequently
included doppelgängers and such shadowy
figures among their characters. There is no
proof anywhere else of these appearances of
his, so we do not know whether any of them
may still be faintly preserved on a brittle
strip of celluloid or whether they are now all
extinguished.
—W. G. Sebald, "Dream Textures: A Brief Note
on Nabokov," 2003

VISIONS OF WORLD LITERATURE(S)

Nabokov had no interest in fitting into someone else's anthology of Russian writers, but provided his own transnational genealogy in the *Onegin*
project and again in the family trees of *Ada*. Nabokov's canon reveals an
implied trajectory for the Russian romantic and modernist novel, extending
from Pushkin to culminate unexpectedly in a late twentieth-century hybrid,
written mostly in English and after fifty years of emigration. *Eugene Onegin*
sought to establish Pushkin as a model for how a great artist could escape
cultural marginalization into the relatively autonomous alterity of art. *Ada*,
Nabokov's final act of alchemy with Russian literature, infects our world with
Antiterra in an attempt to translate and annex the Russian novel to a hybrid,
if English-dominant, canon. More than any of Nabokov's previous or subsequent works, *Ada* seems to seek the final word on Nabokov's precursors,
rival canons, and even on the novel's agonistic competition with rival media.
Nabokov's *Ada* is an imagined library akin to Van Veen's Lucinda Museum.

Despite—or perhaps, because of—the controversy that he unfailingly
inspired in the last two decades of his life, Nabokov has been acknowledged
as the "first among Russian-born literati to attain the 'interliterary stature of
a world writer.'"[1] An unconventional but influential cultural ambassador, he

successfully reimagined the international relevance of the Russian literary tradition, the canon as a complex fabric of intermingled transnational culture, as well as the stylistic and thematic possibilities of the late twentieth-century transnational novel. Russia's ever-liminal position both inside and outside of European culture proves in some sense an advantage; and Nabokov, a model for how other cultural producers might break into and decenter the networks of cultural capital that shape and define canons.

The stakes of my study have been to understand how Nabokov managed to escape the marginal status of a Russian émigré writer to become, in the 1960s and 1970s, the most famous world writer alive; and moreover, how he managed to convince readers that the Russian literary tradition in general was crucial and even central to European and American literatures. In this regard, he resembles less the other famous Russian émigré writers as much as he does the artists and musicians, who had an easier time translating their life's work to European and American soil: the painters Wassily Kandinsky and Marc Chagall, the composer Igor Stravinsky, or the choreographer George Balanchine, all of whom have been defining voices of international modernisms in their respective media.

In his youth, Nabokov had aspired to become a landscape artist, and throughout his life, he placed great emphasis on the visual orientation of his imagination. One of the most famous of synaesthete-writers (or so he claimed), he shares that honor with Proust, Baudelaire, and Rimbaud—although the French poets may have championed synaesthetic visions in "Voyelles" (1857) and "Correspondances" (1871), respectively, without personally experiencing color memory. In interviews, Nabokov often insisted, "I don't think in any language. I think in images" (*Strong Opinions*, 14). He even suggested that his oeuvre might be better conceptualized in terms of visual art, describing the desired final effect of his novels as something like viewing "a picture within a picture: *The Artist's Studio* by Van Bock" (*Strong Opinions*, 73).

I am less concerned with the veracity of such claims than with the strategy they present. It behooves the émigré writer, reliant not only on a foreign language but on his readers' perception of his mastery over that language, to think in images. Nabokov was so often perceived as "not very Russian," or not Russian enough, by fellow émigrés in large part because he refused to be at home only in the Russian language. Instead, he maintained that English might as well have been his first language; and that he could have easily become a "great French writer." I am perfectly willing to believe the latter; but Nabokov's masterful and often outrageous fashioning of his public persona is evident, as is his positioning of himself and his oeuvre outside the bounds of the marginalized émigré and Russia abroad. If he could magically slide between languages and national literary traditions, crossing borders with no need of a Nansen passport, he was free.

But it is even more liberating to think in images than equally well in Russian, English and French. And thus in numerous novels and poems, including the paradigmatic "Ut pictura poesis" that opens this conclusion, Nabokov spoke of stepping across and into the alluring timeless images that he so admired. He persistently probed that painted border: his writings, from the earliest Russian-language works to the final fragments of *The Original of Laura*, are replete with paintings and artist protagonists or antagonists, memorably including Pnin's genius surrogate son Victor Wind and *Laughter in the Dark*'s ominous Axel Rex. Gerard de Vries and D. Barton Johnson have counted over 150 references to painters in Nabokov's oeuvre, even limiting the count to references "either explicit or recognizable."[2] Gavriel Shapiro writes, "Nabokov's turning to the works of the Old Masters in his own writings enabled him to view himself as part and parcel of European cultural continuity and to rightly claim his rich cultural ancestry."[3]

Visual media offer an alternative route out of the language quagmire faced by the émigré aesthetic producer, with their tempting claims of international accessibility. Paintings are accessible to viewers regardless of linguistic background, and in the visual medium it is evident that stylistic practices and innovations cross national borders. In turn, the international language of cinema, as it was declared by Dziga Vertov and other practitioners of the new art in the 1920s, aspired to create a visual Esperanto with the potential to unify the world culturally. Such prophecies have proven equal parts utopian and prescient: film has crossed political, cultural, and linguistic borders to forge unexpected cultural alliances and stylistic hybrids in unprecedented ways throughout the twentieth century, if with different results than Vertov imagined. Pascale Casanova's *World Republic of Letters* deals only with literature for a reason: film and the visual arts cross language borders in ways that interact with, but deeply complicate the cultural capital of powerful literary traditions.

In *Multimedia Modernism*, Julian Murphet reminds us that literary works do not compete with literary works alone, much less quietly coexist with other media:

> It is imperative to offer a revision of the prevailing conception of "media ecologies" as peaceable affairs characterized by the rapid attainment of internal equilibrium . . . Not so, however, in periods of crisis and transition, such as those moments during which new species, or even new genera, emerge to contest for space and resources with the existing life forms. For at such times, ecologies are cast into violent new configurations in which the stereotypical notion of Darwinism comes to the fore: savage competition for resources, sudden mutations, survival of the fittest, extinction of unsuccessful species, and so on.[4]

Building on the metaphor of evolution, Murphet suggests that "convergent differentiation" forces literature especially into a position of "acute medial self-consciousness. It confronts writing with that most powerful of challenges within the new media ecology: acquiring meaningful materiality."[5]

Ada, like Pushkin's *Onegin*, seems to subsume and to crossbreed its sources only to leave them behind. We might recall the postpartum stanza in which Pushkin toyed with returning to *Onegin*: "Insert new pictures into a spacious commodious frame—show us a diorama: the public will come flocking."[6] Other media, transfigured into poetry or prose, suggest new and potentially infinitely productive ways to expand the thematic and stylistic possibilities of verbal narrative. *Ada* is written and not painted or shot, but in a hybrid English that seems to have absorbed Nabokov's other beloved languages, an erudite cosmopolitan's Esperanto. By leaning on an internal gallery of internationally renowned and recognizable works, *Ada* moves further away from the limitations of national canon. We also see an open competition with film as the dominant form of the twentieth century, threatening the status of the novel after the early modernist period. By attempting a kind of filmic prose, *Ada* searches for a way that novels might share the privileges and possibilities of the international language of cinema.

Alongside painting and film, *Ada* finds room besides for murals and mosaic; for the architecture and landscaping of fancy brothels; for comic books, oral storytelling, pulp fiction and its cinematic adaptations; for animated paintings, photography, theater, dance and acrobatic performance; for detailed descriptions of lavish dishes; for microfilms of travel, paintings, and erotica; and numerous invented ways of preserving and re-creating the past, including a vaguely homeopathic use of water to record sound. In his free mixture of high and low forms, a pastiche that pairs Proust with comics, Nabokov comes across as unexpectedly democratic; his readings of the American cultural industry meanwhile echo Frankfurt school Marxist theory.

In *Remediation: Understanding New Media*, Jay David Bolter and Richard Grusin argue that refashioning (allusion, parody, appropriation) within a single medium is

> the one kind of refashioning that literary critics, film critics, and art historians have acknowledged and studied with enthusiasm, for it does not violate the presumed sanctity of the medium, a sanctity that was important to critics earlier in this century, although it is less so now. Refashioning within the medium is a special case of remediation, and it proceeds from the same ambiguous motives of homage and rivalry—what Harold Bloom has called "the anxiety of influence"—as do other remediations.[7]

Through the lenses of narrative and media theory, transnational and world literatures, we find Nabokov's practice to be quite unlike his performatively stiff public provocations. The self-conscious self-fashioning of what I have termed Nabokov's canon, and its emancipatory potentialities for subsequent writers and artists, emerges through the accumulation of rivalries and appropriations.

If one dominant trend in Western culture has been toward greater immediacy,

> hypermediacy has often had to content itself with a secondary, if nonetheless important, status. Sometimes hypermediacy has adopted a playful or subversive attitude, both acknowledging and undercutting the desire for immediacy . . . At the end of the twentieth century, we are in a position to understand hypermediacy as immediacy's opposite number, an alter ego that has never been suppressed fully or for long periods of time.[8]

Remediated, *Ada*'s exuberance simultaneously performs the longing for extreme, even total sensory experience and hypermediation, stressing artificiality and highlighting the novel's form(s). Nabokov thus constructs an edifice for his canon, thereby challenging and even infuriating dominant elites—but in the process, or through his appetite for ever more allusions, analogies, echoes, unexpected connections and equivalences, he sketches a far more culturally fluid world. At the very moment that Nabokov's canon appears triumphantly ascendant, it explodes to include nearly everything that can be seen, remembered, or imagined, collapsing as an illusory category that fails to contain an ever-expanding list of cultural products.

For all the sense of closure that *Ada* may have had for Nabokov, who would never again write anything so indebted to Russian literature, the novel has proven to have an afterlife. His influences are as readily noticeable in popular culture as in highbrow literature, and his novels continue to inspire other forms of four-dimensional art, from film adaptations to an unexpected array of dance, musical, and multimedia creations.[9] We see *Ada*'s afterlife in exegetic projects, such as the multiauthor *AdaOnline* (a form especially appropriate for a novel that presciently resembles hypertext); in poetry, ranging from Cynthia Zarin's English-language collection *The Ada Poems* and the bilingual Russian/English anthology *A Night in Nabokov Hotel*; and even in musical adaptations like the ongoing avant-garde jazz *Tower* albums by Parisian guitarist and composer Marc Ducret.[10] Read in a new context, the layer cake of *Ada* seems far from a dead end, but rather opens rich possibilities for multilingual and transnational invented traditions—perhaps especially online.

In *What Is World Literature?*, David Damrosch suggests that "world literature is not an infinite, ungraspable canon of works but rather a mode of circulation and of reading, a mode that is as applicable to individual works as to bodies of material, available for reading established classics and new discoveries alike."[11] Mads Rosedahl Thomsen in turn argues in *Mapping World Literature: International Canonization and Transnational Literatures*, "It is only within the last decades that the concept of culture has gradually been more and more widely defined as non-essentialist, hybrid and contingent, something that has not been reflected in the practice of literary history, but which in all likelihood is one of the main reasons behind the renewed interest in world literature."[12] Goethe's dream of a world literature, or *Weltliteratur*, has been reimagined for a new era; similarly, Nabokov's works—and Nabokov's endeavors at canon formation—may be read increasingly in such company and context.

NABOKOV'S CHILDREN

Working within the literary medium, Nabokov managed not only to escape marginalization himself, but through his literary output and lifelong aesthetic propaganda campaign, to reconfigure the international cultural playing field. Regardless of the difficulties of reading *Ada* and the critical discord that his late novel provoked, Nabokov managed to conjure in the minds of many readers an alluring vision of Antiterra as a transnational world of arts and letters.

His oeuvre and his transnational status have in turn permeated world literatures and captured the imagination of the Iranian-born Azar Nafisi, Turkish Orhan Pamuk, South African J. M. Coetzee, and the German exile W. G. Sebald, to name only a few contemporary practitioners. Writers who feel distant from the traditional centers of cultural capital find in Nabokov an exceptional source of inspiration, and read him in ways as disparate as do Nafisi, who found in *Lolita* a moving allegory of the subjugation of women (as in her 2003 memoir *Reading Lolita in Tehran*); and Pamuk, who in works like *My Name Is Red* (2000), *The Museum of Innocence* (2008), and *The Naive and the Sentimental Novelist* (2010) argues for the primacy of the visual description in terms often borrowed from Nabokov, but also from the Islamic tradition of illustrating books with ornate miniatures.[13]

The pattern I have traced may help to explain how Nabokov came to serve as an unexpected fountainhead for seemingly disparate (and often overtly political) work: Nabokov's canon vividly shows borders to be permeable across cultures, languages, and media. *Ada*'s remediated paintings, films, and various acrobatics gesture toward a changing cultural world—even as Nabokov claims a central place in the skeletal structure of his own imagining. Rather than merely serving to replace one dominant Anglo-American canon with a slightly more European but equally rigid model, Nabokov's idiosyncratic practice invites similar self-fashioning.

Many contemporary cultural critics set great store by writers who have grown up in Nabokov's museum library, while discounting Nabokov as the relic of an earlier age. But moving against the grain of critical discourse, we can choose to mine Nabokov for unexpectedly emancipatory elements and recast *Ada*'s new world as a forerunner of transnational and world literatures. Now and firmly in the twenty-first century, when so many readers are hybrids and geographical in-betweens, *Ada* more than ever speaks to a reimaginable world.

By the late twentieth and twenty-first century, Nabokov has become as much of a symbolic value to international artists and writers as Pushkin or Joyce had been to him. Nabokov is maddening or enticing, but certainly by now he serves also as a symbol—of a densely allusive and parodic prose style, of an uncompromising stance on aesthetic freedom, and even of a mode of artistic existence. Nabokov has even been accused of ruining a generation of English-language writers, infected by his style and mask of aloof autonomy. However, the list of international and world writers that have paid him homage includes, besides Afizi, Pamuk, Coetzee, and Sebald, also Umberto Eco, Salman Rushdie, Roberto Bolaño, and too many others to list.[14] Many of these authors, despite having vastly different aesthetic, ethical, or political projects of their own, are eager to declare that they are, nevertheless, children of Nabokov. Why should this be the case, if Nabokov represents a time capsule of unseasonable forms? What has Nabokov come to mean for subsequent generations of writers?

I conclude with one vivid example: Nabokov as a visual leitmotif in the work of his unusual and melancholy disciple Sebald. In his own deeply original and meditative anti-novel *The Emigrants* (1992), a work that combines the genres of biography, autobiography, essay, cultural criticism, and fiction, Sebald uses the figure of Nabokov "the butterfly man" as a mysterious recurring leitmotif. The image of the butterfly man speaks at once to Nabokov's innovatively visual mode of writing and to his mythical autonomy. In most cases unnamed but always readily recognizable, Nabokov appears in each of the four life stories that comprise Sebald's novel: the fictionalized biographies of Dr. Henry Selwyn, Paul Bereyter, Ambros Adelwarth, and Max Ferber. The first section establishes Nabokov's importance to the text through a brief but direct reference: Sebald includes among his own snapshots "a photograph of Nabokov in the mountains above Gstaad that I had clipped from a Swiss magazine a few days before."[15] In the second section, Bereyter approaches Mme Landau, the woman who postpones his imminent suicide and who later provides the narrator with the story of his tragedy, when he glimpses her reading *Speak, Memory* on a park bench (*Emigrants*, 43).

But the most moving scenes of *The Emigrants* occur later in the novel. The narrator's great-uncle Ambros Adelwarth voluntarily submits himself to a mental institution, to be slowly destroyed by unnecessary administrations of electroshock therapy. The clinic is in the close vicinity of Ithaca, and the only event that stirs the inmate is the periodic appearance of the butterfly man, who hunts within view of his window. While the dying man watches from inside, "outside the torture chamber, Nabokov dances, making 'curious jumps' with his butterfly net."[16] In her last visit, the narrator's aunt (the narrator may or may not be Sebald's prose persona) uncovers Adelwarth's strange fixation. She joins him at the window:

> The air was coming in from outside and we were looking over the almost motionless trees toward a meadow that reminded me of the Altach marsh when a middle-aged man appeared, holding a white net on a pole in front of him and occasionally taking curious jumps. Uncle Adelwarth stared straight ahead, but he registered my bewilderment all the same, and said: It's the butterfly man, you know. He comes around here quite often. (*Emigrants*, 104)

From the guilt-stricken doctor who participated in the extreme doses of electroshock treatment, the narrator later hears the story of the last day of his great-uncle's life. The doctor, by now in doubt of his own sanity, recounts how for the first time, on that day Adelwarth failed to appear for treatment. When he came to investigate, he found Adelwarth at the window as usual: "When I asked why he had not appeared at the appointed time, he replied (I remember his words exactly): It must have slipped my mind whilst I was waiting for the butterfly man" (*Emigrants*, 115). After that, Adelwarth submits calmly to his final session of treatment, and dies the same day. "I was waiting for the butterfly man" were his last words.

Sebald, who clearly felt the same pressure as Nabokov to expand the novel form, chooses to include visual images in his own works directly, through the enclosed snapshots for which he is well known. In a sense, Sebald builds from what Nabokov had attempted to do in (mostly) prose. However, Sebald not only takes inspiration from Nabokov, but also continually "frames" Nabokov as a still or moving image within *The Emigrants*. Most directly, he pictures Nabokov through the first chapter's clipped photograph, which he includes to ensure that we share his mental picture of the Russian author as an aging but irrepressible Swiss butterfly catcher. But even in the longer prose passage described above, Sebald creates something like an embedded prose-film out of Nabokov's cameo. Adelwarth watches Nabokov make his curious jumps through the frame of the window: we imagine and watch this "footage" with the narrator, equally mesmerized and bewildered as to the secret meaning behind the immortalized motions.

In the final section of *The Emigrants*, the fictional painter Max Ferber hands the narrator his mother's diary, written just prior to her death in the Holocaust in 1941. Max himself has encountered the butterfly man; in fact, he has tried repeatedly but unsuccessfully to paint this specter. It thus comes as no surprise to Sebald's Nabokov-trained readers when Luisa Ferber's cherished memory from girlhood, preserved in that diary, is of witnessing an unknown Russian boy chasing butterflies in Bad Kissingen, accompanied by two refined Russian gentlemen. The boy (we might recognize the scene from *Speak, Memory*) is the very young Nabokov vacationing with his father in the years before the Russian Revolution. Luisa Ferber writes:

> Though everything else around me blurred, I saw that forgotten Russian boy as clearly as anything, leaping about the meadows with his butterfly net; I saw him as a messenger of joy, returning from that distant summer day to open his specimen box and release the most beautiful red admirals, peacock butterflies, brimstones and tortoiseshells to signal my final liberation. (*Emigrants*, 214)

In Luisa's memory, just as through Adelwarth's window, the butterfly boy is captured and framed (this time through focus as "everything else around" blurs) as a moving image. These embedded dream-films haunt Sebald's novel, suggesting another emigrant's solution to the crises of displacement, and of art.

For in Sebald's strange and tragic novel, not one of his emigrants escapes from the past: haunted by history and rootless in any new land, his sensitive and wounded subjects are doomed to wither. At best, they sometimes create works of a quiet and enigmatic beauty and tell their stories— whether through paintings, flower gardens, collections of notes, or chance confessions—before coming to some form of often self-inflicted demise. For them, as perhaps for Sebald, Nabokov symbolizes something both longed-for and impossible: he is the paradigmatic twentieth-century literary émigré to escape historical tragedy and seemingly psychological trauma to find joy and freedom in life as in art.

In each section of *The Emigrants*, Nabokov appears as an image, an instantly recognizable book cover, a veritable short film taking place outside the madhouse window, a haunting encounter, and finally as a lingering childhood memory prior to unimaginable annihilation—all of which invoke Nabokov's practice in his own works. More significantly still, Nabokov, captured at several different ages in Sebald's book, seems to grow younger as the text progresses until at last he is once more a pre-exilic Russian child and a "messenger of joy." Nabokov appears to be so free from the bonds that tie down Sebald's own characters that he even escapes the arrow of time.

Adrian Curtin and Maxim Shrayer have called Nabokov the "exemplary model of the artist-in-exile," and the literary precursor whose work "both complicates and contrasts Sebald's own designs."[17] I suspect that Sebald refuses as well as feels incapable of the butterfly man's freedom. But the recurring image of Nabokov intimates that freedom—from the minefields of history, from the confines of national identity—is somehow possible and even near at hand. Alluring and maddening, Nabokov beckons to the reader with his butterfly net.

Notes

INTRODUCTION

The epigraphs for the introduction are from T. S. Eliot, "Tradition and the Individual Talent," in *Selected Prose of T. S. Eliot*, ed. Frank Kermode (New York: Harcourt, 1975), 38–39; and Stephen Jay Gould, *The Panda's Thumb: More Reflections in Natural History* (New York: Norton, 1980), 84.

1. I summarize the controversy in my second chapter. Part of the exchange between Nabokov, Robert Lowell, and George Steiner over Nabokov's own translation and Lowell's translations of Mandelstam was published in the overtly anticommunist and less overtly CIA-funded *Encounter*, adding ideological layers to the literary debate. See Sylvan Fox, "Stephen Spender Quits *Encounter*," *New York Times*, May 8, 1967.

2. Alexander Gerschenkron, "A Manufactured Monument?," review of Aleksandr Pushkin, *Eugene Onegin: A Novel in Verse*, trans. and commentary Vladimir Nabokov, *Modern Philology* 63 (1966): 340.

3. T. S. Eliot, "The Use of Poetry and the Use of Criticism," in *Selected Prose of T. S. Eliot* (Cambridge, Mass.: Harvard University Press, 1986), 86.

4. As John Guillory writes, "literary culture only very slowly distinguished itself from the clergy and, what is more, continued to form its pedagogic institutions and professional self-representations on the clerical model . . . literary culture continued to *imagine* itself in clerical terms," in *Cultural Capital: The Problem of Literary Canon Formation* (Chicago: University of Chicago Press, 1993), 153.

5. Frederic Jameson, *Postmodernism; or, The Cultural Logic of Late Capitalism* (Durham, N.C.: Duke University Press, 2003), 305.

6. It speaks to Nabokov's success in storming the citadel that the next generation would include him in the list of fathers needing killing. Andreas Huyssen writes, "The ire of the postmodernists was directed not so much against modernism as such, but rather against a certain austere image of 'high modernism,' as advanced by the New Critics and other custodians of modernist culture," in

After the Great Divide: Modernism, Mass Culture, Postmodernism (Blooming-ton: Indiana University Press, 1986), 189.

7. Azade Seyhan, building on Walter Benjamin's "Die Aufgabe des Über-setzers," suggests that the translators too often show greater reverence for the "ar-bitrarily defined higher status" of the "to" language: "Translation should be neither a full linguistic reconstruction nor an appropriation. Rather, it should incorporate the original language's mode of signification. Both the original and the translation should be recognizable as 'fragments of a larger language' [*als Bruchstück einer größeren Sprache*]," in *Writing Outside the Nation* (Princeton, N.J.: Princeton University Press, 2001), 155.

8. Mads Rosendahl Thomsen, *Mapping World Literature: International Can-onization and Transnational Literatures* (London: Continuum, 2008), 83.

9. Gavriel Shapiro, *The Sublime Artist's Studio: Nabokov and Painting* (Evanston, Ill.: Northwestern University Press, 2009), 101.

10. See Ellen E. Berry and Mikhail N. Epstein, *Transcultural Experiments: Russian and American Models of Creative Communication* (New York: Palgrave Macmillan, 1999), 105. Mikhail Epstein, writing about what he terms transcul-ture, urges us to let go of old binaries and look to the world for examples of crea-tive, possibly transcendent new cultural categories.

11. Here I disagree with Edward Said when he writes, "it is necessary to set aside Joyce and Nabokov and even Conrad, who wrote of exile with such pathos, but of exile without cause or rationale. Think instead of the uncountable masses for whom UN agencies have been created, or refugees without urbanity, with only ration cards and agency numbers," in "The Mind of Winter: Reflections on Life in Exile," *Harper's Magazine* (September 1984): 50. Such a position fore-stalls reconsiderations of modernism's roots in exile and displacement. I align myself further with Andreas Huyssen's corrective: "We should abandon the no-tion that a successful attack on elite culture can play a major role in a political and social transformation" today, and "instead we should pay close attention to the ways in which cultural practices and products are linked to the discourses of the political and the social in specific local and national constellations as they de-velop in transnational exchange," in Huyssen, "Geographies of Modernism in a Globalizing World," dedicated to Said's memory, in *Geographies of Modernism: Literatures, Cultures, Spaces*, ed. Peter Brooker and Andrew Thacker (London: Routledge, 2005), 15. Nabokov is starting to "come back in fashion" as a paradig-matic transnational writer, as evidenced by recent work: see Rachel Trousdale, *Nabokov, Rushdie, and the Transnational Imagination: Novels of Exile and Alter-nate Worlds* (New York: Palgrave Macmillan, 2010).

12. John Guillory, "Genesis of the Media Concept," *Critical Inquiry* 36, no. 2 (2010): 360.

13. Franco Moretti, *Signs Taken for Wonders: Essays in the Sociology of Lit-erary Forms* (London: Verso, 1988). See also Eric Hobsbawm: "'Invented tradi-

tion' is taken to mean a set of practices, normally governed by overtly or tacitly accepted rules and of a ritual or symbolic nature, which seek to inculcate certain values and norms of behavior by repetition . . . where possible, they normally attempt to establish continuity with a suitable historic past." Hobsbawm, *The Invention of Tradition*, ed. Eric Hobsbawm and Terence Ranger (Cambridge: Cambridge University Press, 1983), 1.

14. Randal Johnson, "Pierre Bourdieu on Art, Literature, and Culture," in Pierre Bourdieu, *The Field of Cultural Production: Essays on Art and Literature*, ed. Randall Johnson (New York: Columbia University Press, 1993), 10.

15. Bourdieu, *The Field of Cultural Production*, 39.

16. Moretti, *Signs Taken for Wonders*, 276.

17. Ibid., 277.

18. Harold Bloom provocatively popularized the notion of literary family struggle in *The Anxiety of Influence* (1973) and *The Western Canon* (1994): "The aesthetic and the agonistic are one, according to all the ancient Greeks . . . What Homer teaches is a poetics of conflict, a lesson first learned by his rival Hesiod." Bloom, *The Western Canon: The Books and School of the Ages* (New York: Riverhead Trade, 1995), 6. Iurii Tynianov describes literary tradition as "pushing off from what is already known—a struggle." Iu. N. Tynianov, "Dostoevskii i Gogol' (k teorii parodii)," in *Poetika; Istoriia literatury; Kino* (Moscow: Nauka, 1977), 198 (my translation).

19. Tynianov, "Dostoevskii i Gogol'," 199, 211.

20. Viktor Shklovsky, "Art as Technique," in *Russian Formalist Criticism: Four Essays*, ed. Lee T. Lemon and Marion J. Reis (Lincoln: University of Nebraska Press, 1965), 12. See also Graham Roberts, *The Last Soviet Avant-Garde: OBERIU—Fact, Fiction, Metafiction* (Cambridge: Cambridge University Press, 1997), 124.

21. Mikhail Bakhtin, *Formal'nyj metod v literaturovedenii* (New York: Serebrianyi vek, 1982), 44 (my translation). For a discussion of the essay's disputed authorship (P. N. Medvedev or Bakhtin), see Katerina Clark and Michael Holquist, *Mikhail Bakhtin* (Cambridge, Mass.: Harvard University Press, 1984), 146–70.

22. Guillory, *Cultural Capital*, 64.

23. Johnson, "Pierre Bourdieu on Art, Literature, and Culture," 7; see Pierre Bourdieu, *Distinction: A Social Critique of the Judgment of Taste*, trans. Richard Nice (Cambridge, Mass.: Harvard University Press, 1984).

24. Bourdieu, *The Field of Cultural Production*, 72.

25. Ibid., 183, 189.

26. Guillory, *Cultural Capital*, ix.

27. Ibid., 147.

28. Ibid., 168.

29. Ibid., 167.

30. Pascale Casanova, *The World Republic of Letters*, trans. M. B. DeBevoise (Cambridge, Mass.: Harvard University Press, 2004), 4.

31. David Damrosch, *What Is World Literature?* (Princeton, N.J.: Princeton University Press, 2003), 27.

32. René Girard, *Deceit, Desire, and the Novel: Self and Other in Literary Structure*, trans. Yvonne Freccero (Baltimore, Md.: Johns Hopkins University Press, 1965), 1.

33. Girard, *Deceit, Desire*, 15.

34. Marshall Berman, *All That Is Solid Melts into Air: The Experience of Modernity* (New York: Penguin, 1988), 232.

35. Monika Greenleaf, *Pushkin and Romantic Fashion: Fragment, Elegy, Orient, Irony* (Stanford, Calif.: Stanford University Press, 1994), 2. Greenleaf points out that "like Shakespeare, or for that matter Goethe, Dante, Mickiewicz, or any of the other 'first poets' venerated by Romanticism, Pushkin had to be shown to be seminal, the origin without origin, pregnant with all the forms of his culture," ibid., 4.

36. Ibid., 4.

37. Iurii Lotman, *Pushkin: Biografiia pisatelia, stat'i i zametki 1960–1990*, "Evgenii Onegin," kommentarii (St. Petersburg: Iskusstvo SPB, 1995), 412, 420.

38. See Georges Bataille: "What we desire is to bring into a world founded on discontinuity all the continuity such a world can sustain." See his *Erotism: Death and Sensuality*, trans. Mary Dalwood (San Francisco: City Lights Books, 1986), 19.

39. James Wood, "Discussing Nabokov," *Slate* (April 26, 1999): http://www .slate.com/articles/arts/the_book_club/features/1999/discussing_nabokov/_2 .html (accessed 1/5/2015).

CHAPTER ONE

The chapter epigraphs are from Casanova, *World Republic*, 45; and *Dear Bunny, Dear Volodya: The Nabokov-Wilson Letters, 1940–1971*, ed. Simon Karlinsky, rev. ed. (Berkeley: University of California Press, 2001), 73.

1. William Mills Todd III, *Fiction and Society in the Age of Pushkin: Ideology, Institutions, and Narrative* (Cambridge, Mass.: Harvard University Press, 1986), 106.

2. As quoted in Richard Gustafson, "The Metaphor of the Seasons in *Evgenij Onegin*," *Slavic and East European Journal* 6, no. 1 (1962): 6.

3. "Благослови мой долгий труд, / О ты, эпическая муза!" adding humorously, "Довольно. С плеч долой обуза! / Я классицизму отдал честь: / Хоть поздно, а вступленье есть," 7:LV. I give the original from Pushkin's *Polnoe sobranie sochineniii* and Nabokov's 1975 revised translation in each quotation from *Onegin* unless stated otherwise. See Aleksandr Pushkin, *Eugene Onegin:*

A Novel in Verse, trans. and ed. Vladimir Nabokov, rev. ed. (Princeton, N.J.: Princeton University Press, 1975).

4. The most famous expression of this sentiment was the futurists' demand: "Throw Pushkin, Dostoevsky, Tolstoy and the like from the steamship of modernity." Velimir Khlebnikov, Vladimir Mayakovsky, David Burliuk, Aleksei Kruchenykh, Vasilii Kamenskii, Benedikt Livshitz, *A Slap in the Face of Public Taste*, 1912.

5. "Even Pushkin cited Lomonosov's 'discovery' of the Greek heritage of Russian linguistic structures as proof of the poetic superiority of the Russian language." Greenleaf, *Pushkin and Romantic Fashion*, 29, 63.

6. Casanova, *World Republic*, 45.

7. Pierre Bourdieu extended the concept of capital to include cultural, social, and symbolic capital, arguing that cultural and social practices revealed power dynamics akin to those of economics, most famously in his *Distinction*.

8. Casanova, *World Republic*, 4.

9. Ibid., 88.

10. Ibid., 43.

11. Franco Moretti, *Atlas of the European Novel 1800–1900* (London: Verso, 1998), 3.

12. Casanova, *World Republic*, 220. I cite the translation provided in *World Republic*.

13. Ibid., 92.

14. While acknowledging the existence of centripetal and centrifugal cultural forces, Casanova's book underemphasizes the latter. Centers and peripheries are mutually interdependent: the provincial's hunger for the capital is matched by the urban passion for alterity—the lure of the exotic. Furthermore, Casanova never addresses the differences between literary (primarily or entirely language-based) culture and the other arts. The twentieth century dominates her book, but cinema is entirely absent from consideration. One of the most prevalent responses to the "minor language" paradox has been to write poetry in moving images.

15. Casanova considers Joyce "the inventor of a new aesthetic, political, and above all linguistic solution to literary dependence. There is an international genealogy, then, that includes all the great innovators honored as true liberators in the peripheral lands of literary space, a pantheon of great authors regarded as universal classics" (*World Republic*, 327–28). Such a reading reverberates powerfully with Nabokov's transnational genealogy; however, Casanova only mentions Nabokov somewhat in passing, as yet another twentieth-century writer who was forced to change languages to survive.

16. Casanova borrows this term from Valéry Larbaud, Joyce's first editor and translator into French (*World Republic*, 5).

17. Berman, *All That Is Solid*, 232.

18. The spread of the modernism of underdevelopment, in this reading, overlaps with that of socialist politics. Berman's self-conscious outsider is inevitably something of a revolutionary. Thus he stresses Pushkin's putative Decembrism: "In 1832 [Pushkin] began a sequel to his 'novel in verse' *Evgeny Onegin*, in which his aristocratic hero would participate in the December rising. His new canto was written in a code known only to himself" (*All That Is Solid*, 181).

19. For the sake of consistency and continuity with subsequent chapters, I include Nabokov's translation throughout, with exceptions indicated.

20. "Богат, хорош собою, Ленской; / Везде был принят как жених; / Таков обычай деревенской."

21. For Pushkin and Austen, see Catharine Nepomnyashchy, "Jane Austen in Russia: Hidden Presence and Belated Boom," in *The Reception of Jane Austen in Europe*, ed. Anthony Mandal and Brian Southam (London: Continuum, 2007), 334–49.

22. Lotman, *Pushkin*, 428 (my translation).

23. Greenleaf, *Pushkin and Romantic Fashion*, 285.

24. Ibid., 244. While Greenleaf reads *Onegin* as a "deliberately fabricated Romantic fragment" that consistently refuses closure, Lotman has argued that the serial publication of the text, combined with the fact that the author and the epoch changed over the course of the novel, were "circumstances external to Pushkin's original concept. The distinctive characteristics of the novel came together spontaneously and only subsequently were they rendered meaningful by the poet as a conscious principle." Lotman, *Pushkin*, 195.

25. Jan M. Meijer, "The Digressions in *Evgenij Onegin*," in *Dutch Contributions to the Sixth International Congress of Slavists, Prague, 1968*, ed. A. G. F. van Holk (The Hague: Mouton, 1968), 122–52.

26. Lotman, *Pushkin*, 444.

27. Todd, *Fiction and Society*, 124.

28. Ibid., 129.

29. Ibid. Greenleaf adds: "Utterly shaped by the language of novels—*romany*—she sees life as a system of signs, and waits for them to take on the recognizable configuration of some textual 'original.' Hence, her first glimpse of Eugene is a recognition scene: 'Eto on!' (That's him!). . . . Tatiana is always the tense semiotician, parsing Eugene's gestures for his conformity to this or that literary type; conjuring over hot wax and mirrors; conning a book of symbolism . . . able truly to begin perceiving Eugene only by 'reading' the imprint of his thumbnail in the margins of his favorite books. She can 'perceive' only another reader, can interpret only another act of reading." Greenleaf, *Pushkin and Romantic Fashion*, 249.

30. Nabokov argues that the novel is fundamentally unfinished despite its beautiful formal symmetry; Greenleaf claims that as a romantic fragment, *Onegin* is perfectly and permanently unfinished.

31. Todd, *Fiction and Society*, 122.

32. Greenleaf, *Pushkin and Romantic Fashion*, 220.

33. "Цвела, как ландыш потаенный, / Незнаемый в траве глухой / Ни мотыльками, ни пчелой."

34. "Всегда как утро весела."

35. "В чертах у Ольги жизни нет. / Точь-в-точь в Вандиковой Мадонне."

36. "Мой бедный Ленский! изнывая, / Не долго плакала она."

37. "Чуть лишь из пеленок, / Кокетка, ветреный ребенок! / Уж хитрость ведает она, / Уж изменять научена!"

38. "в полном цвете лет."

39. "От хладного разврата света / Еще увянуть не успев."

40. "И всё одно и то же квакать, / Жалеть *о прежнем, о былом*: / Довольно, пойте о другом!"

41. "Стократ блажен, кто предан вере, / Кто, хладный ум угомонив, / Покоится в сердечной неге."

42. "Но жалок тот, кто все предвидит."

43. "мы, враги Гимена, / В домашней жизни зрим один / Ряд утомительных картин, / Роман во вкусе Лафонтена."

44. August Lafontaine (1758–1831), a popular German novelist and contemporary of Goethe.

45. "двухутренний цветок / Увял еще полураскрытый."

46. "Младой певец / Нашел безвременный конец! / Дохнула буря, цвет прекрасный / Увял на утренней заре."

47. "Ни красотой сестры своей, / Ни свежестью ее румяной"; "Она ласкаться не умела"; "Играть и прыгать не хотела."

48. Poets have used the same technique for centuries, whether to describe their beloved or God.

49. "С послушной куклою дитя / Приготовляется шутя / К приличию— закону света" (2:XXVI): "with her obedient doll, the child / prepares in play / for etiquette, law of the *monde*."

50. In fact none of the principal characters have children. The cursory presence of the previous generation suggests some cyclical continuity, but nothing comes next. Only creative production, rather than biological continuity, offers a chance at immortality. Marriage is un-narratable, and Tatiana effectively ends the novel by refusing to commit adultery. See Tony Tanner, *Adultery in the Novel: Contract and Transgression* (Baltimore, Md.: Johns Hopkins University Press, 1979).

51. "Ей рано нравились романы; / Они ей заменяли всё."

52. "в книгах не видал вреда; / Он, не читая никогда, / Их почитал пустой игрушкой."

53. "Теперь с каким она вниманьем / Читает сладостный роман, / С каким живым очарованьем / Пьет обольстительный обман!" By an odd coincidence, Nabokov's reputedly direct ancestor Can Grande della Scalla, prince of Verona,

sheltered Dante during his exile. Dante wrote the *Inferno* and *Purgatorio* in the prince's house, and dedicated *Paradiso* to his benefactor (Vladimir Nabokov, *Strong Opinions* [New York: McGraw-Hill, 1973], 188).

54. "Давно ее воображенье, / Сгорая негой и тоской, / Алкало пищи роковой." See Girard, *Deceit, Desire, and the Novel*, 1–15.

55. As Todd writes, "Disrespect for conventions in *Eugene Onegin* covers a similarly broad range of possibilities, from the creative mixing of genres (a novel in verse) to the fashionable and socially acceptable eccentricity of Eugene (an accomplished dandy) to insultingly casual disregard (Eugene's use of his valet as his second in the duel) to potentially dangerous violation (Tatiana's letter to Eugene)." Todd, *Fiction and Society*, 125.

56. "Татьяна любит не шутя / И предается безусловно / Любви, как милое дитя."

57. "Чтенью предалася / Татьяна жадною душой; / И ей открылся мир иной." Pushkin uses the word *zamok* for castle, which makes Onegin's abode seem even more "borrowed" or Byronic.

58. "младые грации Москвы"; "а впрочем очень недурной."

59. Olga Vainshtein, *Dendi: Moda, literatura, stil' zhizni* (Moscow: Novoe Literaturnoe Obozrenie, 2005), 184 (my translation).

60. "А нынче! . . . / Как с вашим сердцем и умом / Быть чувства мелкого рабом?"

61. "Eugene's development, then, reverses Tatiana's. As she matures in her ability to relate literature and life in a variety of ways, he loses control over the materials of his culture." Todd, *Fiction and Society*, 134.

62. The watch is still popular with today's *monde*, and advertised in journals like the *New Yorker* with references to *Eugene Onegin* and a full-page portrait of Pushkin. Greenleaf notes, "Most clearly emblematic of the passage's mortal pressure is the recurrent ringing of the sleepless, efficient, foreign watch—the metronome that regulates the *perpetuum mobile* of Onegin's dandified existence." Greenleaf, *Pushkin and Romantic Fashion*, 225.

63. "стрелой / Взлетел по мраморным ступеням."

64. "Проснется за полдень, и снова / До утра жизнь его готова, / Однообразна и пестра."

65. "Как *dandy* лондонский . . ."

66. "рано чувства в нем остыли"; "к жизни вовсе охладел."

67. Todd, *Fiction and Society*, 132–33.

68. "Вот как убил он восемь лет, / Утрата жизни лучший цвет."

69. "Мечтам и годам нет возврата; / Не обновлю души моей."

70. "Весна живит его: впервые . . ."

71. "Alas, at various pastimes / I've ruined a lot of life!"; "Увы, на разные забавы / Я много жизни погубил!" (1:XXX).

72. Vainshtein, *Dendi*, 214.

73. "Лорд Байрон прихотью удачной / Облек в унылый романтизм / И безнадежный эгоизм."

74. "Лета к суровой прозе клонят, / Лета шалунью рифму гонят, / И я—со вздохом признаюсь— / За ней ленивей волочусь."

75. "И скоро, скоро бури след / В душе моей совсем утихнет: / Тогда-то я начну писать / Поэму песен в двадцать пять."

76. Craig Cravens, "Lyric and Narrative Consciousness in *Eugene Onegin*," *Slavic and East European Journal* 46, no. 4 (2002): 683. See also Greenleaf: "the polarities contained in the subtitle *A Novel in Verse* are resolved by a dialectical reconciliation of the values of the latter with the former." *Pushkin and Romantic Fashion*, 206. See also Roman Jakobson and Morris Halle, *Fundamentals of Language* (The Hague: Mouton, 1956).

77. "Вперед, вперед, моя исторья!"

78. Cravens, "Lyric and Narrative Consciousness," 688.

79. "Ах, ножки, ножки! где вы ныне?" The Russian terms do not coincide as in English, but are related only metonymically: *nozhka* and *stopa*.

80. Georg Lukács writes: "In the world of distances, all epic verse turns into lyric poetry (*Don Juan* and *Onegin*, although written in verse, belong to the company of the great humorous novels), for, in verse, everything hidden becomes manifest, and the swift flight of verse makes the distance over which prose travels with its deliberate pace as it gradually approaches meaning appear naked, mocked, trampled, or merely a forgotten dream." Lukács, *Theory of the Novel: A Historico-Philosophical Essay on the Forms of Great Epic Literature*, trans. Anna Bostock (Cambridge, Mass.: MIT Press, 1971), 59.

81. Meijer, "The Digressions in *Evgenij Onegin*," 150.

82. Greenleaf, *Pushkin and Romantic Fashion*, 2–3.

83. Here in my literal translation. See also "Therefore, the novel is still unfinished—it's a gold mine. Insert new pictures into a spacious commodious frame—show us a diorama: the public will come flocking, paying you to get in (which will bring you fame and an income)," quoted and translated in Greenleaf, *Pushkin and Romantic Fashion*, 208.

84. "полурусский сосед."

85. "Неполный, слабый перевод, / С живой картины список бледный."

86. "For Russia in the nineteenth century this [the use of French terms] was typical to the highest degree, as the fashionable fops received French fashion journals. And so Pushkin, describing Onegin's costume, did not complain in vain." Vainshtein, *Dendi*, 493.

87. "Не могу . . . // Люблю я очень это слово, / Но не могу перевести; / Оно у нас покамест ново."

88. Pushkin, *Eugene Onegin*, 2:107. I will henceforth cite Nabokov's version of *Eugene Onegin* (both translation and commentary) parenthetically with volume number and page, for example 2:107.

89. "There is no doubt that the schism separated us from the rest of Europe, and that we did not take part in any of the grand events that shook her, but we have had our own mission to fulfill. It is Russia, it is her immense expanses that absorbed the Mongol conquest. The Tatars did not dare to cross our Western borders and leave us at their backs. They turned back to their deserts, and Christian civilization was saved. For this higher end, we had to lead an entirely separate existence, which, while leaving us Christians, nonetheless rendered us completely foreign to the Christian world. . . . You say that the source from which we drew Christianity was impure, that Byzantium was worthy of and inspired contempt, etc.—O my friend, was not Jesus Christ himself born a Jew and was not Jerusalem the fable of nations? Are the gospels any less admirable for it? . . . As regards our historical insignificance, decidedly I cannot agree with you. . . . And don't you find there to be something meaningful in the current position of Russia, something of the sort that may astound a future historian? Do you believe he will situate us outside of Europe? Even though I am devoted to the Emperor personally, I am far from admiring everything that I see around me: as a man of letters, I am irritated; as a man of opinions, I am offended—but I assure you on my honor that I would not exchange my fatherland or wish for any history but that of our ancestors, such as God has given us" (my translation), Pushkin's letter to Chaadaev, *Polnoe sobranie sochineniii A. S. Pushkina v desiat' tomakh* (Leningrad: Nauka, 1977–79), 10:740. The complete original is also available online at http://pushkin.niv.ru/pushkin/pisma/740.htm.

90. For a recent overview, see the three volumes of *Two Hundred Years of Pushkin*, especially vol. 3: *Pushkin's Legacy*, ed. Joe Andrew and Robert Reid, Studies in Slavic Literature and Poetics (Amsterdam: Rodopi, 2003). The point is driven home by Catriona Kelly's *Russian Literature: A Very Short Introduction* (Oxford: Oxford University Press, 2001), which conjures all of Russian literature from a single Pushkin lyric.

91. Tynianov, after describing literary tradition as a struggle, "pushing off from what is already known," notes that with less tempting sources "there is no such contest: these are simply bypassed, with either disavowals or veneration. . . . Precisely such a silent struggle describes the attitude of almost all nineteenth-century Russian literature to Pushkin: evading him, while paying ostensive homage." Tynianov, "Dostoevskii i Gogol'," 198.

92. Iurii Lotman summarizes the interpretation that has itself become canonical: "The narrative principles of *Evgenii Onegin* presented a phenomenon so innovative that the literature of Pushkin's time, for the most part, was incapable of evaluating the scale of his artistic breakthrough." Lotman, *Pushkin*, 412.

93. Greenleaf, *Pushkin and Romantic Fashion*, 4; I give here the full quote first referenced in my introduction.

94. Ibid., 15.

95. With Lotman, Boris Uspensky, William Todd, and many others, Greenleaf writes that Russian culture is marked by "syncretism, the tendency of Russian society and art forms to conflate and play off against each other *simultaneously* 'multiple modeling systems' . . . both indigenous and imported, sometimes up-to-the-minute but more often chronologically out of sync with European fashion." Greenleaf, *Pushkin and Romantic Fashion*, 15–16.

96. Greenleaf, *Pushkin and Romantic Fashion*, 2. William Todd argues that Pushkin fused the "various social images of the writer that the ideology and the institutions of his time offered him: the Russian gentleman amateur, the professional European man of letters, the inspired and autonomous poet of the Romantic movement." Todd, *Fiction and Society*, 109.

97. Lotman, "Chuzhaia rech' v Evgenii Onegine," in *Pushkin*, 412.

98. See Greenleaf, *Pushkin and Romantic Fashion*, 4–6, for an overview of the last two centuries' famous Pushkinists.

99. Ibid., 7.

100. For example, Tynianov describes the difficult semantic bridging performed by the reader/viewer of montage or fragment with examples from cinema and from Pushkin: "Big form in literature is not determined by the number of pages, nor is it determined in cinema by footage. The concept of 'big form' is related to energy, and should be understood in terms of the level of effort expended by the reader or viewer in construal of the work. Pushkin created big form in verse on the basis of digressions. 'Prisoner of the Caucasus' is not any longer than some of Zhukovsky's epistles, but it is big form because the digressions, which are far from the material of the plot, expand the 'space' of the poem to a considerable degree." Tynianov, "On the Foundations of Cinema," trans. Zinaida Breschinsky and Herbert Eagle, in Herbert Eagle, *Russian Formalist Film Theory* (Ann Arbor: Michigan Slavic Publications, 1988), 96.

CHAPTER TWO

Nabokov borrows Pushkin's words "From an article (late 1836 or early 1837)" for the epigraph to his "Translator's Introduction" to *Eugene Onegin*, 1:1. I cite Nabokov's introduction and *Commentary* by volume and page number; to indicate Pushkin's chapters and stanzas, I differentiate by keeping his stanza numbers in Roman numerals. As I stress Nabokov's *Onegin* in this chapter, all quoted verses are given in his English translation.

1. See Brian Boyd, *Vladimir Nabokov: The American Years* (Princeton, N.J.: Princeton University Press, 1991), 318–26.

2. Edmund Wilson, "The Strange Case of Pushkin and Nabokov," *New York Review of Books* 4, no. 12 (July 15, 1965): 3.

3. Ibid., 5.

4. Nabokov's admirers have since mounted defense campaigns. Brian Boyd maintains that *Eugene Onegin* was never intended as a literary translation: Nabokov had originally hoped to publish an interlinear translation with the transliterated Russian. Never meant to stand alone, his version was instead to prove the inimitable value of the original: Pushkin is to Russian as *nothing* is to English. The four volumes are neither replacement nor equivalent, but a glorified set of Cliffs Notes, as suggested by Nabokov's "Translator's Introduction": "Pushkin has likened translators to horses changed at the post-houses of civilization. The greatest reward I can think of is that students may use my work as a pony" (1:x).

5. George Steiner, *After Babel: Aspects of Language and Translation* (Oxford: Oxford University Press, 1998), 332.

6. Richard Rorty suggests that Nabokov deliberately confuses literary with personal immortality throughout his oeuvre: while one might well achieve the former through art, that "immortal" status has no bearing on "the claim that you will actually *be* out there, beyond the walls of time, waiting for dinner guests." Rorty, *Contingency, Irony, and Solidarity* (Cambridge: Cambridge University Press, 1989), 151–52. I return to Rorty's idea in chapter 5.

7. "I shall be remembered by *Lolita* and my work on *Eugene Onegin*," Nabokov stated in a 1967 interview for the *Paris Review*. Included in *Strong Opinions*, 106.

8. Wilson made this accusation in "The Strange Case of Pushkin and Nabokov," the review that effectively ended the Nabokov-Wilson friendship, 3–6. See also the reprinted and amended version in Wilson, *A Window on Russia: For the Use of Foreign Readers* (New York: Farrar, Straus and Giroux, 1972), 209–37.

9. See Clarence Brown's suggestion, "Nabokov's Pushkin and Nabokov's Nabokov," in *Nabokov: The Man and His Work*, ed. L. S. Dembo (Madison: University of Wisconsin Press, 1967), 195. See 195–96 for an eloquent summary of "the barrage" that followed the publication of the travesty-translation.

10. Boyd, *The American Years*, 303.

11. Vladimir Nabokov, *Vladimir Nabokov: Selected Letters 1940–1977*, ed. Dmitri Nabokov and Matthew J. Bruccoli (San Diego, New York, and London: Houghton Mifflin Harcourt, 2012), 216.

12. We might remember the "pressures exerted on Nabokov by the Russian faculty at Wellesley College, where he was teaching, to include Socialist Realist novels in his courses. In several letters, Nabokov expressed his reluctance to compromise on his assertion that 'Communism and its totalitarian rule have prevented the development of authentic literature during these last twenty-five years,' writing to the president of Wellesley College in order to suggest Iurii Olesha and Boris Pasternak as alternatives to Konstantin Simonov and other writers (like Sholokhov) of Socialist Realism," in Norman, *Nabokov, History and the Texture of Time*, 89; Boyd, *The American Years*, 90–91.

13. Seyhan, *Writing Outside the Nation*, 155.

14. Guillory, *Cultural Capital*, 147–48.

15. Guillory writes of "an obsession with the form of the list" in the social, and certainly pedagogical imaginary. Ibid., 35.

16. See Hobsbawm and Ranger, *The Invention of Tradition*.

17. Nabokov's exchange with Sartre, sparked by their mutually unpleasant reviews of *Despair* and *Nausea*, serves as a case study. Sartre gallingly summed up *Despair* as too much like Dostoevsky. Nabokov in turn reviewed Sartre's *Nausea* as derivative of Dostoevsky at his worst: "It belongs to that tense-looking but really very loose type of writing, which has been popularized by many second-raters—Barbusse, Céline, and so forth. Somewhere behind looms Dostoevski at his worst, and still farther back there is old Eugène Sue, to whom the melodramatic Russian owed so much." Nabokov, "Sartre's First Try" (*Strong Opinions*, 228), reprinted from a 1949 article in the *New York Times Book Review*.

18. See Greenleaf, *Pushkin and Romantic Fashion*, 6–7; and Alexandra Smith, *Montaging Pushkin: Pushkin and Visions of Modernity in Russian Twentieth-Century Poetry* (Amsterdam: Rodopi, 2006).

19. Todd writes, "Pushkin's novel has inspired two of the twentieth century's most subtle critics, Vladimir Nabokov and Iurii Lotman, to illuminate its art with encyclopedic commentaries." Todd, *Fiction and Society*, 106. Greenleaf's monograph in turn pushes against Nabokov's *Onegin*. She concludes that "if American critics are joining their voices to, or raising their voices against, the always ongoing indigenous debate about Pushkin, it means that Pushkin has finally reached the world audience that has always been claimed for him." Greenleaf, *Pushkin and Romantic Fashion*, 348—a feat in no small part due to Nabokov's translation and the subsequent controversy.

20. Quoted by Boyd in *The American Years*, 346.

21. In 1937 Nabokov complained about the French indifference to Pushkin: "Tolstoy, who happens to belong to the very same race as Pushkin, or good old Dostoevski, who is vastly inferior, enjoy in France a fame of the same cloth as many native writers. Yet the name of Pushkin, which to us is so replete with music, remains prickly and shabby to the French ear." "Pushkin, or the Real and the Plausible," trans. Dmitri Nabokov, *New York Review of Books* 35, no. 5 (March 31, 1988): 38–42 (originally published in *Nouvelle revue française*, March 1, 1937).

22. Nabokov attacks the Soviet critic N. L. Brodski by name, but adds: "alas, this tendency to generalize and vulgarize the unique fancy of an individual genius has also its advocates in the United States" (*Commentary*, 2:151).

23. Boyd, *The American Years*, 261.

24. I use George Steiner's term here and in subsequent chapters on *Ada, or Ardor*.

25. See Nabokov in 1937: "The greater the number of readers, the less a book is understood; the essence of its truth, as it spreads, seems to evaporate. . . . It is only after the first gleam of its literary fame has tarnished that a work reveals its true character." Nabokov, "Pushkin, or the Real," 42.

26. Nabokov retells his memory of the evening: "I had to replace at the very last moment a Hungarian woman writer, very famous that winter. . . . A number of personal friends of mine, fearing that the sudden illness of the lady and a sudden discourse on Pushkin might result in a suddenly empty house, had done their best to round up the kind of audience they knew I would like to have. The house had, however, a pied aspect since some confusion had occurred among the lady's fans. The Hungarian consul mistook me for her husband, and, as I entered, dashed towards me with the froth of condolence on his lips. Some people left as soon as I started to speak. A source of unforgettable consolation was the sight of Joyce sitting, arms folded and glasses glinting, in the midst of the Hungarian football team." Ibid., 38.

27. Ibid., 39.

28. Ibid., 39.

29. Ibid., 40.

30. Ibid., 41 (italics mine).

31. Ibid., 42.

32. Jorge Luis Borges, "Kafka and His Precursors," in *Labyrinths: Selected Stories and Other Writings*, ed. Donald A. Yates and James E. Irby (New York: New Directions, 2007), 199–201.

33. Nabokov's casual insertion of himself and his family into the Pushkin exegesis has been much remarked upon. One striking moment speaks to the theme of inheritance—here literal, more than literary: after conjecturing that Pushkin fought a duel at the Batovo estate in 1820, Nabokov adds, "The estate of Batovo later belonged to my grandparents, Dmitri Nikolaevich Nabokov, Minister of Justice under Alexander II, and Maria Ferdinandovna, née Baronness von Korff" (*Commentary*, 2:433).

34. Nabokov likewise downplays the modernist "my Pushkin" tradition of which he was well aware. The twentieth century is represented by straw (and flesh) Soviet critics, with only faint traces of the other great writer-Pushkinists such as Aleksandr Blok, Anna Akhmatova, or Vladislav Khodasevich. Again, Nabokov places emphasis on an internationally minded and internationally relevant Pushkin, rather than on the Pushkin of recent Russian tradition.

35. See for example the note: "*Madame Bovary* is finished not only because Emma has killed herself, but because Homais has at last got his decoration. *Ulysses* is finished because everybody in it has fallen asleep. . . . *Anna Karenina* is finished not only because Anna has been crushed by a backing freight train but because Lyovin has found his God. But *Onegin* is not finished" (*Commentary*, 3:311); elsewhere a draft variant of *Onegin's Journey* "reminds one of the Lord Chancellor, equated, though 'M'lud,' with London's 'mud,' in the first chapter (written November 1851) of Dickens' *Bleak House*" (*Commentary*, 3:294).

36. Nabokov sees in Pushkin's choice of words further proof that he read Byron in French: "*romanticheskoy poemi, 'poème romantique,'* as Pichot translated Byron's term 'romount' in Childe-Harold" ("Translator's Introduction," 1:70).

37. See V. M. Zhirmunsky's comparative study, *Bairon i Pushkin: Iz istorii romanticheskoi poemy* (Leningrad: Academia, 1924).

38. Quoted in Greenleaf, *Pushkin and Romantic Fashion*, 10.

39. Greenleaf, *Pushkin and Romantic Fashion*, 2.

40. He must have meant in the first canto alone, Nabokov notes.

41. "What enchants us during the years of love becomes in the years of solitude a source of suffering and regret. One no longer hopes for the turn of the seasons . . . for a beautiful evening at the end of April . . . those things that provoke a need or desire for happiness, are now lethal."

42. "Their life is at times naive and sublime . . . they have the most fantastical ideas about death."

43. "If Richardson has no style . . . he will not survive, because one only lives through style."

44. See also my first epigraph to this chapter.

45. "A bizarre petrified androgyne with the mixed blood of my mother and father"; "my heart is naturally petrified with *ennui* and misery."

46. The 1962 *Pale Fire*, a travesty of annotation, was born out of Nabokov's experience of working on *Onegin* and allowed him to parody his own preoccupations and excesses as imaginative fiction. Kinbote's fantasy kingdom reads as a parody of Nabokov's ideal canon in its synthesis of cultural traditions. See Priscilla Meyer, *Find What the Sailor Has Hidden: Vladimir Nabokov's "Pale Fire"* (Middleton, Conn.: Wesleyan University Press, 1988).

47. The theme "is much too boring to be treated at length. . . . *Ennui* was by 1820 a seasoned cliché of characterization that Pushkin could play with at leisure, on the flowered brink of parody, by transforming West-European formulas into virgin Russian. French literature of the eighteenth and early nineteenth centuries is full of restless young characters suffering from the spleen. It was a convenient device to keep one's hero on the move. Byron endowed it with a new thrill; René, Adolphe, Oberman, and their cosufferers received a transfusion of daemon blood" (*Commentary*, 2:152). See further: "Chateaubriand, 1837 (*Mémoires d'outre-tombe*, ed. Levaillant, pt. II, bk. I, chap. 11): '*Une famille de Renés-poètes et René-prosateurs a pullulé; on n'a plus entendu bourdonner que des phrases lamentables et décousues . . . Il n'y a pas de grimaud . . . qui, à seize ans, n'ait épuisé la vie . . . qui, dans l'abîme de ses pensées, ne se soit livré au 'vague de ses passions.'* Finally—Byron, *Don Juan*, XIII, CI, 5–8: 'For *ennui* is a growth of English root, / Though nameless in our language:—we retort / The fact for words, and let the French translate / That awful yawn which sleep cannot abate'" (*Commentary*, 2:155).

48. "The singer of Childe Harold is of the family of René."

49. Mario Praz, *The Romantic Agony*, trans. Angus Davidson (Oxford: Oxford University Press, 1970), 69, 71.

50. Nabokov stresses that *Onegin* is fundamentally unfinished and highlights one fudged temporal element after another: his point throughout the *Commentary*

is that Pushkin concerned himself with language, and not with history or moral philosophy.

51. Will Norman has recently challenged the anti-historicist bent of Nabokov scholarship, inspired by Nabokov's own "uncompromising stand on the issue of aesthetic autonomy" and "idiosyncratic conception of literary history . . . based on his faith in a constantly evolving tradition of autonomous, formally experimental writers. This tradition develops entirely independently of history, and assumes its own hermetic temporality." Norman, *Nabokov, History and the Texture of Time*, 2–3.

52. Nabokov quotes Brummell's biographer: "Pierce Egan, in his *Life in London* (1821), bk. 1 ch. 3, thus describes the pedigree of a London dandy: 'The DANDY was got by *Vanity* out of *Affectation*—his dam, *Petit-Maître* or *Maccaroni*—his grand-dam, *Fribble*—his great-grand-dam, *Bronze*—his great-great-grand-dam, *Coxcomb*—and his earliest ancestor, FOP.'"

53. Nabokov quotes from Maria Edgeworth's 1809 *Ennui*, chap. 1. The ongoing Breguet advertising campaign still seen in the pages of such journals as the *New Yorker* gives the lines from *Onegin* in white against a full-page portrait of Pushkin: "A dandy on the boulevards . . . / strolling at leisure / until his Breguet, ever vigilant, / reminds him it is midday." The unattributed translation is far from Nabokov's own purposefully awkward version: "til vigilant Bréguet / to him chimes dinner" (*Eugene Onegin*, 1:XV).

54. Onegin's behavior closely follows "that ironically described by an anonymous author in the magazine *Son of the Fatherland (Sïn otechestva)* 20 (1817): "When entering high society, make it your first rule to esteem no one. . . . Be sure never to be surprised; display cold indifference to everything. . . . Make an appearance everywhere, but only for a moment. To every gathering take with you abstraction, boredom; at the theater, yawn, don't pay any attention. . . . In general, make it clear that you don't care for women and despise them" (*Commentary*, 2:90).

55. Irina Reyfman, "The Duel as an Act of Violence," in *Ritualized Violence Russian Style: The Duel in Russian Culture and Literature* (Stanford, Calif.: Stanford University Press, 1999), 15–44.

56. I quote Pushkin, here and elsewhere in this chapter, in Nabokov's translation from the *Commentary*. Pushkin refers in this letter to his infamous political exile in the early 1820s.

57. Sparked by the beetle's noise, Nabokov's notes veer into a wild insect chase through eighteenth- and nineteenth-century poetry, ending with Chateaubriand's translation, *"Les Tombeaux champetres"*: *"On n'entend que le bruit de l'insecte incertain."* Nabokov writes, "—a very uncertain insect, indeed; but then, the Age of Good Taste prohibited one's using the 'specific and low' word *hanneton*. Forty years later the great French writer redeemed this surrender by his excellent translation of *Paradise Lost*" (*Commentary*, 3:83).

58. Nabokov wrote of his Cornell University years that his lectures on literature "irritated or puzzled such students of literature (and their professors) as were accustomed to 'serious' courses replete with 'trends,' and 'schools,' and 'myths,' and 'symbols,' and 'social comment,' and something unspeakably spooky called 'climate of thought'" (*Strong Opinions*, 128).

59. In contrast, we might consider Nabokov's evaluations of Dostoevsky: even *The Double*, which he considered Dostoevsky's most perfect work, he at times calls a "shameless" parody of Gogol. By insisting on Pushkinian parody, Nabokov finds a way to bypass Dostoevsky as a model, and to build an alternative tradition to the rival canon of international Dostoevsky-inspired modernism that might well include Sigmund Freud, Virginia Woolf, the French existentialists, the English modernist poets, and several critical schools as well as literary movements.

60. George Steiner claims that translations introduce "an alternate existence, a 'might have been' or 'is yet to come' into the substance and historical condition of one's own language, literature, and legacy of sensibility. . . . The hermeneutic of import occurs not only across a linguistic-spatial frontier but also requires a motion across time. What ordinary translation tries to do is 'to produce the text which the foreign poet would have written had he been working in one's own speech now, or more or less now.'" Later he clarifies, "The translator labours to secure a natural habitat for the alien presence which he has imported into his own tongue and cultural setting. . . . The foreign text is felt to be not so much an import from abroad (suspect by definition) as it is an element out of one's native past. It has been there 'all along' awaiting reprise. It is really a part of one's own tradition temporarily mislaid." See his *After Babel: Aspects of Language and Translation* (Oxford: Oxford University Press, 1998), 351–52, 365.

CHAPTER THREE

The chapter epigraphs are from Northrop Frye, *Anatomy of Criticism: Four Essays* (Princeton, N.J.: Princeton University Press, 2000), 97; and Vladimir Nabokov, *The Gift* (New York: Vintage, 1991), 98.

1. The interview is quoted in Boyd, *American Years*, 487. Nabokov quotes verbatim Van Veen's description of *his* treatise within the novel, or lends Van a paragraph from his own earlier response: see *Ada*, 562–63.

2. Quoted in the essay "Inspiration," included in Nabokov, *Strong Opinions*, 310.

3. Boyd, *American Years*, 518.

4. George Steiner, "Extraterritorial," *TriQuarterly* 17 (Winter 1970): 124–25.

5. Rorty compares Nabokov with Heidegger in this regard: both peak in the middle and then become truly difficult! Rorty, *Contingency, Irony, and Solidarity*, 161.

6. Michael Wood, *Magician's Doubts: Nabokov and the Risks of Fiction* (Princeton, N.J.: Princeton University Press, 1997), 206.

7. Eric Naiman, *Nabokov, Perversely* (Ithaca, N.Y.: Cornell University Press, 2010), 266.

8. Gerschenkron, "A Manufactured Monument?," 340.

9. I have in mind Roman Jakobson's canonical essay, "On a Generation that Squandered Its Poets," in *Verbal Art, Verbal Sign, Verbal Time* (Minneapolis: University of Minnesota Press, 1985), 111–32.

10. See Frederic Jameson, *Archeaologies of the Future: The Desire Called Utopia and Other Science Fictions* (London: Verso, 2005).

11. Vladimir Nabokov, "On a Book Entitled *Lolita*," in *The Annotated Lolita*, ed. Alfred Appel Jr. (New York: Vintage, 1991), 316–17.

12. Translation as given in Boyd, *American Years*, 490.

13. Boyd, *American Years*, 491.

14. George M. Cummins, "Nabokov's Russian *Lolita*," *Slavic and East European Journal* 21, no. 3 (1977): 354.

15. Ibid., 354. We will see the same effects in reverse in *Ada*.

16. Boyd, *American Years*, 508.

17. George Steiner, another "perfectly normal trilingual child" like Nabokov, draws four basic movements to the hermeneutic of translation in *After Babel: Aspects of Language and Translation* (1975): trust, aggression, incorporation, and retribution. "The commerce between meanings, between poets, which is translation, is preceded by violent and total incursion," he writes: "We plunge into the life, into the integral being of the source attempting (vainly) to break through the Narcissus-image which meets us at the surface and, it may be, continues to meet us at considerable depth." Steiner, *After Babel*, 411. Steiner's four-part hermeneutic of translation echoes Harold Bloom's six revisionary ratios in *The Anxiety of Influence: A Theory of Poetry* (Oxford: Oxford University Press, 1973). In their attempt to model the relation of text B to text A, both writers ultimately turn to the mystical to describe true translation, as true art.

18. See Priscilla Meyer, "Nabokov's Lolita and Pushkin's Onegin—McAdam, McEve and McFate," in *The Achievements of Vladimir Nabokov: Essays, Studies, Reminiscences, and Stories*, ed. George Gibian and Stephen Jay Parker (Ithaca, N.Y.: Cornell University Center for International Studies, 1984). For western European literary allusions, see John Burt Foster Jr., *Nabokov's Art of Memory and European Modernism* (Princeton, N.J.: Princeton University Press, 1993).

19. See George Steiner, "To Traduce or Transfigure: On Modern Verse Translation," *Encounter* 27, no. 2 (August 1966): 48–54; Robert Lowell, "In Defense of George Steiner," *Encounter* (February 1967); Nabokov, "On Adaptation," *New York Review of Books* 13, no. 10 (December 4, 1969). Boyd, who summarizes the entire history on *AdaOnline*, quips that "the portmanteau 'Stonelower' neatly

packs into one word a reverse 'Exegi monumentum,' the Vandals attacking Horace." See http://www.ada.auckland.ac.nz/ada11ann.htm.

20. D. Barton Johnson argues that "the incestuous relationship of Van and Ada is but the final episode in a series of incestuous matings among Veens and Zemskis," in his "Labyrinth of Incest in Nabokov's Ada," *Comparative Literature* 38, no. 3 (1986): 238.

21. In *War and Peace*, Anna Mikhailovna warns Countess Rostova about her son Nikolai's attachment to her penniless ward Sonya with this gruesome phrase. In *Anna Karenina*, Dolly worries about the children's unsupervised games, a moment that *Ada* reinterprets perversely.

22. See Meyer, "Nabokov's *Lolita* and Pushkin's *Onegin*," 179–211.

23. Darkbloom's notes add a gloss for the word "libretto" some 500 pages later: "that of the opera *Eugene Onegin*, a travesty of Pushkin's poem" (*Ada*, 604).

24. See Johnson, "Labyrinth of Incest," 317–18.

25. Umberto Eco devoted his Arthur Miller lecture at New York's PEN festival (May 4, 2009) to the "eternal truth" offered by fictional works that have entered the pubic imagination: "We accept various interpretations and degrees of belief or unbelief in the Bible with tolerance . . . but *it's a fact* that Anna Karenina commits suicide," in my paraphrase. Certain characters, however, like Sherlock Holmes, break free from the texts that birthed them.

26. Johnson writes, "In Nabokov's commentary to *Onegin*, he refers metaphorically to Kiti Scerbackaja as one of Tat'jana's granddaughters [*Eugene Onegin*, II, 504]. In *Ada*, Demon Veen, the children's father, makes passing mention of 'his Aunt Kitty, who married the banker Bolenski after divorcing the dreadful old wencher, Lyovka Tolstoy, the writer.' Thus the literary genealogy is *Eugene Onegin, Anna Karenina, Ada*, or perhaps more aptly Tat'jana, Anna, Ada." In Johnson's "Nabokov's *Ada* and Puškin's *Eugene Onegin*," *Slavic and East European Journal* 15, no. 3 (1971): 319.

27. The "Notes by Vivian Darkbloom" will not allow us to forget the presence of *Onegin*, adding clues and even line references. When Van quotes Ada's translation to their father, he finds the verses "by chance preserved": Darkbloom quotes "'The verses are by chance preserved / I have them, here they are' (*Eugene Onegin*, Six:XXI:1–2)" (*Ada*, 599). The dinner that Marina prepares for Demon includes Persty grapes; the notes add, "Evidently Pushkin's *vinograd*: 'as elongated and transparent / as are the fingers of a girl'" (*Ada*, 599). When Van engages in a scholarly tussle, he warns his school friend, the great Rattner's nephew, "Your uncle has most honest standards . . . but I am going to demolish him soon" (*Ada*, 317). The notes remind us of *Onegin*'s first line: "my uncle has most honest principles," etc. (600).

28. See Meyer, "Nabokov's *Lolita* and Pushkin's *Onegin*," 179–211.

29. See Raúl Ruiz, *Poetics of Cinema: 1 Miscellanies*, trans. Brian Holmes (Paris: Dis Voir, 1995), 9–42.

30. Leland de la Durantaye, "The Pattern of Cruelty and the Cruelty of Pattern in Vladimir Nabokov," *Cambridge Quarterly* 35, no. 4 (2006): 301–26.

31. In a long appendix on Pushkin's African great-grandfather Abram Gannibal, Nabokov ascertains that almost nothing is known about the early life of Pushkin's ancestor, despite generations of scholarly conjecture.

32. Ksana Blank, "The Endless Passage: The Making of a Plot in the Russian Novel" (Ph.D. diss., Columbia University, 1997), 96.

33. Gleb Struve, "Notes on Nabokov as a Russian Writer," in Dembo, ed., *Nabokov: The Man and His Work*, 54. Struve continues: "Nabokov's conception of literature as an artifice, his interest in, and concern with the problems of composition, of pattern, his outspoken contempt for any kind of 'message' in literature, be it social, moral, or religious-philosophical, are all against the grain of the Russian literary tradition. . . . What makes Nabokov even more alien to the Russian literary tradition is his lack of sympathy with, if not interest in, human beings as such" (54).

34. See Pamela Davidson, "The Muse and the Demon in the Poetry of Pushkin, Lermontov, and Blok," in *Russian Literature and Its Demons*, ed. Pamela Davidson (Oxford: Berghahn Books, 2000), 167–214. Nabokov supplemented his translation of Lermontov's *Hero of Our Time* with a sharply evaluative introduction: he found Lermontov's prose sloppier than his poetry, and judged the entire early novel to be very much "of its time"—romantic, but not immortal. See Mikhail Lermontov, *A Hero of Our Time*, trans. and intro. Vladimir Nabokov with Dmitri Nabokov (Ann Arbor, Mich.: Ardis, 1988). For a response to Nabokov's introduction, see Rebecca Stanton, "Talking Back to Nabokov: A Commentary on a Commentary," in "My Nabokov," special issue, *Ulbandus* 10 (2007): 212–21.

35. In his Jane Austen lecture, Nabokov explains that such a heroine, a ward to an aristocratic family, was popular in the eighteenth- and nineteenth-century novel. Joseph Frank provides a succinct summary of Nabokov's reading: such a ward character serves "a variety of narratological purposes. Her alien status evokes pathos, she can enter into a love affair with the son of the family . . . Dickens, Dostoevsky and Tolstoy all used the same convention, and Nabokov remarks that the prototype of these 'quiet maidens is, of course, Cinderella. Dependent, helpless, friendless, neglected, forgotten—and then marrying the hero,'" Joseph Frank, "Lectures on Literature," in *Garland Companion to Vladimir Nabokov*, ed. Vladimir E. Alexandrov (New York: Garland, 1995), 237. By that logic, Van is the Cinderella at Ardis, observing the manor with an outsider's eyes, and then entering into a love triangle with both the family's daughters.

36. "various things so sad and so tender, that my entire Heart was melting."

37. Appel picks up on the recurrence of allusions to Byron and Chateaubriand and writes in a telling footnote, "Chateaubriand and Byron are to *Ada* what Poe and Mérimée are to *Lolita*." Appel, *"Ada* Described," in *Nabokov:*

Criticism, Reminiscences, Translations, and Tributes, ed. Alfred Appel Jr. and Charles Newman (Evanston, Ill.: Northwestern University Press, 1970), 180.

38. Cancogni also finds Chateaubriand to be one of the "most pervasive presences" in *Ada*. She adds: "Chateaubriand's *Memoires* are not the only recollections reflected by *Ada*. Proust's . . . *À la recherche du temps perdu* also plays an important role in the intertextual network of the novel." Cancogni, *Mirage in the Mirror: Nabokov's Ada and Its French Pre-Texts* (New York: Garland Publishing, 1985), 278.

39. Is this Nabokov's subtle revenge for that vague translation *"insecte incertain,"* mentioned in his *Onegin Commentary*? See *Eugene Onegin*, 3:83, and my note 57 in the previous chapter. Nabokov criticized Chateaubriand for his loose phrasing in *"Les Tombeaux champêtres,"* attributing his lack of specificity to the influence of the eighteenth-century's "good taste."

40. Darkbloom's notes patiently explain that Ada "liked crossing orchids: she crosses here two French authors, Baudelaire and Chateaubriand" (*Ada*, 595).

41. Nabokov must have been frustrated indeed by his audience's lack of memory to attach such Cliffs Notes to subsequent additions: "p. 138. *Ma soeur te souvient-il encore*: first line of the third sextet of Chateaubriand's *Romance à Hélène* (*'Combien j'ai douce souvenance'*) composed to an Auvergne tune that he heard during a trip to Mont Dore in 1805 and later inserted in his novella *Le Dernier Abencerage*. The final (fifth) sextet begins with *'Oh! qui me rendra mon Hélène. Et ma montagne et le grand chène'*)—one of the leitmotivs of the present novel . . . p. 139. Lucile: the name of Chateaubriand's actual sister (*Ada*, 596)." In contrast, Nabokov only points out Byron to his Anglophone readers when otherwise obscured in Russian or French, or by an especially wild pun, for example, *bayronka* and *le beau ténébreux* as quoted above (*Ada*, 602, 604).

42. I assume the latter to be a crossed reference to Algernon Swinburne's 1866 poem "Dolores," about the vampiric and poisonous eponymous "Lady of Pain." Ada resembles Dolores at several of her most femme fatale moments in the novel, but adds always a dose of Nabokovian humor. Nabokov seems to have more sympathy for the romantics than for their decadent heirs.

43. Chillon's Castle, known from Byron's 1816 poem "The Prisoner of Chillon," is in fact only three kilometers from Montreux, Switzerland.

44. Appel calls *Ada* a summary of the "sufferings wrought by freedom . . . Nabokov's critique of Romanticism. *Don Juan's Last Fling* is no idle title." Alfred Appel Jr., *Nabokov's Dark Cinema* (New York: Oxford University Press, 1974), 50.

45. Carl Proffer calls the sentence Tolstoyan. Cancogni challenges him: "Though Proffer might well be right, we find his example inadequate, if not unconvincing, and particularly so when set next to another passage (by another author) whose echo we followed: 'Quand on partit de Tostes, au mois de Mars, madame Bovary était enceinte.' Aside from obvious, if improbable, semantic parallels, this

passage from *Madame Bovary* also happens, like the one from *Ada*, to close the first part of the novel." Cancogni, *Mirage in the Mirror*, 259. A French scholar finds Flaubert in *Ada*; a Slavist, Tolstoy.

46. Compare Harold Bloom's battle lines in such books as *The Western Canon* and *Genius: A Mosaic of One Hundred Exemplary Creative Minds* (New York: Warner Books, 2002). A striking American-Russian parallel is the lingering insistence of intellectuals from both cultures on a "Western" (rather than French, or German) canon: both are anxious to define a list of great books in such a way as to be included.

47. Peter Burger, *Theory of the Avant-Garde*, trans. Michael Shaw (Minneapolis: University of Minnesota Press, 1984).

48. Eric Naiman describes this phenomenon with wit and hilarity in *Nabokov, Perversely*.

49. Galya Diment suggests that Nabokov "feared being reduced to a sum total of other writers' influences to the same degree which he feared being dwarfed as an individual by simplistic formulas of mass Freudianism." Diment, "Strong Opinions," in *Garland Companion to Vladimir Nabokov*, 691. Yet the *Garland Companion* contains no fewer than twenty-three articles with the title "Nabokov and Writer X." *Ada* is full of feints—against poor translators and transfigurers; against Freudians (try reading an unintended family romance into this "family romance"!); and against influence-hunters through sheer wealth of intercut allusions. See also Nabokov's famous rejoinder to William Rowe's sexo-symbolic reading: "One may wonder if it was worth Mr. Rowe's time to exhibit erotic bits picked out of *Lolita* or *Ada*—a process rather like looking for allusions to aquatic mammals in *Moby Dick*" (*SO*, 304).

50. Naiman writes, "So many of the quibbles in *Ada* are sexual that in its own attitude toward language the narration captures the avidity of its heroes for intercourse. . . . the book sets impressive standards for lexical nymphomania and satyriasis." Naiman, *Nabokov, Perversely*, 249.

51. Ellen Pifer writes that the entire "world of *Ada* has been made strange by art, its landscape saturated with an atmosphere of make-believe. . . . The artifice is more intricately contrived, the self-conscious allusions more densely woven than in any previous, or subsequent, novel by Nabokov." Pifer, *Nabokov and the Novel* (Cambridge, Mass.: Harvard University Press, 1980), 132. Bobbie Ann Mason, another of the book's early champions, turns to film and photography to explain the novel. The setting is "like a photo with multiple exposures"; the novel is like Bergman's *Persona*, which "shows the cameraman to the audience at the end of the film as a reminder that it was all imaginary." Mason, *Nabokov's Garden: A Guide to "Ada"* (Ann Arbor, Mich.: Ardis, 1974), 43, 142.

52. Mariia Virolainen, "Mimikriia rechi ('Evgenii Onegin' Pushkina i 'Ada' Nabokova)," in *Rech' i molchanie: Siuzhety i mify russkoi slovesnosti* (St. Petersburg: Amfora, 2003), 400 (my translation).

53. See Johnson, "Nabokov's *Ada* and Puškin's *Eugene Onegin*," and "The Labyrinth of Incest in Nabokov's *Ada.*"

54. Virolainen, "Mimikriia rechi," 406.

55. Nabokovians tend away from Roland Barthes's more radical conception of any given text as a "compendium of intersecting codes," or from Julia Kristeva's post-structuralist theory of intertextuality, where "the text is no longer legitimately to be understood as the discrete product of a stable, originating consciousness." See Cancogni, *Mirage in the Mirror*, 46; and Michael Glynn, *Vladimir Nabokov: Bergsonian and Russian Formalist Influences in His Novels* (New York: Palgrave Macmillan, 2007), 1.

56. Cancogni, *Mirage in the Mirror*, 308, quoting the *Princeton Encyclopedia of Poetry and Poetics*.

57. Emphasis mine. Proffer places the majority of the references to Russian authors in the first group; presumably, if Nabokov aims to create a shared literary culture with his English-language readers, he has cause to be most insistent on the Russian authors. Carl R. Proffer, "*Ada* as Wonderland: A Glossary of Allusions to Russian Literature," in *A Book of Things about Vladimir Nabokov*, ed. Carl R. Proffer (Ann Arbor, Mich.: Ardis, 1974), 250.

58. Alfred Appel Jr., introduction to *The Annotated Lolita* by Vladimir Nabokov (New York: Vintage, 1991), lvi.

59. Alfred Appel Jr., "*Lolita*: The Springboard of Parody," in Dembo, ed., *Nabokov: The Man and His Work*, 114. See also Patricia Merivale, "The Flaunting of Artifice in Vladimir Nabokov and Jorge Luis Borges," in *Nabokov: The Man and His Work*, 209. In turn, Alexander Dolinin argues that "almost any phrase [in *Lolita* especially] might be decoded as an 'auto-meta-descriptor' referring to the text itself," in "Nabokov's Time Doubling: From *The Gift* to *Lolita*," *Nabokov Studies* 2 (1995): 3–40. See also Dolinin, "Nabokov as a Russian Writer," in *The Cambridge Companion to Nabokov*, ed. Julian W. Connolly (Cambridge: Cambridge University Press, 2005), 49–64; Dolinin, "Don't Ride by, Re-reader," *Nabokovian* 25 (1990): 37–40.

60. See: "The difficulty in the majority of Nabokov's allusions lies not in discovering their source but in discovering their part in the patterns of hidden recurrence and in the elusive structuring of the novels." Brian Boyd, *Nabokov's "Ada": The Place of Consciousness* (Ann Arbor, Mich.: Ardis, 1985), 8.

61. Pekka Tammi, *Russian Subtexts in Nabokov's Fiction: Four Essays* (Tampere, Finland: Tampere University Press, 1999), 6. Taranovsky's most often-quoted dictum states: "If an investigator finds a subtitle '*Pindaricheskii otryvok*' in the first printing [of Mandelstam's poem], it means that he must re-read Pindar's odes," repeated in Tammi, *Russian Subtexts*, 10.

62. The phrase is taken from *The Gift*, just as Appel's beloved phrase "the springboard of parody" is lifted from *Sebastian Knight*.

63. Tammi, *Russian Subtexts*, 35.

64. Tammi, *Russian Subtexts*, 54. Of *Ada*, the most exaggeratedly allusive of all Nabokov's work, Tammi writes: "*Ada* abounds with quotations, thematic echoes, and stylistic parodies of Tolstoy. . . . That attributes of Tolstoy's style derive from (and are inferior to) Flaubert is a pervasive claim in Nabokov's writing. In his lecture on *Anna Karenina* Nabokov said that 'the structure of [Tolstoy's novel] is of a more conventional kind, although the book was written twenty years later than Flaubert's *Madame Bovary*' (*Lectures on Literature*, 2:147). Compare also: 'that lorgnette I found afterwards in the hands of Madame Bovary, and later Anna Karenin had it'" (*Speak, Memory*, 202), 55–56.

65. Cancogni, *Mirage in the Mirror*, 6–7. Cancogni focuses on Nabokov's French sources, but she too catches the centrality of Pushkin to Nabokov's oeuvre: "Pushkin's poetry lends familiar colors to unfamiliar landscapes" (17).

66. Ibid., 185. "Reality, in my opinion, need be no more than a springboard."

67. Ibid., 6.

68. Michael Wood, "Nabokov's Late Fiction," in *Cambridge Companion to Nabokov*, 201.

69. See Naiman's *Nabokov, Perversely*; Norman's *Nabokov, History and the Texture of Time*; Martin Hägglund's *Dying for Time: Proust, Woolf, Nabokov* (Cambridge, Mass.: Harvard University Press, 2012); Duncan White's *Nabokov and His Books: Between Late Modernism and the Literary Marketplace* (Oxford: Oxford University Press, forthcoming).

70. Guillory, "The Genesis of the Media Concept," 358. Guillory defends Benjamin, finding in his reading a more subtle dialectic than what Adorno could then see.

71. The classical *tartarus* is another name for Hades. See Shakespeare's usage: "he's in Tartar limbo, worse than hell," from *The Comedy of Errors*, act 4, scene 2.

CHAPTER FOUR

The first chapter epigraph was translated by Nabokov in Vladimir Nabokov, *Lectures on Literature*, ed. Fredson Bowers (New York: Harcourt/Bruccoli Clark, 1980), 211. The second is from Vladimir Nabokov, *Strong Opinions*, 173.

1. J. E. Rivers, "Proust, Nabokov and *Ada*," in *Critical Essays on Vladimir Nabokov*, ed. Phyllis A. Roth (Boston: G. K. Hall, 1984), 138–39.

2. Proust's Charlus deteriorates mentally throughout *À la recherche*, a clue to the reader of *Pale Fire*. The characters of *À la recherche* in turn model themselves on earlier literature (see Girard, *Deceit, Desire, and the Novel*, 193–228). I also detect in Kinbote an echo of harmless Mr. Dick from *David Copperfield*, whose mania involves slipping into the first person in a colossal treatise on Charles the First of England.

3. John Updike comments that even in Nabokov's "first published interview, in 1932, to a correspondent for a Riga newspaper," he denied "any German influ-

ence on his work during the Berlin years, [responding] 'One might more properly speak about a French influence: I love Flaubert and Proust'" (Nabokov, *Lectures on Literature*, "Introduction," xx).

4. Here as in the *Pale Fire* pastiche, Nabokov mentions Cocteau: "Jean Cocteau has called the work 'A giant miniature, full of mirages, of superimposed gardens, of games conducted between space and time'" (*Lectures on Literature*, 208). Note the suggestive resemblance to the mirages, games, and superimposed cinematic gardens of *Ada*.

5. Leona Toker writes that "Nabokov mentions Bergson among poets and novelists who were his 'top favorites' between the two World Wars" in "Nabokov and Bergson," in *Garland Companion to Vladimir Nabokov*, 367. See also Michael Glynn, *Bergsonian and Russian Formalist Influences*, 57.

6. See Foster, *Nabokov's Art of Memory and European Modernism*, 87. See also Gerard de Vries and D. Barton Johnson: "Colours are essential in the intricate patterns Nabokov invented, to which they contribute mythological, conventional, and cultural connotations," in *Nabokov and the Art of Painting* (Amsterdam: Amsterdam University Press, 2006), 20.

7. Nabokov adds that there is another reason of a "private kind" for this flourish: the author seeks to disguise his sexual proclivities behind classically lovely lads and ladies (*Lectures on Literature*, 228). Nabokov consistently takes Proust to task for modeling his Albertine on an Albert. See Rivers, "Albertine escapes not only from the limits of gender but from any attempt to categorize and contain her" ("Proust, Nabokov and *Ada*," 141).

8. See also: "One essential difference exists between the Proustian and the Joycean methods of approaching their characters. Joyce takes a complete and absolute character, God-known, Joyce-known, then breaks it up into fragments and scatters these fragments over the space-time of his book. The good rereader gathers these puzzle pieces and gradually puts them together. On the other hand, Proust contends that a character, a personality, is never known as an absolute but always as a comparative one. He does not chop it up but shows it as it exists through the notions about it of other characters" (*Lectures on Literature*, 217).

9. Nabokov's analysis of Tolstoy in the *Lectures on Russian Literature* finds the most magical aspect of *Anna Karenina* to be the perfect rendering of "real time": readers feel the novel's events to take place at just the pace of life—a brilliant illusion achieved through stylistic manipulation.

10. See also: "These characters cross and recross each other's trails in a most intricate counterpoint—a monstrous development of Flaubert's counterpoint themes . . . in *Madame Bovary*" (*Lectures on Literature*, 330).

11. Molly has the more apparent insight in Episode 18: "O Jamesy let me up out of this." James Joyce, *Ulysses* (New York: Vintage, 1990), 769.

12. Durantaye, "Pattern of Cruelty," 306.

Notes to Pages 108–111

13. Colleen Lamos writes that "sexual energies and identifications that, for male subjects, were (and are) coded as deviant" characterize the works of the writers "who are widely regarded as the major figures of literary modernism." Lamos, *Deviant Modernism: Sexual and Textual Errancy in T. S. Eliot, James Joyce, and Marcel Proust* (Cambridge: Cambridge University Press, 1998), 1. Compare Mario Praz, quoting Novalis's aphorism: "'It is strange that the true source of cruelty should be desire'" (*Romantic Agony*, 28).

14. Clearly, these lists are ideologically as well as aesthetically motivated: the only German-language writer Nabokov would admit to admiring after World War II was Kafka, a Czech Jew.

15. See the episodes "Mademoiselle O" and "Lantern Slides"; Nabokov's childhood love Colette; and especially Francophile Uncle Ruka. Foster notes, "Ruka's own French writings (74), his *belle époque* affluence, and his homosexuality all recall Proust; and in the Russian variant Nabokov even specifies that his uncle looked like Proust" ("Nabokov and Proust," in *Garland Companion to Vladimir Nabokov*, 478).

16. Rivers, "Proust, Nabokov and *Ada*," 147. See also Foster, "Nabokov and Proust," 480.

17. Cancogni, *Mirage in the Mirror*, 199.

18. See Shapiro, *The Sublime Artist's Studio*; and de Vries and Johnson, *Nabokov and the Art of Painting*.

19. Cancogni, *Mirage in the Mirror*, 282.

20. By Joyce's poem, Ada seems to mean the final lines from the Anna Livia Plurabelle chapter of *Finnegans Wake*: "I feel as old as yonder elm. A tale told of Shaun or Shem? All Livia's daughter-sons. Dark hawks hear us. Night! Night! My ho head halls. I feel as heavy as yonder stone. Tell me of John or Shaun? Who were Shem and Shaun the living sons or daughters of? Night now! Tell me, tell me, tell me, elm! Night night! Telmetale of stem or stone. Beside the rivering waters of, hitherandthithering waters of. Night!" James Joyce, *Finnegans Wake* (Middlesex, Eng.: Penguin, 1983), 215–16. Boyd notes that this was the section Joyce recorded in his own voice, and quotes from *Strong Opinions*: "A formless and dull mass of phony folklore, a cold pudding of a book, a persistent snore in the next room . . . only the infrequent snatches of heavenly intonations redeem it from utter insipidity," http://www.ada.auckland.ac.nz/ada18ann.htm. The altered title *Les Malheurs de Swann* suggests Comtesse de Ségur's *Les Malheurs de Sophie*, a text familiar to both the young Nabokov and young Marcel.

21. Darkbloom glosses, "lime tea." See Cancogni, *Mirage in the Mirror*, 283. When the protagonist of *Look at the Harlequins!*, Nabokov's last complete novel originally published in 1974, "remembers" writing a novel very much like *Ada*, it is the children's light-and-shadow games that he recalls: "The hideous suspicion that even *Ardis*, my most private book, soaked in reality, saturated with sun flecks, might be an unconscious imitation of another's unearthly art, that suspi-

196

cion might come later." Vladimir Nabokov, *Look at the Harlequins!* (New York: Vintage, 1990), 234.

22. Rivers, "Proust, Nabokov and *Ada*," 135.

23. *AdaOnline*, notes to 1.2, http://www.ada.auckland.ac.nz/ada12ann.htm. See also Rivers, "Proust, Nabokov and *Ada*"; and Foster, *Nabokov's Art of Memory*, 480. Boyd, Rivers, and Foster all find *Ada* a fundamentally more optimistic portrait of romantic love than that offered in *À la recherche*.

24. It is their parents' darkly romantic example that robs Van and Ada of mother and father, respectively, and from growing up as siblings. As James Wood points out, Nabokov's characters simultaneously do and do not ask to be "recognized" as real people. We alternately feel uneasy and do not care at all about Van and Ada's incest: in the end, these characters are only Nabokov's children. James Wood, *How Fiction Works* (New York: Farrar, Straus and Giroux, 2008).

25. See Rivers, "Proust, Nabokov and *Ada*," 146. Trousdale writes of Nabokov's transnational synthesis: "Despite its many flaws, Antiterra provides a model for world-fashioning writers through its translation of the private world of Van's childhood into a public world with history, geography, and a literary tradition in which the reader can participate," Trousdale, *Nabokov, Rushdie and the Transnational Imagination*, 69.

26. See Rivers, "Proust, Nabokov and *Ada*," 152–53; and Cancogni, *Mirage in the Mirror*, 285–86.

27. Compare Proust's feasts: "The cooking abilities of Françoise are beautifully brought into juxtaposition with the artistic carving of the quatrefoils on the porches of thirteenth-century cathedrals . . . This cream of chocolate was as 'light and fleeting' as an 'occasional piece' of music'" (Nabokov, *Lectures on Literature*, 227).

28. See also "One Spencer Muldoon, born eyeless, aged forty, single, friendless, and the third blind character in this chronicle, had been known to hallucinate during fits of violent paranoia" (*Ada*, 468). Boyd notes that Ada and Lucette echo "St. Adelia and St. Lucy, both of whom are depicted as having their eyes plucked out: St. Adelia, by herself, to reject her own lustfulness, and St. Lucy, by others, for refusing to marry when she insisted on remaining a virgin." See *AdaOnline*, http://www.ada.auckland.ac.nz/ada15ann.htm.

29. Compare the lorgnette stolen from a Mayne Reid western heroine that Nabokov "found afterward in the hands of Madame Bovary, and later Anna Karenin had it, and then it passed into the possession of Chekhov's Lady with the Lapdog and was lost by her on the pier at Yalta" (*Speak Memory*, 202).

30. Kim's surname, shared with the Empress Josephine, suggests one of the many reversals of fortune that take place on Antiterra: African Americans and Russians make up the world's privileged groups, whereas the Beauharnais family and the occasional German composer work as servants or penniless tutors.

31. Young Ada translates François Coppée's "Matin d'Octobre" with a telling creative neologism: "Their fall is gentle. The leavesdropper / Can follow each"

(*Ada*, 247). The narrator's voice repeats her wordplay when a "stray ardilla daintily leavesdrops" on Ada and Van in the Edenic shattal tree.

32. See *AdaOnline* and the Kyoto Reading Circle notes, "Annotations to *Ada* (7)," May 2005, http://vnjapan.s141.xrea.com/main/ada/index.html.

33. "So far as Flaubertian intoxication is concerned, I cannot recommend enough to writers the purging, exorcising virtue of pastiche. When we finish a book, we not only wish to continue living with the characters, with Mme de Beauseant and Frederic Moreau, but also our interior voice, disciplined during the entire reading process to follow the rhythm of Balzac or Flaubert, wants to continue speaking like them. It is necessary to take a moment, to let the pedal prolong the sound; that is to say, to write a voluntary pastiche, after which one can return to being original, and not make one's entire life an involuntary pastiche" (Cancogni quotes Proust from "*À propos du style de Flaubert*" in *Mirage in the Mirror*, 208). Cancogni argues that *Ada*'s pastiches pass through Proust when they echo Flaubert. Part 3 begins with: "He traveled, he studied, he taught. He contemplated the pyramids. . . . He went shooting. . . . He learned to appreciate the singular little thrill" (*Ada*, 449). This closely echoes *L'Éducation sentimentale*, and precisely those intonations that Proust singles out for admiration in *Contre Sainte-Beuve; see* Cancogni, *Mirage in the Mirror*, 261.

34. See Sebastian Knight's literary manifesto in Nabokov's first English-language novel (originally published in 1941): "I am going to show you not the painting of a landscape, but the painting of different ways of painting a certain landscape, and I trust that their harmonious fusion will disclose the landscape as I intend you to see it." Vladimir Nabokov, *The Real Life of Sebastian Knight* (New York: Vintage, 1992), 95. For images that inspired Nabokov's description of Lucette at the Paris bar, see Henri de Toulouse-Lautrec's *Divan Japonais* (1892–93), and the Barton & Guestier wines advertisement in the *New Yorker* (March 23, 1963), reproduced in de Vries and Johnson, *Nabokov and the Art of Painting*, 116–17.

35. Joyce, *Ulysses*, 4. "Algy" refers to Algernon Swinburne (1837–1909): "I will go back to the great sweet mother, / Mother and lover of men, the sea" ("The Triumph of Time," lines 257–58); "*Epi oinopa pontoon*" is the Homeric formula "over the wine-dark sea." See also *AdaOnline* regarding this passage: http://www.ada.auckland.ac.nz/ada11ann.htm.

36. Boyd remarks that Nabokov's *Ada* "often couples Proust and Joyce (see I.1: 8–9, I.27: 169.33)," and that Marina's bath conjures the "painting of *The Bath of the Nymph* which Joyce associates with Molly's infidelity to Bloom in *Ulysses*)." See *AdaOnline*, http://www.ada.auckland.ac.nz/ada11ann.htm.

37. Jansy Berndt de Souza Mello (NABOKOV-L Archives, April 25, 2004) notes that "Nabokov here pays tribute to James Joyce, whose Stephen Dedalus . . . is a version of Joyce himself (and a pseudonym Joyce himself used as a young writer) . . . the description of Van upside down reflects Nabokov's

images in his Cornell and Harvard lectures in praise of Joyce's stylistic shifts in *Ulysses*."

38. Episode 2 in *Ulysses* is infected by the question-and-answers of Stephen Dedalus's teaching, including a reference to Tarentum (Van's legs are "hoisted like a Tarentine sail"). Inevitably such adjectives in *Ada* lead somewhere: "You, Cochrane, what city sent for him?" and so on. Joyce, *Ulysses*, 24.

39. The phrase was used by D. J. Enright in an early review of *Ada*. See his "Pun-Up," *Listener*, October 2, 1969, 457–58. Nabokov responded in the Darkbloom notes, stressing the wealth of allusions and pastiches in *Ada*, pointing to many sources besides the Irish grandmaster.

40. Nabokov stresses this point in his Tolstoy lecture in *Lectures on Russian Literature*, as well as on Joyce in *Lectures on Literature*. In 1967 and while working on *Ada*, Nabokov wrote in his foreword to the newly translated *King, Queen, Knave*: "I must admit I was a little surprised to find in my Russian text so many '*monologue intérieur*' passages—no relation to *Ulysses*, which I hardly knew at the time; but of course I had been exposed since tender boyhood to *Anna Karenin*, which contains a whole scene consisting of those intonations, Eden-new a hundred years ago, now well used" (*King, Queen, Knave*, trans. Dmitri Nabokov in collaboration with the author [New York: McGraw-Hill, 1968], x).

41. See Boyd, *Nabokov's "Ada,"* 54. Boyd stresses the Joycean subtext as linked with the theme of virginity (flower, deflower) and hence with Lucette. His ethical/aesthetic reading of *Ada* suggests that all future Joycean allusions should draw our attention to the hidden fate of Lucette.

42. The two projects, *Ada* and the *Wake*, have a good deal in common: Joyce was also accused of "having created in the *Wake* the ultimate private language." Andrew Schmitz, "The Penman and the Postal-Carrier: Preordained Rivalry in Joyce's *Finnegans Wake*," in *Agonistics: Arenas of Creative Control*, ed. Janet Lungstrum and Elizabeth Sauer (New York: State University of New York Press, 1997), 248. One review of *Ada* puts it: "Strangely, over the work as a whole is cast the shadow of Joyce's *Finnegans Wake*. Nabokov dismissed Joyce's last novel as a failed experiment; but the theme of incest; the imitation of parents by their children; the uncertain, alternating identity of the narrator(s); the part played by the book itself in its own story; all recall Joyce's work. There is even a chapter challenging Jung's approach to the interpretation of dreams . . . It's almost as if Nabokov is trying to correct Joyce's mistake." Stephen Crowe, "A Fairy Tale for Grown-Ups: *Ada or Ardor*," *UrbanTree*, http://urbarbo.blogspot.com/2009/05/fairy-tale-for-grown-ups-nabokovs-ada.html.

43. Durantaye, "The Pattern of Cruelty," 306.

44. Ibid.

45. In *L'Éducation sentimentale*, Frédéric meets the news of his lost fortune with the words, "Ruiné, dépouillé, perdu!" See Cancogni, *Mirage in the Mirror*, 265.

46. The leather *fartuk* ends up as his last name, in typical Van-memoir fashion, as well as a rather silly punning identification with the previous coachman Ben Wright. Trofim and Blanche have a blind child, presumably due to her venereal disease. The "sore of Eros" echoes the risks of incest and inbreeding.

47. Appel seems a likely model for *Ada*'s fictional editor Oranger, who may or may not have tampered with the "text," and who has been rewarded in this world or some other with Violet Knox.

48. "When in early September Van Veen left Manhattan for Lute, he was pregnant" (*Ada*, 325). We know from two pages earlier that young Ada included in her graduation album a clever pastiche "mimicking Tolstoy's paragraph rhythm and chapter closings" (*Ada*, 323).

49. The final paragraphs of *Ada*, like John Ray Jr.'s "Foreword" to *Lolita*, contrast the sparkling prose of the admitted villain with the tin ear of conventional style (and morality).

50. See Martin Hägglund, "Writing: Nabokov," in *Dying for Time: Proust, Woolf, Nabokov* (Cambridge, Mass.: Harvard University Press, 2012), 106.

51. We visualize Narcissus, but the Veens suggest throughout that "Vaniada" are divided halves of the same spiritual being, as in Aristophanes's myth of androgynes as the source of erotic longing from Plato's *Symposium*. Their blue and red edits include a short tiff on the subject: "Sorry, no—if people remembered the same they would not be different people. That's-how-it-went. But we are not 'different'!" (*Ada*, 120). The troubling remainder in this vision is Lucette, who repeats black-and-white Ada's beauty but in color. Ada's sister-in-law even comments tastelessly that dead Lucette's "prettiness seemed to complement Ada's, the two halves forming together something like perfect beauty, in the Platonic sense" (*Ada*, 518).

52. Trousdale writes, "It is striking how many transnational novels deal with incest and monstrosity . . . Failures of fertility are generally linked to failed past attempts at making a real place for an imaginary community." Trousdale, *Nabokov, Rushdie and the Transnational Imagination*, 166.

53. In a forthcoming study, I compare the "two Vladimirs," Nabokov and Sorokin, finding parallels between *Lolita* and *The Thirtieth Love of Marina* (1995), and likewise *Ada* and *Roman* (or *The Novel*, 1994).

54. Jameson, *Postmodernism*, 305. See also Will Norman's "Swiss Time: Cold War Pastoral in Late Nabokov," in *Nabokov, History, and the Texture of Time* (New York: Routledge, 2012).

CHAPTER FIVE

The chapter epigraph is from Borges, "Kafka and His Precursors," 199, 201.

1. Trousdale discovers different Zenos in *Ada*: the Brothers Zeno, whose sixteenth-century travel narrative joins many other references to Renaissance

explorers in Nabokov's novel. See Trousdale, *Nabokov, Rushdie, and the Transnational Imagination*, 58.

2. The proliferation of rabbit names in *Ada* (Doctors Lapiner, Krolik, Lagosse, etc.) may be related. From Darkbloom's notes: "for some obscure but not unattractive reason, most of the physicians in the book turn out to bear names connected with rabbits" (*Ada*, 591). Achilles races the tortoise like the hare; we think too of the proverbial reproductive habits of rabbits.

3. Appel notes the regressive sequence, but does not make the connection to Zeno or Bergson: "*Ada* is almost two times as long as any previous Nabokov novel. Although its highly allusive first half constitutes a coherently organized Museum of the Novel (Austen to *Ada*), an array of the exhausted possibilities any practitioner must now confront, the second half of the book poses too many problems. . . . Ada is often undermined by impossibly hermetic and gratuitous encrustations" (*Nabokov's Dark Cinema*, 48).

4. Boyd writes, "far from exhibiting any failure of control Ada is not only one of the most morally stringent of novels but is perhaps the most rigorously planned" (Boyd, *Nabokov's "Ada,"* ix).

5. There is a suggestive parallel between the work Van is best known for and Nabokov's *Lolita* in the wake of Stanley Kubrick's film.

6. Boyd, *American Years*, 487. After *Ada*'s publication, Nabokov curbed interpreters by insisting that Van's theory of time had "no existence beyond the fabric of one part of the novel *Ada*." He rebuked Jeffrey Leonard by stating that Veen's Time is "something quite different from what Proust called 'lost time' . . . And finally I owe no debt whatsoever . . . to the famous Argentine essayist [Borges] . . . Mr. Leonard would have lost less of it had he gone straight to Berkeley and Bergson" (*Strong Opinions*, 289–90).

7. Nabokov was quick to respond to accusations that Van was modeled after himself, and he never forgave John Updike the ungallant suggestion that "bitchy and lewd Ada" might resemble Vera. See John Updike, "Van Loves Ada, Ada Loves Van," *New Yorker*, August 2, 1969, 67–75. "The more gifted and talkative one's characters are, the greater the chances of their resembling the author in tone or tint of mind," Nabokov protested: "I am not really aware of any special similarities—just as one is not aware of sharing mannerisms with a detestable kinsman. I loathe Van Veen" (*Strong Opinions*, 120).

8. See Glynn, *Bergsonian and Russian Formalist Influences*, 55; and Hilary L. Fink, *Bergson and Russian Modernism, 1900–1930* (Evanston, Ill.: Northwestern University Press, 1999).

9. Ramin Jahanbegloo, *Berlin Conversations with Isaiah* (London: Peter Halban, 1991), 8.

10. Bergson's literary approach to philosophy marks one strain of Continental philosophy, including Benjamin and the Frankfurt school, and later Derrida, Deleuze, and the French deconstruction critics. See Valentine Moulard-

Leonard, *Bergson-Deleuze Encounters: Transcendental Experience and the Thought of the Virtual* (Albany: State University of New York Press, 2008); and Keith Robinson, *Deleuze, Whitehead, Bergson: Rhizomatic Connections* (London: Palgrave Macmillan, 2009).

11. See Glynn, *Bergsonian and Russian Formalist Influences*, 55. Bertrand Russell in his *History of Western Philosophy* called the Bergsonian moment a "revolt against reason," marking the sharp division between this particular strain of Continental philosophy and the developing Anglo-American analytic school. Russell, *A History of Western Philosophy, and Its Connection with Political and Social Circumstances from the Earliest Times to the Present Day* (New York: Simon and Schuster, 1945), 791.

12. Bergson, *Time and Free Will*, repr. in *Henri Bergson: Key Writings*, ed. Keith Ansell-Pearson and John Mullarkey (New York: Continuum, 2002), 65–66.

13. Bergson, *Creative Mind*, in *Henri Bergson: Key Writings*, 255. Nabokov's hostility to Plato may have Bergsonian roots. See Richard Rorty: "[Nabokov] wanted to say that idiosyncratic imagery, of the sort he was good at, rather than the kind of generalizing ideas which Plato was good at, is what opens the gates of immortality. . . . Nabokov runs together literary with personal immortality. If only the former is at stake, then, indeed, Plato was wrong, and Nabokov, Heidegger and Derrida are right. If you want to be remembered by future generations, go in for poetry rather than mathematics." Rorty, *Contingency, Irony, and Solidarity*, 151–52.

14. Bergson, *Creative Mind*, 257.

15. Gayatri Spivak uses "trace" in her translations of Derrida, for "the reader must remind himself of at least the track, even the spoor" in the French word *trace*. Gayatri Chakravorty Spivak, translator's preface to *Of Grammatology* by Jacques Derrida (Baltimore, Md.: Johns Hopkins University Press, 1976), xvii.

16. Bergson, *Time and Free Will*, in *Henri Bergson: Key Writings*, 77.

17. Bergson, *Creative Evolution*, in *Henri Bergson: Key Writings*, 176.

18. Bergson, *Creative Evolution*, 173.

19. Vladimir Nabokov, *Speak, Memory* (New York: Vintage, 1989), 20.

20. As Eric Naiman puts it, "There is Freud and there are vulgar Freudians, and Freud was occasionally one of them"; the same can be said of Nabokov and vulgar Nabokovians. Naiman, *Nabokov, Perversely*, 266–67.

21. Glynn, *Bergsonian and Russian Formalist Influences*, 68.

22. Bergson, *Matter and Memory*, in *Henri Bergson: Key Writings*, 125.

23. Bergson, *Creative Evolution*, 171.

24. Bergson, *The Creative Mind*, 262–63.

25. Bergson, *Time and Free Will*, 74–75.

26. *Axel's Castle* is structured around six case studies, resembling structurally as well as thematically Walter Pater's famous treatise, *The Renaissance*.

27. If seventeenth-century science "presented the universe as a mechanism [and] caused people to draw the conclusion that man was something apart from nature, something introduced into the universe from outside and remaining alien to all that he found," the romantic poet feels "the falsity of this assumption . . . that what we are and what we see, what we hear, what we feel and what we smell, are inextricably related, that all are involved in the same great entity. . . . The Romantic poet, then, with his turbid or opalescent language, his sympathies and passions which cause him to merge with his surroundings, is the prophet of a new insight into nature: he is describing things as they really are; and a revolution in the imagery of poetry is in reality a revolution in metaphysics." Edmund Wilson, *Axel's Castle: A Study in Imaginative Literature of 1870–1930* (New York: Farrar, Strauss and Giroux, 2004), 6.

28. Ibid., 18.

29. Ibid., 126.

30. The fictional prose stylist Bergotte in *À la recherche* is deeply moved by a painting he sees in old age, and exclaims that he should have written all his books just like that perfect patch of color. Nabokov chooses a moment where Proust beautifully illustrates Bergson's ideas on art and representations of reality.

31. Toker, "Nabokov and Bergson," 367. See also Stephen Blackwell, *Zina's Paradox: The Figured Reader in "The Gift"* (New York: Peter Lang, 2000).

32. Toker, "Nabokov and Bergson," 370.

33. Glynn, *Bergsonian and Russian Formalist Influences*, 57. Wilson considered Joyce and Proust to share a broadly understood symbolist sensibility precisely through the influence of Bergson; many Russian and French symbolist poets were avid Bergsonians.

34. Foster, *Nabokov's Art of Memory*, 83.

35. Ibid., 84.

36. Ibid., 83, paraphrased from Bergson's 1903 *Introduction to Metaphysics*.

37. Walter Benjamin, *Illuminations*, ed. Hannah Arendt, trans. Harry Zohn (New York: Schocken, 1969), 157.

38. See Trousdale, *Nabokov, Rushdie, and the Transnational Imagination*, 80–81; and Hägglund, *Dying for Time: Proust, Woolf, Nabokov*, 94–98.

39. Rorty writes that Nabokov often tries to tie in a "highly unfashionable concern for metaphysical immortality together with the more respectable notion of literary immortality" (*Contingency, Irony, and Solidarity*, 150). In *Ada*, Nabokov ascribes just such a conflation of aesthetics and metaphysics to the Veens, distancing himself in the process.

40. Aleksey Sklyarenko (NABOKOV-L April 2004) suggests a model for the L catastrophe in "La Pointe," a 1900s Russian science-fiction story by Konstantin Sluchevsky. It is quite possible that Nabokov borrowed the bare bones of his stories from pulp sources, as Sklyarenko and Michael Maar suggest. Nabokov had

a Shakespearean talent for transforming pedestrian narratives, adding poetry by removing motive and exposition.

41. Boyd finds one such metonymic slide in the scene where Van makes his way from the train station to Ardis and back again; without exchanging his ride for a mount, Van suddenly appears on horseback (Boyd, *Nabokov's "Ada,"* 11).

42. At least three times in the novel, Van is aware that in some other world, he has just died. With an eye to Nabokov's 1930 novel *The Eye*, we could read what follows each incident as postmortem delusion.

43. Humbert's precursor in the 1939 Russian-language novella *The Enchanter* (*Volshebnik*) wears a watch with no hands, a recurring motif throughout the story.

44. Hägglund coins the term "chronolibidinal" for such desires in *Dying for Time*.

45. "Cinematography can provide us with a plausible impression of movement by stringing together static images and animating them. However, we are not experiencing motion itself but immobile images, rendered mobile in order to produce an abstraction of motion." See Glynn, *Bergsonian and Russian Formalist Influences*, 72.

46. Boyd, *American Years*, 585.

47. Barbara Wyllie, *Nabokov at the Movies: Film Perspectives in Fiction* (Jefferson, N.C.: McFarland, 2003), 10.

48. The third film in *Ada* is yet another adaptation, of Mlle Larivière's *Enfants Maudits*, a melodramatic incestuous love story and another alternate version of Van and Ada's memoir. Nabokov must have also had in mind Jean Cocteau's incest-driven novel *Les Enfants terribles* (1929), and Jean-Pierre Melville's film adaptation (1950).

49. Nabokov, *Annotated Lolita*, 32.

50. Compare Onegin and Tatiana; Frédéric and Mme Arnoux in *L'Éducation sentimentale*, and so on.

51. Compare with Van's admission, "Ought to begin dating every page of the manuscript: Should be kinder to my unknown dreamers" (*Ada*, 122).

52. See Cancogni, *Mirage in the Mirror*, 61.

53. Ibid., 101.

54. Ibid., 69.

55. Ibid., 143–44.

56. Marie-Laure Ryan, *Narrative across Media: The Languages of Storytelling* (Lincoln: University of Nebraska Press, 2004), 10.

CONCLUSION

A note on the first epigraph: I give the last two stanzas here. Nabokov dedicated the poem to his early drawing master Mstislav Dobuzhinsky, after seeing his exhibition in Berlin in 1926. Trans. Dmitri Nabokov, in *Nabokovian* 51 (Fall 2009): 28–31.

The second epigraph is from W. G. Sebald, *Campto Santo*, ed. Sven Meyer, trans. Anthea Bell (London: Hamilton, 2005), 143.

1. Shapiro, *Sublime Artist's Studio*, 101.

2. De Vries and Johnson, *Nabokov and the Art of Painting*, 19.

3. Shapiro, *Sublime Artist's Studio*, 189. I address the other media in *Ada* and the role of the novel in a changing media ecology more fully in an article dedicated to that topic: "Nabokov's Moving Images," in *Nabokov in Context*, ed. David Bethea and Siggy Frank (Oxford: Oxford University Press, forthcoming).

4. Julian Murphet, *Multimedia Modernism: Literature and the Anglo-American Avant-Garde* (Cambridge: Cambridge University Press, 2009), 13.

5. Ibid., 30.

6. "Вставляй в просторную, вместительную раму / Картины новые—открой нам диораму: / Привалит публика . . ." (quoted and translated in Greenleaf, *Pushkin and Romantic Fashion*, 208).

7. Jay David Bolter and Richard Grusin, *Remediation: Understanding New Media* (Cambridge, Mass.: MIT Press, 200), 49.

8. Bolter and Grusin, *Remediation*, 34. See also Clement Greenberg: "Realistic, illusionist art had dissembled the medium, using art to conceal art. Modernism used art to call attention to art." Greenberg, "Modernist Painting," in *The New Art: A Critical Anthology*, ed. Gregory Battock (New York: E. P. Dutton, 1973), 68–69.

9. As Yuri Leving writes, "The last years of the twentieth century were marked by a bull market in screen adaptations of Vladimir Nabokov's novels, including a new *Lolita* (1997) and a feature-length version of *The Luzhin Defense* (2000) . . . Not only the power of the author's imagination but also certain narrative mechanisms render the Nabokovian discourse suitable for translation into the cinema idiom." See his "Filming Nabokov: On the Visual Poetics of the Text," *Russian Studies in Literature* 40, no. 3 (Summer 2004): 6.

10. Cyntha Zarin, *The Ada Poems* (New York: Knopf, 2010); Anatoly Kudriavitsky, ed., *A Night in Nabokov Hotel: 20 Contemporary Poets from Russia* (Dublin: Dedalus, 2007).

11. Damrosch, *What Is World Literature?*, 5. See also John Pizer, *The Idea of World Literature: History and Pedagogical Practice* (Baton Rouge: Louisiana State University Press, 2006); Christopher Prendergast, ed., *Debating World Literature* (London: Verso, 2004); and the important corrective by Emily Apter, *Against World Literature: On the Politics of Untranslatability* (London: Verso, 2013).

12. Thomsen, *Mapping World Literature*, 3.

13. See Azar Nafisi, *Reading Lolita in Tehran: A Memoir in Books* (New York: Random House, 2003); and Orhan Pamuk, *The Naive and the Sentimental Novelist*, trans. Nazim Dikba (Cambridge, Mass.: Harvard University Press, 2010).

14. On Nabokov and Rushdie, see Trousdale, *Nabokov, Rushdie, and the Transnational Imagination*.

15. W. G. Sebald, *The Emigrants*, trans. Michael Hulse (New York: New Directions, 1996), 16.

16. Adrian Curtin and Maxim D. Shrayer, "Netting the Butterfly Man: The Significance of Vladimir Nabokov in W. G. Sebald's *The Emigrants*," *Religion and the Arts* 9, no. 3 (2005): 272. See also Leland de la Durantaye, "The Facts of Fiction; or, The Figure of Vladimir Nabokov in W. G. Sebald," *Comparative Literature Studies* 45, no. 4 (2008): 425–45.

17. Curtin and Shrayer, "Netting the Butterfly Man," 277.

Bibliography

PRIMARY SOURCES

Works by Vladimir Nabokov

Nabokov, Vladimir. *Ada, or Ardor: A Family Chronicle*. New York: Vintage International, 1990. Reprint of the 1969 edition by McGraw-Hill. Page references are to the Vintage edition.

———. *The Annotated Lolita*. Edited by Alfred Appel Jr. New York: Vintage, 1991.

———. *Bend Sinister*. New York: Vintage International, 1990.

———. *Conclusive Evidence*. New York: Harper, 1951.

———. *Dear Bunny, Dear Volodya: The Nabokov-Wilson Letters, 1940–1971*. Edited by Simon Karlinsky. Berkeley: University of California Press, 2001.

———. *Despair*. New York: Vintage, 1989.

———. *Drugie berega*. New York: Chekhov Publishing House, 1954.

———. *The Enchanter*. New York: Putnam, 1986.

———. *The Eye*. New York: Vintage, 1990.

———. *The Gift*. New York: Vintage, 1991.

———. *Glory*. New York: Vintage, 1991.

———. *Invitation to a Beheading*. New York: Vintage, 1989.

———. *King, Queen, Knave*. New York: Vintage, 1989.

———. *Laughter in the Dark*. New York: New Directions, 2006. Originally published in 1938.

———. *Lectures on Literature*. New York: Harcourt Brace Jovanovich/Bruccoli Clark, 1980.

———. *Lectures on Russian Literature*. New York: Harcourt Brace Jovanovich/Bruccoli Clark, 1981.

———. *Lolita*. New York: Vintage, 1989. Originally published in 1955.

———. *Lolita*. Translated into Russian by Vladimir Nabokov. Moscow: Eksmo-Press, 2001.

———. *Lolita: A Screenplay*. New York: McGraw-Hill, 1974.

———. *Look at the Harlequins!* New York: Vintage, 1990.

———. *The Luzhin Defense*. New York: Vintage, 1990. Originally published in 1964 as *The Defense*.

———. *Mary*. New York: Vintage, 1989.

———. "On Adaptation." *New York Review of Books*, 13, no. 10 (December 4, 1969).

———. *The Original of Laura*. Edited by Dmitri Nabokov. New York: Knopf, 2009.

———. *Pale Fire*. New York: Vintage, 1989. Originally published in 1962.

———. *Pnin*. New York: Vintage, 1991. Originally published in 1957.

———. *Poems and Problems*. New York: McGraw-Hill, 1971.

———. "Pushkin, or the Real and the Plausible." Translated by Dmitri Nabokov. *New York Review of Books* 35, no. 5 (March 31, 1988): 38–42. Originally published in *Nouvelle revue française* (March 1937).

———. *The Real Life of Sebastian Knight*. New York: Vintage, 1992.

———. *Vladimir Nabokov: Selected Letters 1940–1977*. Edited by Dmitri Nabokov and Matthew J. Bruccoli. San Diego, New York, and London: Houghton Mifflin Harcourt, 2012.

———. *Speak, Memory*. New York: Vintage, 1989. Originally published in 1966.

———. *Strong Opinions*. New York: Vintage, 1990. Originally published in 1973.

———. *Stikhi*. Ann Arbor, Mich.: Ardis, 1979.

———. *Transparent Things*. New York: Vintage, 1989. Originally published in 1972.

———. "Ut pictura poesis." Translated by Dmitri Nabokov. *Nabokovian* 51 (Fall 2009): 28–31.

Works by Aleksandr Pushkin

Pushkin, Aleksandr. *Eugene Onegin: A Novel in Verse*. 4 vols. Edited and translated by Vladimir Nabokov. Revised edition, Princeton, N.J.: Princeton University Press, 1975.

———. *Polnoe sobranie sochineniii A. S. Pushkina v Pushkina v desiat' tomakh*. Leningrad: Nauka, 1977–79.

SECONDARY SOURCES

Secondary Sources on Nabokov

Alexandrov, Vladimir E., ed. *Garland Companion to Vladimir Nabokov*. New York: Garland, 1995.

———. *Nabokov's Otherworld*. Princeton, N.J.: Princeton University Press, 1991.

Allan, Nina. *Madness, Death and Disease in the Fiction of Vladimir Nabokov*. Birmingham, UK: Dept. of Russian Language and Literature, University of Birmingham, 1994.

Alter, Robert. "*Ada,* or the Perils of Paradise." In Quennell, *Vladimir Nabokov,* 103–18.

Appel, Alfred, Jr. "*Ada* Described." *Triquarterly* 17, Special Issue on Nabokov (Winter 1970): 160–86. Reprinted in Appel, *Nabokov: Criticism.* Page numbers refer to the *Triquarterly* version.

———. Introduction to *The Annotated Lolita,* by Vladimir Nabokov. New York: Vintage, 1991.

———. "*Lolita:* The Springboard of Parody." In Dembo, *Nabokov,* 106–43.

———. *Nabokov's Dark Cinema.* New York: Oxford University Press, 1974.

Appel, Alfred, Jr., and Charles Newman, eds. *Nabokov: Criticism, Reminiscences, Translations, and Tributes.* Evanston, Ill.: Northwestern University Press, 1970. Originally published as *Triquarterly* 17, Special Issue on Nabokov (Winter 1970).

Bayley, John. "Under Cover of Decadence: Nabokov as an Evangelist and Guide to the Russian Classics." In Quennell, *Vladimir Nabokov,* 42–58.

Beaujour, Elizabeth Klosty. "Bilingualism." In Alexandrov, *Garland Companion,* 37–43.

———. "Translation and Self-Translation." In Alexandrov, *Garland Companion,* 714–24.

Bethea, David M. "Izgnanie kak ukhod v kokon: Obraz babochki u Nabokova i Brodskogo." *Russkaia Literatura* (St. Petersburg) 3 (1991): 167–75.

———. "Sologub, Nabokov, and the Limits of Decadent Aesthetics." *Russian Review* 63, no. 1 (January 2004): 48–62.

Blackwell, Stephen. *Zina's Paradox: The Figured Reader in "The Gift."* New York: Peter Lang, 2000.

Bloom, Harold, ed. *Vladimir Nabokov's Lolita.* New York: Chelsea House Publishers, 1987.

Boyd, Brian. "Ada." In Alexandrov, *Garland Companion,* 3–18.

———. "*Ada,* the Bog and the Garden; or, Straw, Fluff, and Peat: Sources and Places in *Ada.*" *Nabokov Studies* 8 (2004): 107–33.

———. "Annotations to *Ada.*" *Nabokovian* 30 (Spring 1993). Full text with Boyd's annotations is available as *AdaOnline,* http://www.ada.auckland.ac.nz/.

———. "Nabokov at Cornell." In Gibian, *Achievements of Vladimir Nabokov,* 119–44.

———. *Nabokov's Ada: The Place of Consciousness.* Ann Arbor, Mich.: Ardis, 1985. Christchurch, New Zealand: Cybereditions, 2001.

———. *Vladimir Nabokov: The American Years.* Princeton, N.J.: Princeton University Press, 1991.

———. *Vladimir Nabokov: The Russian Years.* Princeton, N.J.: Princeton University Press, 1990.

Bozovic, Marijeta, ed. "My Nabokov." Special issue, *Ulbandus* 10 (2007).

Brown, Clarence. "Little Girl Migrates (Nabokov)." *New Republic,* January 20, 1968, 19–20.

———. "Nabokov's Pushkin and Nabokov's Nabokov." In Dembo, *Nabokov,* 195–208.

Brown, Edward J. "Review: Nabokov and Pushkin (with Comments on New Translations of Eugene Onegin)." *Slavic Review* 24, no. 4 (December 1965): 688–701.

———. "Review: Round Two: Nabokov versus Pushkin." *Slavic Review* 36, no. 1 (March 1977): 101–5.

Buhks, Nora. *Eshafot v khrustal'nom dvortse: O russkikh romanakh V. Nabokova.* Moscow: Novoe literaturnoe obozrenie, 1998.

Cancogni, Annapaola. *The Mirage in the Mirror: Nabokov's Ada and Its French Pre-Texts.* New York: Garland Publishing, 1985.

———. "Nabokov and Chateaubriand." In Alexandrov, *Garland Companion,* 382–88.

Clark, Beverly L. "Dark Ada, Light Lucette, and Van." *Studies in American Fiction* 12 (1984): 79–86.

Connolly, Julian W., ed. *The Cambridge Companion to Nabokov.* Cambridge: Cambridge University Press, 2005.

Crowe, Stephen. "A Fairy Tale for Grown-Ups: *Ada or Ardor.*" *UrbanTree.* http://urbarbo.blogspot.com/2009/05/fairy-tale-for-grown-ups-nabokovs-ada.html.

Couturier, Maurice. "Nabokov and Flaubert." In Alexandrov, *Garland Companion,* 405–12.

Cummins, George M. "Nabokov's Russian *Lolita.*" *Slavic and East European Journal* 21, no. 3 (Autumn 1977): 354–65.

Curtin, Adrian, and Maxim D. Shrayer. "Netting the Butterfly Man: The Significance of Vladimir Nabokov in W. G. Sebald's *The Emigrants.*" *Religion and the Arts* 9, nos. 3–4 (2005): 258–83.

Davidson, James A. "Some Thoughts on Hitchcock and Nabokov." http://www.imagesjournal.com/issue03/features/hitchnab1.htm.

Davidson, Pamela. "The Muse and the Demon in the Poetry of Pushkin, Lermontov, and Blok." In *Russian Literature and Its Demons,* edited by Pamela Davidson, 167–214. Oxford: Berghahn Books, 2000.

Davydov, Sergei. "Nabokov and Pushkin." In Alexandrov, *Garland Companion,* 482–96.

Dembo, L. S., ed. *Nabokov: The Man and His Work.* Madison: University of Wisconsin Press, 1967. Originally published as *Wisconsin Studies in Contemporary Literature* 8, no. 2, Special Issue on Nabokov (Spring 1967).

Diment, Galya. "English as Sanctuary: Nabokov's and Brodsky's Autobiographical Writings." *Slavic and East European Journal* 37, no. 3 (Autumn 1993): 346–61.

———. "Strong Opinions." In Alexandrov, *Garland Companion,* 691.

Dolinin, Alexander. "Don't Ride by, Re-reader." *Nabokovian* 25 (1990): 37–40.

———. *"Eugene Onegin."* In Alexandrov, *Garland Companion*, 117–30.

———. *Istinnaia zhizn' pisatelia Sirina: Raboty o Nabokove*. St. Petersburg: Akademicheskii proekt, 2004.

———. *"Lolita* in Russian." In Alexandrov, *Garland Companion*, 221–30.

———. "Nabokov as a Russian Writer." In Connolly, *Cambridge Companion*, 49–64.

———. "Nabokov's Time Doubling: From *The Gift* to *Lolita*." *Nabokov Studies* 2 (1995): 3–40.

Durantaye, Leland de la. "The Facts of Fiction; or, The Figure of Vladimir Nabokov in W. G. Sebald." *Comparative Literature Studies* 45, no. 4 (2008): 425–45.

———. "The Pattern of Cruelty and the Cruelty of Pattern in Vladimir Nabokov." *Cambridge Quarterly* 35, no. 4 (2006): 301–26.

———. *Style Is Matter: The Moral Art of Vladimir Nabokov*. Ithaca, N.Y.: Cornell University Press, 2007.

Enright, D. J. "Pun-up." *Listener,* October 2, 1969, 457–58.

Field, Andrew. *Vladimir Nabokov: The Life and Work of Vladimir Nabokov*. New York: Crown, 1986.

Foster, John Burt, Jr. "Nabokov and Proust." In Alexandrov, *Garland Companion*, 472–81.

———. "Nabokov and Tolstoy." In Alexandrov, *Garland Companion*, 518–28.

———. "Nabokov before Proust: The Paradox of Anticipatory Memory." *Slavic and East European Journal* 33, no. 1 (Spring 1989): 78–94.

———. *Nabokov's Art of Memory and European Modernism*. Princeton, N.J.: Princeton University Press, 1993.

Frank, Joseph. "Lectures on Literature." In Alexandrov, *Garland Companion*, 234–58.

Gerschenkron, Alexander. "A Manufactured Monument?" *Modern Philology* 63 (1966): 336–47.

Gibian, George, and Stephen Jay Parker, eds. *The Achievements of Vladimir Nabokov: Essays, Studies, Reminiscences, and Stories*. Ithaca, N.Y.: Cornell University Center for International Studies, 1984.

Glynn, Michael. *Vladimir Nabokov: Bergsonian and Russian Formalist Influences in His Novels*. New York: Palgrave Macmillan, 2007.

Grabes, Herbert. *Fictitious Biographies: Vladimir Nabokov's English Novels*. The Hague: Mouton, 1977.

Grayson, Jane. *Nabokov Translated: A Comparison of Nabokov's Russian and English Prose*. Oxford: Oxford University Press, 1977.

Grishakova, Marina. *The Models of Space, Time and Vision in V. Nabokov's Fiction: Narrative Strategies and Cultural Frames*. Tartu Semiotics Library 5. Tartu, Estonia: Tartu University Press, 2006. http://www.kriso.ee/cgi-bin/shop/9949113067.html.

Hägglund, Martin. *Dying for Time: Proust, Woolf, Nabokov.* Cambridge, Mass.: Harvard University Press, 2012.

Hayles, N. Katherine. "Ambivalence: Symmetry, Asymmetry, and the Physics of Time Reversal in Nabokov's *Ada.*" In *The Cosmic Web: Scientific Field Models and Literary Strategies in the Twentieth Century,* 111–38. Ithaca, N.Y.: Cornell University Press, 1984.

Hodgart, Matthew. "Review." *New York Review of Books,* May 22, 1969, 3–4.

Izmirlieva, Valentina. "Nabokov and Casanova; or, Lolita and Zaïre." In *Poetics, Self, Place: Essays in Honor of Lisa Crone,* edited by Nicole Boudreau, Sarah Krive, and Catherine O'Neil, 630–47. Bloomington, Ind.: Slavica Publishers, 2007.

———. "Nabokov vs. Casanova: An Affair of Honor." In "My Nabokov," edited by Marijeta Bozovic. Special issue, *Ulbandus* 10 (2007): 8–24.

Johnson, D. Barton. "The Labyrinth of Incest in Nabokov's *Ada.*" *Comparative Literature* 38, no. 3 (Summer 1986): 224–55.

———. "'L'Inconnue de la Seine' and Nabokov's Naiads." *Comparative Literature* 44, no. 3 (Summer 1992): 225–48.

———. "Nabokov's *Ada* and Pushkin's *Eugene Onegin.*" *Slavic and East European Journal* 15, no. 3 (Autumn 1971): 316–23.

Karlinsky, Simon. "Illusion, Reality and Parody in Nabokov's Plays." In Dembo, *Nabokov,* 183–94.

———. "Nabokov's Novel *Dar* as a Work of Literary Criticism: A Structural Analysis." *Slavic and East European Journal* 7, no. 3 (Autumn 1963): 284–90.

Karlinsky, Simon, and Alfred Appel, Jr., eds. *The Bitter Air of Exile: Russian Writers in the West, 1922–1972.* Berkeley: University of California Press, 1977.

Kaufman, Linda. "Framing Lolita: Is There a Woman in the Text?" In *Refiguring the Father: New Feminist Readings of Patriarchy,* edited by Patricia Yaeger and Beth Kowaleski-Wallace, 131–50. Carbondale: Southern Illinois University Press, 1989.

Kiš, Danilo. "Une riche nostalgie (Nabokov)." *Magazine littéraire* 233 (1986): 35–37.

Kudriavitsky, Anatoly, ed. *A Night in Nabokov Hotel: 20 Contemporary Poets from Russia.* Dublin: Dedalus, 2007.

Kurganov, Efim. *Lolita i Ada.* St. Petersburg: Iz-vo zhurnala "Zvezda," 2001.

Kyoto Reading Circle notes. "Annotations to *Ada* (7)." May 2005. http://vnjapan .s141.xrea.com/main/ada/index.html.

Lee, L. L. "Vladimir Nabokov's Great Spiral of Being." *Western Humanities Review* 18 (1964): 225–36.

Leonard, Jeffrey. "In Place of Lost Time: *Ada.*" *TriQuarterly* 17 (Winter 1970): 136–46.

Leving, Yuri. "Filming Nabokov: On the Visual Poetics of the Text." *Russian Studies in Literature* 40, no. 3 (Summer 2004): 6–31.

Lilly, Mark. "Nabokov Homo Ludens." In Quennell, *Vladimir Nabokov,* 88–102.

Lipovetsky, Mark. "The Discursive Wars: Cultural Narratology of Nabokov's *Lolita.*" *Amsterdam International Electronic Journal for Cultural Narratology* 1 (Spring 2005). http://cf.hum.uva.nl/narratology/s05_index.htm.

Lodge, David. "Review: *Keys to Lolita.*" *Modern Language Review* 65, no. 3 (July 1970): 618.

Long, Michael. *Marvell and Nabokov: Childhood and Arcadia.* Oxford: Clarendon, 1984.

Lowell, Robert. "In Defense of George Steiner," *Encounter* (February 1967).

Maar, Michael. *Speak, Nabokov.* Translated by Ross Benjamin. London: Verso, 2009.

———. *The Two Lolitas.* Edited by Perry Anderson. London: Verso, 2005.

Mason, Bobbie Ann. *Nabokov's Garden: A Guide to Ada.* Ann Arbor, Mich.: Ardis, 1974.

McLean, Hugh. "*Lectures on Russian Literature.*" In Alexandrov, *Garland Companion,* 258–74.

Merivale, Patricia. "The Flaunting of Artifice in Nabokov and Jorge Luis Borges." In Dembo, *Nabokov,* 209–24.

Meyer, Priscilla. *Find What the Sailor Has Hidden: Vladimir Nabokov's "Pale Fire."* Middletown, Conn.: Wesleyan University Press, 1988.

———. "Nabokov's Lolita and Pushkin's Onegin—McAdam, McEve and McFate." In Gibian and Parker, *Achievements of Vladimir Nabokov,* 179–211.

Moynahan, Julian. "*Lolita* and Related Memories." *Triquarterly* 17, Special Issue on Nabokov (Winter 1970): 247–53. Reprinted in Appel, *Nabokov: Criticism.* Page numbers refer to the *Triquarterly* version.

———. "Nabokov and Joyce." In Alexandrov, *Garland Companion,* 433–44.

Muliarchik, A. S. *Russkaia proza Vladimira Nabokova.* Moscow: Izdatel'stvo Moskovskogo universiteta, 1997.

Nabokov, Dmitri. "Translating with Nabokov." In Gibian, *Achievements of Vladimir Nabokov,* 145–77.

NABOKOV-L. Vladimir Nabokov Forum Archives. http://listserv.ucsb.edu/archives/nabokv-l.html.

Naiman, Eric. *Nabokov, Perversely.* Ithaca, N.Y.: Cornell University Press, 2010.

Nassar, Joseph Michael. "The Russian in Nabokov's English Novels." Ph.D. diss., State University of New York at Binghamton, 1977.

Nicol, Charles, and J. E. Rivers. *Nabokov's Fifth Arc.* Austin: University of Texas Press, 1982.

Nivat, Georges. "Nabokov and Dostoevsky." In Alexandrov, *Garland Companion,* 398–402.

———. "*Speak, Memory.*" In Alexandrov, *Garland Companion,* 672–85.

Norman, Will. *Nabokov, History and the Texture of Time.* New York: Routledge, 2012.

Oates, Joyce Carol. "A Personal View of Nabokov." *Saturday Review of the Arts* 1 (January 1973): 36–37.

Packman, David. *Vladimir Nabokov: The Structure of Literary Desire.* Columbia: University of Missouri Press, 1982.

Parker, Dorothy. "Sex—Without the Asterisks." *Esquire* 50, no. 4 (October 1958): 102–3.

Pifer, Ellen. "Dark Paradise: Shades of Heaven and Hell in *Ada.*" *Modern Fiction Studies* 25, no. 3 (1979): 481–99.

———. *Nabokov and the Novel.* Cambridge, Mass.: Harvard University Press, 1980.

———. *Nabokov's Garden: A Guide to "Ada."* Ann Arbor, Mich.: Ardis, 1974.

Poulin, Isabelle. *Vladimir Nabokov lecteur de l'autre.* Bordeaux: Presses Universitaires de Bordeaux, 2005.

Proffer, Carl. "*Ada* as Wonderland: A Glossary of Allusions to Russian Literature." In Proffer, *Book of Things*, 249–79.

———, ed. *A Book of Things about Vladimir Nabokov.* Ann Arbor, Mich.: Ardis, 1974.

———. *Keys to Lolita.* Bloomington: Indiana University Press, 1978.

Quennell, Peter, ed. *Vladimir Nabokov: His Life, His Work, His World; A Tribute.* New York: Morrow, 1980.

Rivers, J. E. "Proust, Nabokov and *Ada.*" In *Critical Essays on Vladimir Nabokov*, edited by Phyllis A. Roth, 138–39. Boston: G. K. Hall, 1984.

Rivers, J. E., and Charles Nicol, eds. *Nabokov's Fifth Arc: Nabokov and Others on His Life's Work.* Austin: University of Texas Press, 1982.

Rosengrant, Judson. "Nabokov, Onegin, and the Theory of Translation." *Slavic and East European Journal* 38, no. 1 (Spring 1994): 13–27.

Roth, Phyllis A., ed. *Critical Essays on Vladimir Nabokov.* Boston: G. K. Hall, 1984.

Rougemont, Denis de. "Nouvelles métamorphoses de Tristan." *Preuves* 96 (1959): 14–27.

Rowe, William Woodin. *Nabokov and Others: Patterns in Russian Literature.* Ann Arbor, Mich.: Ardis, 1979.

Russian Literature Triquarterly 17 (1991). Special Issue on Nabokov.

Safariants, Rita. "Literary Bilingualism and Code-Switching in Vladimir Nabokov's *Ada.*" In "My Nabokov," edited by Marijeta Bozovic. Special issue, *Ulbandus* 10 (2007): 192–211.

Sartre, Jean-Paul. Review of *La Méprise* [*Despair*] by Vladimir Nabokov. In *Nabokov: The Critical Heritage*, edited by Norman Page, 65–66. London: Routledge, 1997.

Schiff, Stacy. *Véra (Mrs. Vladimir Nabokov).* New York: Random House, 1999.

Shapiro, Gavriel. *The Sublime Artist's Studio: Nabokov and Painting.* Evanston, Ill.: Northwestern University Press, 2009.

Shloss, Carol. "*Speak, Memory:* The Aristocracy of Art." In Rivers, *Nabokov's Fifth Arc*, 224–29.

Shrayer, Maxim D. "The Poetics of Vladimir Nabokov's Short Stories, with Reference to Anton Chekhov and Ivan Bunin." Ph.D. diss., Yale, Spring 1995.

Shute, Jennifer P. "Nabokov and Freud." In Alexandrov, *Garland Companion*, 412–20.

Smith, Gerald S. "Notes on Prosody." In Alexandrov, *Garland Companion*, 561–66.

Stanton, Rebecca. "Talking Back to Nabokov: A Commentary on a Commentary." In "My Nabokov," edited by Marijeta Bozovic. Special issue, *Ulbandus* 10 (2007): 212–21.

Steiner, George. "Extraterritorial." *TriQuarterly* 17 (Winter 1970): 119–28.

———. *Extraterritorial: Papers on Literature and the Language of Revolution*. Harmondsworth, Eng.: Penguin, 1975.

———. "To Traduce or Transfigure: On Modern Verse Translation." *Encounter* 27, no. 2 (August 1966): 48–54.

Straumann, Barbara. *Figurations of Exile in Hitchcock and Nabokov*. Edinburgh: Edinburgh University Press, 2009.

Struve, Gleb. "Notes on Nabokov as a Russian Writer." In Dembo, *Nabokov*, 45–56.

Stuart, Dabney. "*Laughter in the Dark*: The Novel as Film." In *Nabokov: Dimensions of Parody*, 87–113. Baton Rouge: Louisiana University Press, 1978.

Tammi, Pekka. *Russian Subtexts in Nabokov's Fiction: Four Essays*. Tampere, Finland: Tampere University Press, 1999.

Toker, Leona. "Nabokov and Bergson." In Alexandrov, *Garland Companion*, 367–73.

Trilling, Lionel. "The Last Lover: Vladimir Nabokov's *Lolita*." *Encounter* 11 (1958): 9–19.

Trousdale, Rachel. *Nabokov, Rushdie, and the Transnational Imagination: Novels of Exile and Alternate Worlds*. New York: Palgrave Macmillan, 2010.

Trubikhina, Julia. "Struggle for the Narrative: Nabokov and Kubrick's Collaboration on the *Lolita* Screenplay." In "My Nabokov," edited by Marijeta Bozovic. Special issue, *Ulbandus* 10 (2007): 149–72.

Updike, John. "Van Loves Ada, Ada Loves Van." Review of *Ada* by Vladimir Nabokov. *New Yorker*, August 2, 1969, 67–75.

Virolainen, Mariia. "Mimikriia rechi ('Evgenii Onegin' Pushkina i 'Ada' Nabokova)." In *Rech' i molchanie: Siuzhety i mify russkoi slovesnosti*, 400–411. St. Petersburg: Amphora, 2003.

"Vladimir Nabokov: The Art of Fiction." Special Issue, *Paris Review* 40 (Summer-Fall 1967).

Vries, Gerard de, and D. Barton Johnson. *Nabokov and the Art of Painting*. Amsterdam: Amsterdam University Press, 2006.

Warner, Nicholas O. "The Footnote as Literary Genre: Nabokov's Commentaries to Lermontov and Pushkin." *Slavic and East European Journal* 30, no. 2 (Summer 1986): 167–82.

White, Duncan. *Nabokov and His Books: Between Late Modernism and the Literary Marketplace*. Oxford: Oxford University Press, forthcoming.

Wilson, Edmund. "The Strange Case of Pushkin and Nabokov." *New York Review of Books* 4, no. 12 (July 15, 1965): 1–11.

Wood, James. "Discussing Nabokov." *Slate* (April 26, 1999): http://www.slate.com/articles/arts/the_book_club/features/1999/discussing_nabokov/_2.html.

Wood, Michael. *The Magician's Doubts: Nabokov and the Risks of Fiction.* Princeton, N.J.: Princeton University Press, 1997.

———. "Nabokov's Late Fiction." In Connolly, *Cambridge Companion*, 200–214.

Wyllie, Barbara. *Nabokov at the Movies: Film Perspectives in Fiction.* Jefferson, N.C.: McFarland, 2003.

Zimmer, Dieter E. "Vladimir Nabokov: A Bibliography of Criticism." With additions by Jeff Edmunds. *Zembla* web page. http://www.libraries.psu.edu/iasweb/nabokov/.

Zunshine, Lisa, ed. *Nabokov at the Limits: Redrawing Critical Boundaries.* New York: Garland, 1999.

Zverev, Aleksei. "Nabokov, Updike, and American Literature." Translated by Anna K. Primrose. In Alexandrov, *Garland Companion*, 536–48.

Secondary Sources on Pushkin

Andrew, Joe, and Robert Reid, eds. *Two Hundred Years of Pushkin*. Studies in Slavic Literature and Poetics. Amsterdam: Editions Rodopi B.V., 2003.

Blank, Ksana. "The Endless Passage: The Making of a Plot in the Russian Novel." Ph.D. diss., Columbia University, 1997.

Cravens, Craig. "Lyric and Narrative Consciousness in *Eugene Onegin*." *Slavic and East European Journal* 46, no. 4 (Winter 2002): 683–709.

Eikhenbaum, Boris. *O proze*. Leningrad: Khudozhestvennaia literatura, 1969.

Gasparov, Boris. "Eugene Onegin in the Age of Realism." In *Five Operas and a Symphony*, 58–94. New Haven, Conn.: Yale University Press, 2005.

Greenleaf, Monika. *Pushkin and Romantic Fashion: Fragment, Elegy, Orient, Irony*. Stanford, Calif.: Stanford University Press, 1994.

———. "Tynianov, Pushkin and the Fragment: Through the Lens of Montage." In *Cultural Mythologies of Russian Modernism: From the Golden Age to the Silver Age*, edited by Boris Gasparov, Robert Hughes, and Irina Paperno, 264–92. Berkeley: University of California Press, 1992.

Gustafson, Richard F. "The Metaphor of the Seasons in *Evgenij Onegin*." *SEEJ* 6, no. 1 (Spring 1962): 6–20.

Hoisington, Sonia. *Russian Views of Pushkin's "Eugene Onegin."* Bloomington: Indiana University Press, 1988.

Iakubovich, D. P. "Antichnost' v tvorchestve Pushkina." *Vremennik Pushkinskoi kommissii* 6 (1941): 92–93.

Jakobson, Roman, and Morris Halle. *Fundamentals of Language*. The Hague: Mouton, 1956.

———. "On a Generation That Squandered Its Poets." In *Verbal Art, Verbal Sign, Verbal Time*, 111–32. Minneapolis: University of Minnesota Press, 1985.

Kelly, Catriona. *A Short Introduction to Russian Literature*. Oxford: Oxford University Press, 2001.

Khodasevich, Vladimir. *Poeticheskoe khoziaistvo Pushkina*. Leningrad: Mysel', 1924.

Levitt, Marcus C. "Pushkin in 1899." In *Cultural Mythologies of Russian Modernism: From the Golden Age to the Silver Age*, edited by Boris Gasparov, Robert Hughes, and Irina Paperno, 183–203. Berkeley: University of California Press, 1992.

Lotman, Iurii. *Pushkin: Biografiia pisatelia; Stat'i i zametki 1960–1990; "Evgenii Onegin," Kommentarii*. St. Petersburg: Iskusstvo-SPB, 2005.

Meijer, Jan M. "The Digressions in 'Evgenii Onegin.'" In *Dutch Contributions to the Sixth International Congress of Slavists*, edited by A. G. F. Van Holk, 122–52. The Hague: Mouton, 1968.

Nepomnyashchy, Catharine. "Jane Austen in Russia: Hidden Presence and Belated Boom." In *The Reception of Jane Austen in Russia*, edited by Anthony Mandal and Brian Southam, 334–49. London: Continuum, 2007.

Reyfman, Irina. "The Duel as an Act of Violence." In *Ritualized Violence Russian Style: The Duel in Russian Culture and Literature*, 15–44. Stanford, Calif.: Stanford University Press, 1999.

Rosenshield, Gary. *Pushkin and the Genres of Madness: The Masterpieces of 1833*. Madison: University of Wisconsin Press, 2003.

Sandler, Stephanie. *Distant Pleasures: Alexander Pushkin and the Writing of Exile*. Stanford, Calif.: Stanford University Press, 1989.

Shklovsky, Viktor. "Art as Technique." In *Russian Formalist Criticism: Four Essays*, edited by Lee T. Lemon and Marion J. Reis. Lincoln: University of Nebraska Press, 1965.

———. "'Evgenii Onegin' (Pushkin i Stern)." In *Ocherki po poetike Pushkina*. Berlin: Epokha, 1923.

———. *Zametki o proze Pushkina*. Moscow: Sovetskii pisatel', 1937.

Smith, Alexandra. *Montaging Pushkin: Pushkin and Visions of Modernity in the Twentieth Century*. Amsterdam: Editions Rodopi B.V., 2006.

Stil'man, L. N. "Problemy literaturnykh zhanrov i traditsii v 'Evgenii Onegine' Pushkina: K voprosu perekhoda ot romantizma k realizmu." In *American Contributions to the Fourth International Congress of Slavists*. The Hague: Mouton, 1958.

Todd, William, III. *The Familiar Letter as a Literary Genre in the Age of Pushkin*. Princeton, N.J.: Princeton University Press, 1976.

———. *Fiction and Society in the Age of Pushkin: Ideology, Institutions, and Narrative*. Cambridge, Mass.: Harvard University Press, 1986.

Tynianov, Iury. *The Problem of Verse Language*. Translated by Michael Sosa and Brent Harvey. Ann Arbor, Mich.: Ardis, 1981.

Vainshtein, Ol'ga. *Dendi: Moda, literatura, stil' zhizni*. Moscow: Novoe literaturnoe obozrenie, 2006.

Wolff, Tatiana, ed. and trans. *Pushkin on Literature*. Stanford, Calif.: Stanford University Press, 1986.

Zhirmunsky, V. M. *Bairon i Pushkin*. Leningrad: Academia, 1924.

Additional Sources

Adorno, Theodor, and Max Horkheimer, *The Dialectic of Enlightenment*. Stanford, Calif.: Stanford University Press, 2002.

Apter, Emily. *Against World Literature: On the Politics of Untranslatability*. London: Verso, 2013.

Arnheim, Rudolf. *Visual Thinking*. Berkeley: University of California Press, 1969.

Bakhtin, Mikhail. *Formal'nyj metod v literaturovedenii*. New York: Serebrianyi vek, 1982.

Bataille, Georges. *Erotism: Death and Sensuality*. Translated by Mary Dalwood. San Francisco: City Lights Books, 1986.

Battock, Gregory, ed. *The New Art: A Critical Anthology*. New York: E. P. Dutton, 1973.

Beagle, Peter S. *The Garden of Earthly Delights*. London: Pan Books, 1982.

Beaujour, Elizabeth. *Alien Tongues: Bilingual Russian Writers of the "First" Emigration*. Ithaca, N.Y.: Cornell University Press, 1989.

Benjamin, Walter. *Illuminations*. Edited by Hannah Arendt. Translated by Harry Zohn. New York: Schocken, 1969.

Bergson, Henri. *Henri Bergson: Key Writings*. Edited by Keith Ansell Pearson and John Mullarkey. New York: Continuum, 2002.

Berman, Marshall. *All That Is Solid Melts into Air: The Experience of Modernity*. New York: Penguin, 1988.

Berry, Ellen E., and Mikhail Epstein. *Transcultural Experiments: Russian and American Models of Creative Communication*. New York: Palgrave Macmillan, 1999.

Bloch, Ernst. *The Principle of Hope*. Vol. 2. Translated by Neville Plaice, Stephen Plaice, and Paul Knight. Cambridge, Mass.: MIT Press, 2000.

Bloom, Harold. *The Anxiety of Influence: A Theory of Poetry*. Oxford: Oxford University Press, 1997.

———. *Genius: A Mosaic of One Hundred Exemplary Creative Minds*. New York: Warner Books, 2002.

———. *The Western Canon: The Books and School of the Ages*. New York: Riverhead Trade, 1995.

Bolter, David Jay, and Richard Grusin. *Remediation: Understanding New Media.* Cambridge, Mass.: MIT Press, 2000.

Borges, Jorge Luis. "Kafka and His Precursors." In *Labyrinths,* edited by Donald A. Yates and James E. Irby, 199–201. New York: New Directions, 2007.

Bourdieu, Pierre. *Distinction: A Social Critique of the Judgment of Taste.* Translated by Richard Nice. Cambridge, Mass.: Harvard University Press, 1987.

Brooker, Peter, and Andrew Thacker, eds. *Geographies of Modernism: Literatures, Cultures, Spaces.* London: Routledge, 2005.

Brooks, Peter. *Reading for the Plot: Design and Intention in Narrative.* Cambridge, Mass.: Harvard University Press, 1984.

Bürger, Peter. *Theory of the Avant-Garde.* Translated by Michael Shaw. Minneapolis: University of Minnesota Press, 1984.

Burgin, Diana Lewis. *Richard Burgin: A Life in Verse.* Bloomington, Ind.: Slavica, 1989.

Burrus, Virginia. *The Sex Lives of Saints: An Erotics of Ancient Hagiography.* Philadelphia: University of Pennsylvania Press, 2004.

Casanova, Pascale. *The World Republic of Letters.* Translated by M. B. DeBevoise. Cambridge, Mass.: Harvard University Press, 2007.

Clark, Katerina, and Michael Holquist. *Mikhail Bakhtin.* Cambridge, Mass.: Harvard University Press, 1984.

Clark, Kenneth. *What Is a Masterpiece?* New York: Thames and Hudson, 1992.

Coetzee, J. M. *Disgrace.* New York: Penguin, 2000.

Culler, Jonathan. *Literary Theory: A Very Short Introduction.* New York: Oxford University Press, 1997.

———. *Structuralist Poetics.* London: Routledge and Kegan Paul, 1975.

Damrosch, David. *What Is World Literature?* Princeton, N.J.: Princeton University Press, 2003.

Derrida, Jacques. *Of Grammatology.* Translated by Gayatri Chakravorty Spivak. Baltimore, Md.: Johns Hopkins University Press, 1976.

Eagle, Herbert. *Russian Formalist Film Theory.* Ann Arbor: Michigan Slavic Publications, 1988.

Eco, Umberto. "Arthur Miller Lecture," New York PEN Festival, May 4, 2009.

———. "Granita." In *Misreadings,* 7–14. Orlando, Fla.: Harcourt, 1993.

Eliot, T. S. *The Sacred Wood: Essays on Poetry and Criticism.* London: Methuen, 1976.

———. "The Uses of Poetry and the Uses of Criticism." In *The Selected Prose of T. S. Eliot.* Cambridge, Mass.: Harvard University Press, 1986.

Fink, Hilary L. *Bergson and Russian Modernism, 1900–1930.* Evanston, Ill.: Northwestern University Press, 1999.

Fox, Sylvan. "Stephen Spender Quits *Encounter.*" *New York Times,* May 8, 1967.

Freeborn, Richard. "The Classic Russian Novel." In *Reference Guide to Russian Literature,* edited by Neil Cornwell. London: Fitzroy, Dearborn, 1998.

Frye, Northrop. *The Anatomy of Criticism*. Princeton, N.J.: Princeton University Press, 2000.

Ginzburg, Lydia. *On Psychological Prose*. Translated by Judson Rosengrant. Princeton, N.J.: Princeton University Press, 1991.

Girard, René. *Deceit, Desire and The Novel: Self and Other in Literary Structure*. Translated by Yvonne Freccero. Baltimore, Md.: Johns Hopkins University Press, 1965.

Gould, Stephen Jay. *The Panda's Thumb: More Reflections in Natural History*. New York: Norton, 1980.

Grafton, Anthony. *The Footnote: A Curious History*. London: Faber and Faber, 1997.

Groys, Boris. *The Total Art of Stalinism: Avant-Garde, Aesthetic Dictatorship, and Beyond*. Princeton, N.J.: Princeton University Press, 1992.

Guillory, John. *Cultural Capital: The Problem of Literary Canon Formation*. Chicago: University of Chicago Press, 1993.

———. "Genesis of the Media Concept." *Critical Inquiry* 36, no. 2 (Winter 2012): 321–62.

Hobsbawm, Eric, and Terence Ranger, eds. *The Invention of Tradition*. Cambridge: Cambridge University Press, 1983.

Huyseen, Andreas. *After the Great Divide: Modernism, Mass Culture, Postmodernism*. Bloomington: Indiana University Press, 1986.

———. "Geographies of Modernism in a Globalizing World." In *Geographies of Modernism*, ed. Peter Brooker and Andrew Thacker.

Iser, Wolfgang. *The Act of Reading: A Theory of Aesthetic Response*. London: Routledge and Kegan Paul, 1978.

———. *The Implied Reader: Patterns of Communication in Prose and Fiction from Bunyan to Beckett*. Baltimore, Md.: Johns Hopkins University Press, 1987.

Jahanbegloo, Ramin. *Conversations with Isaiah Berlin*. London: Peter Halban, 1991.

Jameson, Frederic. *Archaeologies of the Future: The Desire Called Utopia and Other Science Fictions*. London: Verso, 2005.

———. *Postmodernism; or, The Cultural Logic of Late Capitalism*. Durham, N.C.: Duke University Press, 2003.

Johnson, Lee McKay. *The Metaphor of Painting: Essays on Baudelaire, Ruskin, Proust, and Pater*. Ann Arbor, Mich.: UMI Research, 1980.

Johnson, Randal. "Pierre Bourdieu on Art, Literature, and Culture." In Pierre Bourdieu, *The Field of Cultural Production: Essays on Art and Literature*, ed. Randall Johnson. New York: Columbia University Press, 1993.

Joyce, James. *Finnegans Wake*. Middlesex, Eng.: Penguin, 1983.

———. *Ulysses*. New York: Vintage, 1990.

Lamos, Colleen. *Deviant Modernism: Sexual and Textual Errancy in T. S. Eliot, James Joyce, and Marcel Proust*. Cambridge: Cambridge University Press, 1998.

Lermontov, Mikhail. *A Hero of Our Time*. Translated and with introduction by Vladimir Nabokov, with Dmitri Nabokov. Ann Arbor, Mich.: Ardis, 1988.

Lethem, Jonathan. "The Ecstasy of Influence: A Plagiarism." *Harper's Magazine*, February 2007, 59–71.

Lipovetsky, Mark. "Russian Literary Postmodernism in the 1990s." *Slavonic and East European Review* 79, no. 1 (January 2001): 31–50.

Lotman, I. M. *The Structure of the Artistic Text*. Translated by Ronald Vroon and Gail Vroon. Ann Arbor: University of Michigan Press.

Lukács, Georg. *Theory of the Novel*. Translated by Anna Bostock. Cambridge, Mass.: MIT Press, 1971.

Lungstrum, Janet, and Elizabeth Sauer, eds. *Agonistics: Arenas of Creative Control*. New York: State University of New York Press, 1997.

Monaco, James. *How to Read a Film: The Art, Technology, Language, History, and Theory of Film and Media*. Revised edition. New York: Oxford University Press, 1981.

Moretti, Franco. *Atlas of the European Novel 1800–1900*. London: Verso, 1998.

———. *Signs Taken for Wonders: Essays in the Sociology of Literary Forms*. London: Verso, 1988.

Moulard-Leonard, Valentine. *Bergson-Deleuze Encounters: Transcendental Experience and the Thought of the Virtual*. Albany: State University of New York Press, 2008.

Murphet, Julian. *Multimedia Modernism: Literature and the Anglo-American Avant-Garde*. Cambridge: Cambridge University Press, 2009.

Nafisi, Azar. *Reading Lolita in Tehran: A Memoir in Books*. New York: Random House, 2003.

Nietzsche, Friedrich. "Homer's Contest." In Lungstrum and Sauer, *Agonistics*, 35–45. New York: State University of New York Press, 1997.

Pamuk, Orhan. *My Name Is Red*. Translated by Erdag Göknar. New York: Vintage, 2002.

———. *The Museum of Innocence*. Translated by Maureen Freely. New York: Alfred A. Knopf, 2009.

———. *The Naive and the Sentimental Novelist*. Translated by Nazim Dikba. Cambridge, Mass.: Harvard University Press, 2010.

Panofsky, Erwin. *Meaning in the Visual Arts*. Chicago: University of Chicago Press, 1983.

Paperno, Irina, and Joan Grossman, eds. *Creating Life: The Aesthetic Utopia of Russian Modernism*. Stanford, Calif.: Stanford University Press, 1994.

Pater, Walter. *The Renaissance: Studies in Art and Poetry*. Mineola, N.Y.: Dover, 2005.

Perloff, Marjorie. *21st Century Modernism: The "New" Poetics*. Malden, Mass.: Blackwell, 2002.

Pizer, John. *The Idea of World Literature: History and Pedagogical Practice.* Baton Rouge: Louisiana State University Press, 2006.

Pratt, Mary Louise. *Imperial Eyes: Travel Writing and Transculturation.* London: Routledge, 1992.

Praz, Mario. *The Romantic Irony.* Translated by Angus Davidson. Oxford: Oxford University Press, 1970.

Prendergast, Christopher, ed. *Debating World Literature.* London: Verso, 2004.

Proust, Marcel. *In Search of Lost Time.* Translated by C. K. Moncrieff and Terrence Kilmartin. Revised by D. J. Enright. New York: Modern Library, 2003.

Roberts, Graham. *The Last Soviet Avant-Garde: OBERIU—Fact, Fiction, Metafiction.* Cambridge: Cambridge University Press, 1997.

Robinson, Keith. *Deleuze, Whitehead, Bergson: Rhizomatic Connections.* London: Palgrave Macmillan, 2009.

Rorty, Richard. *Contingency, Irony and Solidarity.* Cambridge: Cambridge University Press, 1989.

Rougemont, Denis de. *Love Declared: Essays on the Myths of Love.* Translated by Richard Howard. New York: Pantheon, 1961.

———. *Love in the Western World.* Translated by Montgomery Belgion. Princeton, N.J.: Princeton University Press, 1983.

Ruiz, Raul. *Poetics of Cinema.* Paris: Dis Voir, 1995.

Russell, Bertrand. *A History of Western Philosophy, and Its Connection with Political and Social Circumstances from the Earliest Times to the Present Day.* New York: Simon and Schuster, 1945.

Ryan, Marie-Laure. *Narrative across Media: The Languages of Storytelling.* Lincoln: University of Nebraska Press, 2004.

Said, Edward. "The Mind of Winter: Reflections on Life in Exile." *Harper's Magazine,* September 1984, 49–55.

Schmitz, Andrew. "The Penman and the Postal-Carrier: Preordained Rivalry in Joyce's *Finnegans Wake.*" In Lungstrum and Sauer, *Agonistics,* 240–55.

Sebald, W. G. "Dream Textures: A Brief Note on Nabokov." In Sebald, *Campto Santo,* edited by Sven Meyer, translated by Anthea Bell. London: Hamilton, 2005.

———. *The Emigrants.* Translated by Michael Hulse. New York: New Directions, 1996.

Seth, Vikram. *The Golden Gate.* New York: Vintage, 1991.

Seyhan, Azade. *Writing Outside the Nation.* Princeton, N.J.: Princeton University Press, 2001.

Sorokin, Vladimir. *Roman.* Moscow: BSG Press, 2000.

Steiner, George. *After Babel: Aspects of Language and Translation.* Oxford: Oxford University Press, 1998.

Tanner, Tony. *Adultery in the Novel: Contract and Transgression.* Baltimore, Md.: Johns Hopkins University Press, 1979.

Thomsen, Mads Rosendahl. *Mapping World Literature: International Canonization and Transnational Literatures*. London: Continuum, 2008.

Tynianov, I. N. *Arkhaisty i novatory*. Petrograd: Priboi, 1929.

———. "Dostoevskii i Gogol' (k teorii parodii)." In *Poetika; Istoriia literatury; Kino*. Moscow: Nauka, 1977.

———. "On the Foundations of Cinema." Translated by Zinaida Breschinsky and Herbert Eagle. In Herbert Eagle, ed. *Russian Formalist Film Theory*. Ann Arbor: Michigan Slavic Publications, 1988.

Wilson, Edmund. *Axel's Castle*. New York: Farrar, Straus and Giroux, 2004. Originally published 1931.

———. *A Window on Russia*. New York: Farrar, Straus and Giroux, 1972.

Wood, James. *How Fiction Works*. New York: Farrar, Straus and Giroux, 2008.

Zarin, Cyntha. *The Ada Poems*. New York: Knopf, 2010.

Index

Index

Hobsbawm, Eric, 172n13
Horkheimer, Max, 6
Housman, A. E., 99
Huyssen, Andreas, 171n6, 172n11

Jakobson, Roman, 36, 45, 46
James, Henry, 119
Jameson, Frederic, 4, 130
Johnson, D. Barton, 91, 162, 189n20, 189n26
Joyce, James, 5, 13, 19, 51, 54, 88–89, 93,
    94–95, 99–100, 127–28, 136, 139, 142,
    158; in *Ada*, 99, 111, 113, 119–28,
    198nn36–37, 199nn40–42; Casanova
    on, 175n15; characterization, 195n8; at
    Nabokov lecture, 51, 184n26
  WORKS: *Finnegans Wake*, 3, 13, 73, 106,
    111, 122–23, 127, 128, 139, 196n20,
    199n42; *A Portrait of the Artist as
    a Young Man*, 128; *Ulysses*, 16, 80,
    85, 94, 99–100, 103–9, 119–22,
    124, 127–28, 184n35, 195n11,
    198nn36–37, 199n38
Jung, Carl G., 139, 199n42

Kafka, Franz, 99, 109, 196n14; Borges on,
    53, 89, 131
Kandinsky, Wassily, 5, 161
Katenin, Pavel, 58
Keats, John, 64
Khodasevich, Vladimir, 42, 48, 184n34
Kristeva, Julia, 10, 193n55
Kubrick, Stanley, 75, 150, 201n5
Küchelbecker, Wilhelm, 67

Lafontaine, August, 27, 177n44
Lamos, Colleen, 196n13
Lautréamont, Comte de, 119
Leigh, Augusta, 86
Leonard, Jeffrey, 201n6
Lermontov, Mikhail, 85, 93, 190n34
Leving, Yuri, 205n9
Lomonosov, Mikhail, 175n5
Lotman, Iurii, 11, 23, 24, 42, 59, 176n24,
    180n92, 183n19
Lovelace, Ada (née Byron), 85, 86
Lowell, Robert, 45, 75, 76–77, 171n1
Lukács, Georg, 179n80

Mandelstam, Osip, 42, 45, 48, 75, 76, 93,
    171n1

Manet, Édouard, 126
Manley, Delarivier, 118
Marvell, Andrew, 85
Marxist theory, 8, 163
Mason, Bobbie Ann, 192n51
Maturin, Charles, 59
Maupassant, Guy de, 118
media theory, 6, 43, 162–64
Meijer, Jan, 24, 37
Mercanton, James, 123
Mérimée, Prosper, 93–94, 150
Meyer, Priscilla, 82
Mickiewicz, Adam, 42
Milton, John, 44, 85
modernism: Bergson's influence on, 13,
    136, 158; Dostoevsky's influence on,
    187n59; early Russian literature and,
    10, 11, 17, 19, 40, 49, 83; Greenberg
    on, 205n8; Nabokov and, 4, 6, 8–9,
    13, 48, 106, 107–8, 128–30, 158; post-
    modernists vs., 171n6; roots in exile
    and displacement, 172n11; sexual de-
    viancy and, 108, 196n13; Wilson on,
    141
modernity, 9, 18
Moretti, Franco, 6–7, 18
Morini, Simona, 127
Murphet, Julian, 162–63

Nabokov, Dmitri, 153
Nabokov, Vera, 72, 75, 97, 201n7
Nabokov, Vladimir: academic career, 46,
    90, 182n12, 187n58; allegory aversion,
    99, 104; allusions function, 91–95, 130,
    157, 192n50, 193n60; ambition, 46; on
    anti-novels, 97, 129; cosmopolitanism,
    84, 163; critics and readers relation-
    ship, 90–91; fame, 5, 72–73, 160–61,
    165; Francophilia, 10, 19; on genius,
    99, 103, 108, 119; on German litera-
    ture, 194n3, 196n14; influence, 164,
    165–66; on literary popularity, 183n25;
    Pushkin affinity, 45–46, 48–49, 84, 89,
    194n65; Russian language relationship,
    74–75; stream of consciousness tech-
    nique, 104–7, 119, 123, 126, 199n40;
    as transnational writer, 161, 164–66,
    172n11, 197n25; "un-Russianness,"
    84, 190n33; visual orientation, 161–62,
    195n6, 198n34. *See also* Byron, Lord;

Index

Parny, Évariste de Forges, Vicomte de, 54
Pichot, Amédée, 44, 56, 58, 184n36
Pifer, Ellen, 192n51
Plato, 137, 200n50, 202n13
Pope, Alexander, 64, 65
Pound, Ezra, 47, 109, 122
Praz, Mario, 62, 196n13
Proffer, Carl, 92–93, 191n45, 193n57
Proust, Marcel, 5, 13, 54, 88, 94–95, 97–
    104, 106–22, 127–29, 127, 157–58,
    161, 196n15; *Ada* and, 78, 85, 102,
    109–19, 120, 121–22, 128–29, 136,
    146, 153, 191n38, 201n6; Bergson and,
    136, 141, 158, 203n30; characteriza-
    tion, 195n8; *Pale Fire* and, 97–98, 102,
    194n2; on pastiche, 118, 198n33
Pushkin, Aleksandr, 10–11, 15–17, 20–43,
    85, 128, 160, 174n35, 175n5, 181n96;
    avant-garde reaction against, 17,
    175n4; "big form" in, 181n100; Chaa-
    daev letter, 40–41, 180n89; on Chateau-
    briand, 44; Decembrism, 176n18;
    defense of *EO*, 67–68; Francophilia,
    10, 19; French indifference to,
    183n21; influence (and "my Push-
    kin" tradition), 41–43, 48–49, 70, 141,
    180n91, 184n34; personal qualities,
    51–52; on translators, 44, 182n4
WORKS:
Caucasian Prisoner, The, 57, 181n100
"Demon, The," 85
Evgenii Onegin, 4, 5, 11–12, 15–17,
    20–40, 42, 48–49, 176n24, 183n19;
    in *Ada*, 76, 77, 78–82, 85, 91–92,
    150, 189n27; adaptations, 50, 51–52;
    artifice in, 11, 15–16; belatedness in,
    12, 17, 20–21, 63–64, 96; Breguet
    watch, 12, 31, 65, 178n62, 186n53;
    critical reception, 37, 41, 42, 67,
    132, 180n92; disrespect for conven-
    tions, 178n55; dueling in, 65–66;
    fashion in, 25–34, 39, 64, 65–68, 70,
    96, 179n86; floral imagery, 21, 26–28,
    31–33; foreign influences, 16, 17,
    24, 26–27, 35–36, 38–40, 53–54,
    84, 88; Lensky's role, 22, 27–28, 34,
    66; meta-literary aspects, 11, 16–17,
    24, 33, 34–41, 43, 63, 66–67, 78,
    83; Muse figure, 33; narrator in, 16,
    23–24, 26–28, 31, 33–34, 35–36,
    38–39; novels in, 28–29, 38, 53,
    59–60; Olga's role, 26–27, 34; One-
    gin's role, 23–24, 31–33, 35, 39,
    186n54; polylingualism, 38–39;
    pursuit motif, 15–16, 64, 79, 155;
    restraint in, 32, 81; serial publica-
    tion, 37, 67, 155, 176n24; stanza
    form, 21, 36, 70; Tatiana's role, 24,
    28–32, 80, 157–58, 176n29, 177n50,
    178n61; time and timeliness in,
    16–17, 20–25, 27, 31–33, 36–37,
    62–65, 147; unfinished state, 25,
    37–38, 163, 176n30, 179n83, 184n35,
    185n50; verse novel form, 54–55,
    178n55, 179n76, 179n80. *See also*
    Nabokov, Vladimir: *Eugene Onegin*
"Exegi monumentum," 68, 69, 189n19
"Grapes," 92, 117, 189n27
Gypsies, The, 57, 94
Queen of Spades, The, 51
Rusalka, 84
Stone Guest, The, 88

Racine, Jean, 60
refashioning, 163
Reid, Mayne, 197n29
Repin, Ilya, 50
Richardson, Samuel, 29, 38, 60, 185n43
Rimbaud, Arthur, 75, 85, 161
Rivers, J. E., 97, 112
romanticism, 17, 35, 42, 61, 62, 141,
    203n27; Nabokov and, 47, 52, 72,
    85–86, 191n42, 191n44
Rorty, Richard, 73, 182n6, 187n5, 202n13,
    203n39
Rousseau, Jean-Jacques, 38, 54
Rowe, William, 192n49
Ruiz, Raúl, 82
Rushdie, Salman, 166
Russell, Bertrand, 202n11
Russian Formalism. *See* Formalism
Russian literature: belated development,
    10, 17, 19–20, 38, 40–42, 49, 68, 88,
    96; proletarian novels, 60; superfluous
    man figure, 49; syncretisn, 181n95
Ryan, Marie-Laure, 157

Said, Edward, 73, 172n11
Sand, George, 118
Sartre, Jean-Paul, 45, 48, 183n17